PROPHETS, POETS, PRIESTS, and KINGS

The Old Testament Story

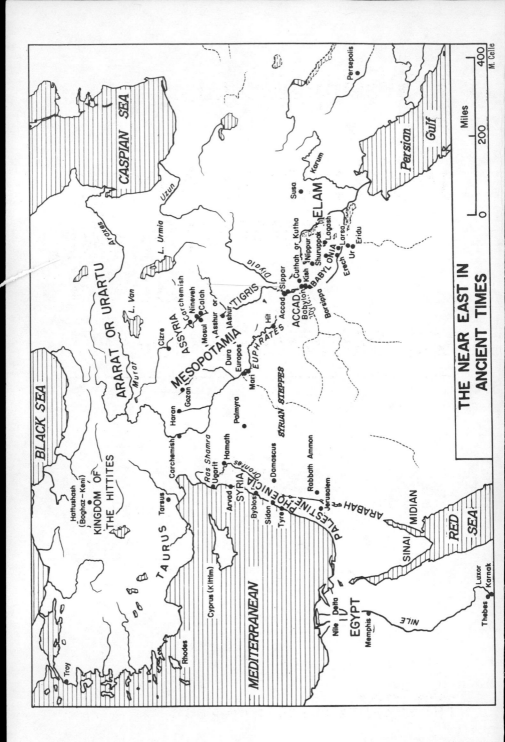

THE NEAR EAST IN
ANCIENT TIMES

M. Celle

Miles

0   200   400

F. Washington Jarvis

PROPHETS, POETS, PRIESTS, and KINGS

The Old Testament Story

A Crossroad Book
THE SEABURY PRESS · NEW YORK

The Seabury Press
815 Second Avenue
New York, N.Y. 10017

ACKNOWLEDGMENTS
Grateful acknowledgment is extended to the following publishers for permission to quote from the copyrighted material listed:

SCM Press Ltd.—*The Book of Daniel* by E. W. Heaton.
Charles Scribner's Sons—*Personalities of the Old Testament* by Fleming James.

Illustrations from *The Jerusalem Bible,* copyright © 1966 by Darton, Longman & Todd Ltd. (London) and Doubleday & Company, Inc. (Garden City, New York). Used by permission of the publishers.

Quotations from the Holy Scriptures are from The New English Bible, copyright 1961, 1970 by the Delegates of the Oxford University Press and the Syndics of the Cambridge University Press.

Library of Congress Cataloging in Publication Data
Jarvis, Frank Washington, 1939–
    Prophets, poets, priests, and kings.

    "A Crossroad book."
    1. Bible.   O.T.—Criticism, interpretation, etc.
I. Title.
BS1171.2.J37   220.6   73–17900
ISBN 0–8164–2089–0 (cloth)
ISBN 0–8164–2586–8 (paper)

With gratitude to my grandparents

GEORGE PATTERSON CRANDALL
NELLIE C. VAN BUREN CRANDALL
FRANK WASHINGTON JARVIS
RUTH WILSON JARVIS

"O God, we have heard with our ears, and
our fathers have declared unto us, the noble
works that thou didst in their days, and in
the old time before them."

ACKNOWLEDGMENTS

For three years several hundred students at University School have been victims of earlier versions of this book. They have shown no reluctance to criticize! I owe them—most of all—apologies and thanks.

My colleagues, the Rev. W. Chave McCracken, Dr. Richard A. Hawley, and Rabbi Arthur Lelyveld, have offered useful suggestions on several chapters. My dear friend Mrs. Nathaniel W. Baker has read the entire manuscript with consummate critical care. I am grateful beyond expression to the Rev. Dr. Frank Halliday Ferris, saint of the Lord and hero of the Faith, whose insight and wise counsel deepened and enriched this book significantly.

The grand prize for endurance goes to Mrs. R. Wallace Hutson who has typed and retyped this book. In trying circumstances her patience and gentle kindness have never failed.

Finally, I am deeply grateful to Robert Gilday of the Seabury Press who has helped and encouraged me all along the way.

Feast of St. James of Jerusalem   F. WASHINGTON JARVIS
1973

A PERSONAL NOTE

Throughout my life I have been urged repeatedly to "read the Bible." Time and again with the best intentions I set out to do so. As I plodded my way through the first few difficult, double-columned, fine-printed pages, I soon found myself glancing ahead at the seemingly endless narrative, wondering how many years it would take me to read it all.

At times, fortified by the self-admonition that it was "good for me," I persisted for forty or fifty pages. But, truth to tell, I found the effort uninteresting and joyless. And usually sooner rather than later the Bible found its way back onto the shelf.

Over the last ten years, as a parish clergyman and teacher, I have come to the conclusion that my experience is typical. I know very few people who "read the Bible" and of those few who do almost none reads anything in the *Old* Testament except the psalms.

Years ago Voltaire wrote, "The Bible is of all books the most celebrated and the most unknown." Almost everyone has a Bible; many have several; but few read it.

In the last ten years I have gradually (and only gradually, I am sorry to say) begun to discover the riches which lie buried in the pages of the Old Testament. I use the word "buried" advisedly because only with determination and the aid of abridged Bibles and commentaries was I able to uncover for myself some of the treasure hidden within the Old Testament.

The Old Testament is very long. Its books are not in chronological order. Much of it is difficult to understand. Much of it is of little interest or value.

This book attempts to present, in a concise and ordered way, the principal events and ideas of the Old Testament.

There are many versions of the Bible and there are innumerable commentaries on its various books. I have tried to present in a single volume the most significant Old Testament passages along with simple commentary.

I am not an Old Testament scholar. I am indebted to a galaxy of scholars whose writings have helped me understand more fully the Old Testament story. Anyone who "knows" the Old Testament will have his own opinions about what its most important ideas and events are. I have found it difficult to decide which of the great Old Testament "moments" to include in this book. Interpretations of various Biblical passages differ from scholar to scholar, and I have usually deliberately avoided scholarly debate simply by opting for one view. At the back of this book is a list of books on the Old Testament which I hope the reader will pursue. In them he will discover richer and deeper insights than are possible in this introductory book.

CONTENTS

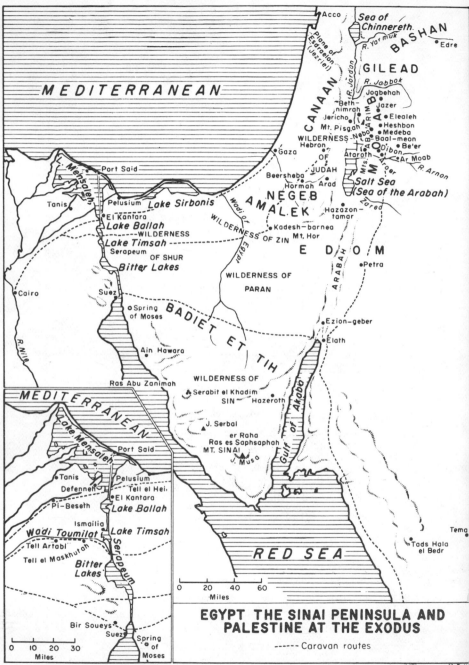

MEDITERRANEAN

Acco

Sea of Chinnereth

BASHAN

Edre

Plane of Esdraelon (Jezrael)

R. Yarmuk

GILEAD

R. Jordan

R. Jabbok

Jogbehah

Beth-nimrah

Jazer

C A N A A N

Jericho

Mt. Pisgah

Elealeh

Heshbon

Medeba

Nebo

Baal-meon

WILDERNESS OF

Hebron

Be'er

Ataroth

D'ibon

M O A B

Ar Moab

Gaza

JUDAH

Aroer

R. Arnon

Port Said

Lake Mensaleh

Beersheba

NEGEB

Salt Sea (Sea of the Arabah)

Tanis

Pelusium

Lake Sirbonis

Hormah

Arad

El Kantara

Lake Ballah

AMALEK

WILDERNESS

Lake Timsah

Hazazon-tamar

Serapeum

OF SHUR

Wadi of Egypt

Kadesh-barnea

Mt. Hor

Zored

Bitter Lakes

WILDERNESS OF ZIN

E D O M

Cairo

Suez

BADIET ET TIH

WILDERNESS OF PARAN

Petra

R. Nile

Spring of Moses

Ezion-geber

Ain Hawara

Elath

Ras Abu Zanimah

WILDERNESS OF

Gulf of Akaba

Serabit el Khadim

SIN

Hazeroth

J. Serbal

er Raha

Ras es Saphsaphah

MT. SINAI

J. Musa

Tema

RED SEA

Tads Hala el Bedr

MEDITERRANEAN

Lake Mensaleh

Port Said

Tanis

Pelusium

Defenneh

Tell el Hei

El Kantara

Pi-Beseth

Lake Ballah

Ismailia

Lake Timsah

Wadi Toumilat

Tell Artabl

Serapeum

Tell el Maskhutah

Bitter Lakes

Bir Soueys

Suez

Spring of Moses

0   10   20   30
Miles

0   20   40   60
Miles

EGYPT THE SINAI PENINSULA AND PALESTINE AT THE EXODUS

------- Caravan routes

M. Cell

INTRODUCTION

Before the reader plunges into the Old Testament story, he may wish to deal briefly with a few important general questions: What is the Old Testament and where did it come from? What do we mean by the word "God" and what kind of language do men use to describe their experience of God?

Our word Bible comes from the Greek words *ta biblia* which mean "the books." The Old Testament is a collection of books by a number of different men who lived between 950 and 165 B.C. in a tiny, politically inconsequential nation sandwiched precariously between what were at the time the world's superpowers. These men—with varying abilities and insights—were struggling to perceive, in the events of their own lives, what life is all about.

They were searching for what we and people in every age have sought to discover: the meaning and purpose of human existence.

Libraries are filled with man's insights into the mystery of life. Philosopher after philosopher arises to speak to people of his own time, then fades into the shadows where only historians preserve his thoughts. Amazingly, however, the insights of the ancient Israelites remain a best seller 2500 years after being written, a phenomenal vitality rivaled in human experience only by the New Testament.

IS GOD PERSONAL?

One conviction unites the very different men whose writings make up the Old Testament: the conviction that they have experienced in their own lives a transcendent personal Being who gives order and purpose to the universe and who involves himself in human affairs.

The Old Testament is about God. It is not a collection of abstract philosophical speculations about the nature of the Deity.

It is a book written by men who believe that they have experienced God active in the events of their own lives and the life of their nation. The experience the Old Testament writers seek to share is that the Creator of all things has, in concrete events in human experience, revealed himself and his purpose for the universe he has created, that now in the present he seeks to enter into relationship with us, and that in relationship to him we can discover the meaning of life.

For several generations men have shied away from the biblical concept of a personal, caring God. If they accept any idea of God, they have been inclined to conceive of him as impersonal, as the Force or Principle or Energy which is the source and basis of the impersonal forces we call "natural laws." To speak of God as personal has seemed naive or childish. Somehow abstract and impersonal categories have seemed more scientific, more sophisticated.

The last few years, however, have seen this tendency reversed. One of the achievements of the evolutionary process is human personality. Therefore, the Originator and Sustainer of that process (if such there be) must at least be capable of personality (though he is far more than simply a person). If the highest achievement of the evolutionary process is human personality, then when we want to describe the Force which caused the whole process, we must turn to personal language as the highest category of language we possess to describe that Force.

There are, of course, dangers involved in describing God in personal terms. Early in its history Israel sometimes lapsed into describing God as if he were only a big man. The Israelites could use rather crude anthropomorphisms (picturing God as a man) and anthropopathisms (endowing God with human emotions). Genesis, for example, pictures God "walking in the garden in the cool of the day" (3:8), "smelling a soothing odour" (8:21), and coming down from heaven to see what men on earth were doing (11:5). As they grew in philosophic sophistication, however, the Israelites were more careful to avoid language which made God appear to be merely a powerful man. Yet they never impoverished their understanding of God by speaking of him in impersonal or abstract terms. Israel's faith was (and is) that at the heart of things there is a vividly personal Being who cares.

IS THE OLD TESTAMENT TRUE?

The Old Testament has a beautiful and inspiring message. But the question inevitably arises whether or not it is *true*. A sixth-grader, for example, can tell you that the two (quite different) accounts of the creation of the world at the beginning of the Bible are not "true." Science shows us that the world was created not thousands but millions of years ago and that it was not created in six days. How can anyone believe Jonah was swallowed by a whale and lived to tell about it? If the Bible is such a great book—if it's supposedly "the word of God"—why is it wrong? And who wants to believe in a God who commands one of his prophets (Elisha) to undertake the wholesale slaughter of those who worship another god? If some parts of the Bible are wrong and other parts immoral, why should we bother to consider the remainder?

The answer to these questions is, of course, that God did not dictate the Bible. The Old Testament is a collection of books by an array of authors who have varying perceptive abilities, viewpoints, insights, and interests. It is a library containing every imaginable sort of literature: historical narrative, legal codes, poetry, protests, myths, legends, fiction, ritual regulations, fantasy, sermons, and love songs. Parts of the Old Testament are boring; parts of it are intellectually and morally worthless.

The Old Testament's various authors are human. Each has his own abilities, prejudices, and interests. We may treat the Old Testament writers as we might treat witnesses in a court of law. We know that witnesses often view the same event in startlingly different ways. Some witnesses are more perceptive or articulate or reliable than others. But taken together their testimony gives us a fairly clear picture of what happened. Each Old Testament author is trying to witness in his own way to what he believes is God's disclosure of himself to men. The Bible may be called "God's word" or "holy" only in that it is a collection of books *about* God. But God didn't write it and the people who did had all the limitations which go with being human.

Some of the Old Testament is straight historical narrative, and archeological study more and more confirms the accuracy and veracity of the Old Testament's picture and chronology. But much of the Old Testament is trying to convey realities which simply cannot be expressed in factual prose. Its writers time and time again turn to allegory, symbolism, and hyperbole in an effort to convey the *significance* of what they felt or saw. We use such language ourselves. The student "bombs a test." We have a "blast" at a party. A girl is "swept off her feet" by a boy who "loses his head" over her. It rains "cats and dogs." And an alcoholic goes "on the wagon." Obviously none of these things literally happens, none is literally true. But no one in his right mind would deny that, while these statements are not literally true, they are true in that they convey the significance of what happened.

When we try to describe a great emotional experience or insight, language is even more inadequate. The language of lovers is filled with images and symbols, with words which cannot be taken literally. We inevitably turn to poetic language (even though not usually to poetry itself) when we try to describe an experience which moves us deeply. In fact, in describing personal relationships and great emotional experiences, the imaginative, metaphorical language of poetry is far more adequate than abstract or literal language.

So not all truth is expressed in literal terms. Shakespeare's expression of love in one of his sonnets is just as "true" as the manual that goes with a power-lawn mower. The Old Testament authors found factual narrative only partially adequate when they sought to express their experience of God. They often turned to poetic and imaginative language when they wanted to convey the significance of an experience. If men find poetic language barely adequate to describe sunsets, love affairs, and symphonies, they naturally have difficulty coming up with human terms adequate to describe the experience of an infinite and transcendent Being. We should, then, expect to see some wrenchings of language when we turn to the Old Testament. And we do.

The symbols of one age are not necessarily those of another. The grandmother of the boy who "bombed the test" may find it difficult to understand what the boy is talking about. If the grandmother wants to understand her grandson, she will inquire about what his symbols mean. If we are interested in understanding Israel's experience, we shall not find it difficult to come to grips with the symbolic language in which it is expressed.

WHERE DID THE BIBLE COME FROM?

In the ancient world information was passed by word of mouth. Writing materials were expensive and difficult to obtain, books were almost unknown, and only a tiny percentage of the population could read or write.

Business and legal affairs were undertaken by the spoken word without the benefit of written records. Memory was therefore vital in trade and law and, in fact, in virtually every aspect of life.

Likewise, ancient peoples had no written records of the past and depended on the spoken word to preserve memories of the past from one generation to another.

Historians and anthropologists tell us that the oral traditions of ancient (non-literary) people are therefore highly trustworthy. Necessity made them develop keen memories. We must remember also that thy did not live, as we do, in a world overwhelmed by written, spoken, and visual media, noise, and instant access.

By 950 B.C., a small group of men emerged in Israel who could read and write. When they undertook the writing down of Israel's early history, they had a massive body of oral stories—passed down the centuries by word of mouth—to draw upon.

Over the centuries, as the Israelite tribes had gathered for their annual reunions, the stories of their national family's past were told aloud and reminiscences shared. The officiants at the shrines where the tribes held their reunions bore special responsibility for preserving with great accuracy the stories of Israel's past. They memorized these stories and retold them in exactly the same words year after year at the reunions. Any modern adult who has read a familiar story to a pre-literate child can tell you how quickly the child will notice and object to even small omissions and changes which the reader might make in the story. We have every reason to believe, for the same reason, that Israel's oral traditions were preserved with remarkable accuracy.

Our Bible's first five books ("the Pentateuch") come from four principal strands of oral tradition. These strands were written down and combined between 950 and 425 B.C. Each of the strands originates from a different time and place and has its own particular emphases and interests. Reading the first five books of the Bible today, scholars can identify each of the four strands.

They call each by a letter: J, E, D, and P. We need not go into the particular interests of each of these strands of oral traditions; each will be discussed in this book in relation to the time in which it was written down. (See chapters 10, 14, and 15.)

Like us, the Israelites viewed the past from the vantage point of the present. They remembered from the past those events which seemed to point toward the present. Looking back they often discerned a sense of direction, purpose, or pattern of behavior in the past which people living in the past did not themselves perceive.

Certain great events colored Israel's understanding of its past. The Israelites' escape from Egypt at the Exodus, their conquest of Canaan, and their development as a nation, made them a distinctive and self-conscious community. Looking back to their earlier history before the Exodus, they naturally picked out certain events (which led up to the Exodus, and which prepared Israel for it) as especially significant. The Israelites also occasionally endowed their ancestors with more insight and foresight than they really possessed.

IS ISRAEL'S EARLIEST HISTORY TRUSTWORTHY?

We should perhaps pause here to consider for a moment the special problems which arise in connection with Israel's history before the Exodus. The stories of these earliest times (roughly the period 1750–1600 B.C.) are found in chapters 12–50 of Genesis. They focus on four distinctive fathers of the nation, the "patriarchs" Abraham, Isaac, Jacob, and Joseph.

Legends gathered around these historical figures the way they later did around the heroes of our own nation. Stories circulated in the nineteenth century, for example, of Abe Lincoln walking ten miles back and forth to school each day in the snow. We know these stories are not "true," but they demonstrate in an exaggerated way the truth that Lincoln's childhood was rough and that his rise to greatness was difficult. We must remember that legends arise around great men because they are great men. Though some of the patriarchal stories may be legendary (not literally true), they nevertheless express real truth about the patriarchs' significance.

The accounts of the patriarchal period were not written down until 650 to 850 years after the patriarchs lived. Since those who wrote down the oral traditions were members of what was by then a distinctive nation with a distinctive religion, these writers to some extent projected their own national and religious identity onto the past. The patriarchs were probably important only within their own tribes, but later historians pictured them as national leaders. Although the patriarchs may have had no direct relation to one another and may have come from quite different tribes and times, later historians show Israel's history to be a single progression from one patriarch to another, father to son.

History is never objective since every historian must select what to write about on the basis of what he thinks is important. In reading the work of any historian—modern or ancient—we must recognize that he has a particular point of view. We must certainly bear this in mind as we read Israel's historians. They make no claim to impartiality. They see even their earliest ancestors as deeply aware of Israel's distinctive national destiny as God's chosen people.

On the other hand, we must not underestimate the historical accuracy of the Old Testament accounts of the patriarchal period. Modern archeological study confirms the picture of patriarchal times found in Genesis. Anthropological study teaches us the high value we can place on the oral tradition of non-literary people. Finally, Genesis' own candid recital of Israel's failures and mistakes indicates that we are reading history remarkably free of the sort of arrogance which falsifies and distorts.

WHAT'S IN IT FOR ME?

We do not turn to the Old Testament because we are interested in ancient history. Nor are we interested in reading about the once active deity described by the schoolboy: "God is a very old man, with a long gray beard, who lives in heaven. He used to do all sorts of great things a long time ago when he was younger. But now he is retired and mainly just rests on his throne."

We turn to the Old Testament in the hope of finding something of present value for our lives. The Old Testament writers do not claim to have all the answers. They do not pretend to have the final word about the meaning of life. They do claim, however, that God has revealed himself clearly enough for us to know him and respond to him in a way that can give our lives meaning and value. The Old Testament records the insights which a remarkably perceptive people had about the same living, personal God who is disclosing himself to us right now.

One of the most comforting things about the Old Testament is its remarkable honesty about the Israelites' half-hearted response to God. It is not a book about superhumans who suddenly "saw the light" and were instantly transformed into models of virtue. It is about real people like ourselves, living in a real world, trying to make ends meet, trying to live decent lives, trying to discover what it all means.

This book has a simple purpose: to look at some of the situations in ancient Israel in which men perceived something of the meaning of things, in which men encountered God in the midst of everyday life, and to look at some of the ways in which they dared—however falteringly and incompletely—to respond to him.

Perhaps, like men and women of other generations, we too shall discover in the Old Testament something of value as we search for the meaning of our lives in our time.

Chapter 1

ABRAHAM

The scene of Israel's early history is the "Fertile Crescent" of rich, well-watered land that runs along the Tigris and Euphrates Rivers, the Mediterranean Sea along the coast of modern Israel and down the Nile River in Egypt. In this area man first became civilized.

The earliest significant figure in Israel's story is Abram. Though he came originally from Ur, we first encounter him as a tribal sheik living in Harran, a city between the northern reaches of the Tigris and Euphrates Rivers. Israel's story begins about 1750 B.C. with Abram's decision to leave the settled security of town life and to embark on a search for a new home for his people. Like our ancestors who sought the promise of a new life in a new land, Abram dared to give up what was certain and to take his wife Sarai and nephew Lot, his dependents and his herds, and seek what was promising and yet uncertain.

Looking back hundreds of years later, the Jews felt Abram had been "called" by God. Their account is quite literal: God simply tells Abram to move and he does. We do not know what form the "call" took, but we do know that Abram and his tribal family believed they were called and that they responded by setting out as travelers in tents in search of a new land.

The Lord said to Abram, 'Leave your own country, your kinsmen, and your father's house, and go to a country that I will show you. I will make you into a great nation, I will bless you and make your name so great that it shall be used in blessings:

Those that bless you I will bless,
those that curse you, I will execrate.
All the families on earth
will pray to be blessed as you are blessed.'

And so Abram set out as the Lord had bidden him, and Lot went with him. He took his wife Sarai, his nephew Lot, all the property they had collected, and all the dependants they had acquired in Harran, and they started on their journey to Canaan. When they arrived, Abram passed through the country to the sanctuary at Shechem. There the Lord appeared to Abram and said, 'I give this land to your descendants.' So Abram built an altar there to the Lord who had appeared to him. Thence he went on to the hill-country east of Bethel and pitched his tent between Bethel on the west and Ai on the east. There he built an altar to the Lord and invoked the Lord by name. Thus Abram journeyed by stages towards the Negeb.   [Gen. 12:1–9, abridged]

Though Abram is promised land and blessing, the price for receiving the promise is costly: "Leave your country, your kinsmen, and your father's house." God chooses Abram not to indulge him, but to lay a burdensome responsibility on him.

Perhaps the most striking thing about Abram's (and Israel's) call is that neither Abram nor his descendants ever advanced any reason as to why God might have chosen *them:* no effort is ever made to demonstrate that Abram or his people were somehow specially deserving. From the beginning of Israel's experience onward, "goodness" seems to be defined in terms of how well a man takes advantage of the opportunities for growth, insight, and service which are offered to him.

Archeologists tell us that in this period groups of nomads (called Habiru) were wandering with herds and families throughout the Fertile Crescent. One of these Habiru groups was Abram's tribe, the Hebrews. Like the immigrants who in modern times left Europe in search of a new life in America, or those who pioneered the American West, the Hebrews had to endure many hardships and trials as they sought a new land for themselves.

After lengthy sojourns including a trip to Egypt during a plague, Abram's tribe finally arrived at what they believed was the land of promise (roughly, modern Israel). Here they immediately became entangled in a family squabble. Because he was childless, Abram had taken his nephew Lot with him to be his heir. But since pasture land and water were scarce in the new land, Abram's herdsmen quarreled with Lot's over the limited resources which were available.

Abram went up from Egypt into the Negeb, he and his wife and all that he had, and Lot went with him. Abram was now very rich in cattle and in silver and gold. From the Negeb he journeyed by stages to Bethel. Now Lot was travelling with Abram, and he too possessed sheep and cattle and tents. The land could not support them both together; for their livestock were so numerous that they could not settle in the same district, and there were quarrels between Abram's herdsmen and Lot's. The Canaanites and the Perizzites were then living in the land. So Abram said to Lot, 'Let there be no quarrelling between us, between my herdsmen and yours; for we are close kinsmen. The whole country is there in front of you; let us part company. If you go left, I will go right; if you go right, I will go left.' Lot looked up and saw how well-watered the whole Plain of the Jordan was; all the way to Zoar it was like the Garden of the Lord, like the land of Egypt. So Lot chose all the Plain of the Jordan and took the road on the east side. Thus they parted company. Abram settled in the land of Canaan; but Lot settled among the cities of the Plain and pitched his tents near Sodom.

After Lot and Abram had parted, the Lord said to Abram, 'Raise your eyes and look into the distance from the place where you are, north and south, east and west. All the land you can see I will give to you and to your descendants for ever. I will make your descendants countless as the dust of the earth; if anyone could count the dust upon the ground, then he could count your descendants. Now go through the length and breadth of the land, for I give it to you.' So Abram moved his tent and settled by the terebinths of Mamre at Hebron; and there he built an altar to the Lord.   [Gen. 13:1–18, abridged]

Though, as senior, Abram has the right of first choice, he generously offers first choice to Lot. Lot selfishly chooses the best for himself. (Genesis later recounts how Lot became so immersed in seeking worldly goods that he was destroyed by them.) Later generations saw Abram and Lot as demonstrating man's contradictory nature: Lot shows man's inherent selfishness while Abram illustrates man's capacity for generosity.

GOD'S PROMISE TO ABRAM

The impressions we form on first meeting a person are different from our insights into that person as we get to know him better. The same is true for the Hebrews' understanding of God. At this point they understood him to be just the God of their tribe, not the God of the whole universe. They were not monotheists (believers in one God), but henotheists (they believed that there was only one god *for their tribe*, while other tribes had their own gods). Though, as we discussed in the Introduction, man's understanding and description of God cannot help but be anthropomorphic and anthropopathic, the Hebrews' understanding of God at this point was primitively so. God appears as a rather frightening, powerful man. He eats, rejoices, becomes angry, and makes deals.

The Hebrews understood their relationship with God as a "covenant" (bargain). In return for God's guidance and protection, the Hebrews were expected to live by certain standards of behavior.

When Abram was ninety-nine years old, the Lord appeared to him and said, 'I am God Almighty. Live always in my presence and be perfect, so that I may set my covenant between myself and you and multiply your descendants.' Abram threw himself down on his face, and God spoke with him and said, 'I make this covenant, and I make it with you: you shall be the father of a host of nations.'   [Gen. 17:1–4]

God is concerned not just with Israel, but ultimately with all nations. Abraham and his nation are the means by which God will bring all men to himself.

'Your name shall no longer be Abram, your name shall be Abraham, for I make you father of a host of nations.'   [Gen. 17:5]

Abram means "High Father" while Abraham means "Father of a Multitude." The change of name is the sign of the changed (deeper) relationship which Abraham has with God as a result of God's covenant with him.

'I will make you exceedingly fruitful; I will make nations out of you, and kings shall spring from you. I will fulfil my covenant between myself and you and your descendants after you, generation after generation, an everlasting covenant, to be your God, yours and your descendants' after you. As an everlasting possession I will give you and your descendants after you the land in which you now are aliens, all the land of Canaan, and I will be God to your descendants.'   [Gen. 17:6–8]

The Hebrews' obligation under the new covenant agreement is ethical: they are "to live always in my presence and be perfect."

Unlike other ancient peoples, the Hebrews understood that commitment to their God had automatic implications about the way they lived. Belief and ethics were to them inseparable.

The outward symbol of this new relationship is circumcision. In that it involves the organ by which a man brings new life into being, circumcision is an effective outward sign for an agreement made not only with Abraham and his tribe, but with all their decendants.

God said to Abraham, 'For your part, you must keep my covenant, you and your descendants after you, generation by generation. This is how you shall keep my covenant between myself and you and your descendants after you: circumcise yourselves, every male among you.'
[Gen. 17:9–10]

A great sadness clouded Abraham's life: he and his wife Sarah were childless. Earlier they had chosen Lot to be their heir, but he had left them. Later Abraham, in accordance with ancient custom, had conceived a son (Ishmael) by Sarah's maid Hagar. Now that they were old, Abraham and Sarah knew that they could have no children of their own. We can imagine their incredulity, therefore, when they discovered, in the strange incident which follows, that Sarah was to give birth to a child. Three strangers appear at Abraham's tent. Abraham receives them with characteristic generosity and, in so doing, mysteriously receives God as his guest.

As Abraham was sitting at the opening of his tent in the heat of the day, he looked up and saw three men standing in front of him. When he saw them, he ran from the opening of his tent to meet them and bowed low to the ground. 'Sirs,' he said, 'if I have deserved your favour, do not pass by my humble self without a visit. Let me send for some water so that you may wash your feet and rest under a tree; and let me fetch a little food so that you may refresh yourselves. Afterwards you may continue the journey which has brought you my way.' They said, 'Do by all means as you say.' So Abraham hurried into the tent to Sarah and said, 'Take three measures of flour quickly, knead it and make some cakes.' Then Abraham ran to the cattle, chose a fine tender calf and gave it to a servant, who hurriedly prepared it. He took curds and milk and the calf he had prepared, set it before them, and waited on them himself under the tree while they ate. They asked him where Sarah his wife

was, and he said, 'There, in the tent.' The stranger said, 'About this time
next year I will be sure to come back to you, and Sarah your wife shall
have a son.' Now Sarah was listening at the opening of the tent, and
he was close beside it. Both Abraham and Sarah had grown very old,
and Sarah was past the age of child-bearing. So Sarah laughed to herself and said, 'I am past bearing children now that I am out of my time,
and my husband is old.' The Lord said to Abraham, 'Why did Sarah
laugh and say, "Shall I indeed bear a child when I am old?" Is anything impossible for the Lord? In due season I will come back to you,
about this time next year, and Sarah shall have a son.' Sarah lied because she was frightened, and denied that she had laughed; but he
said, 'Yes, you did laugh.'   [Gen. 18:1b–15]

Sarah compounds her guilt by lying. Most people—including ourselves—have a tendency to idealize the ancestors and heroes of
their nation. This story is a good example of the remarkable
candor with which the Hebrews spoke of their ancestors' imperfections.

SODOM AND GOMORRAH

Abraham generously offers to guide the strangers to the next
step on their journey: Sodom and Gomorrah, cities notorious
throughout the area for their immorality.

The men set out and looked down towards Sodom, and Abraham
went with them to start them on their way. The Lord thought to himself,
'Shall I conceal from Abraham what I intend to do? He will become a
great and powerful nation, and all nations on earth will pray to be
blessed as he is blessed. I have taken care of him on purpose that he
may charge his sons and family after him to conform to the way of
the Lord and to do what is right and just; thus I shall fulfil all that I have
promised for him.' So the Lord said, 'There is a great outcry over Sodom
and Gomorrah; their sin is very grave. I must go down and see whether
their deeds warrant the outcry which has reached me. I am resolved to
know the truth.'   [Gen. 18:16–21]

Note the anthropomorphic description of God: he is indecisive
("Shall I tell Abraham?") and has to visit the cities in order to
see them. In the conversation with Abraham which follows, God
is perceived as a tough wheeler-dealer with whom man must try
to drive a hard bargain.

When the men turned and went towards Sodom, Abraham remained standing before the Lord. Abraham drew near him and said, 'Wilt thou really sweep away good and bad together? Suppose there are fifty good men in the city; wilt thou really sweep it away, and not pardon the place because of the fifty good men? Far be it from thee to do this —to kill good and bad together; for then the good would suffer with the bad. Far be it from thee. Shall not the judge of all the earth do what is just?' The Lord said, 'If I find in the city of Sodom fifty good men, I will pardon the whole place for their sake.' Abraham replied, 'May I presume to speak to the Lord, dust and ashes that I am: suppose there are five short of the fifty good men? Wilt thou destroy the whole city for a mere five men?' He said, 'If I find forty-five there I will not destroy it.' Abraham spoke again, 'Suppose forty can be found there?'; and he said, 'For the sake of the forty I will not do it.' Then Abraham said, 'Please do not be angry, O Lord, if I speak again: suppose thirty can be found there?' He answered, 'If I find thirty there I will not do it.' Abraham continued, 'May I presume to speak to the Lord: suppose twenty can be found there?' He replied, 'For the sake of the twenty I will not destroy it.' Abraham said, 'I pray thee not to be angry, O Lord, if I speak just once more: suppose ten can be found there?' He said, 'For the sake of the ten I will not destroy it.' When the Lord had finished talking with Abraham, he left him, and Abraham returned home.

[Gen. 18:22–33]

Despite its glaringly anthropopathic description of God, this story has tremendous significance. On one level it illustrates how the goodness of a few can have dramatic effects on the lives of many. On a deeper level, however, Abraham's question of God ("Shall not the judge of the earth do what is just?") springs from a great insight: God must be *at least* as moral—as just—as man. Even the sophisticated Greeks centuries later believed in gods whose lives were characterized by immoral antics. For the Hebrews, apparently from the start, God and morality were inseparable.

Apparently not even ten righteous men could be found and the cities were destroyed. God's "angels" (the word means messengers; there is no reason to think they had wings or white robes or were different from human beings) now appear to investigate Sodom, Lot's home town.

The two angels came to Sodom in the evening, and Lot was sitting in the gateway of the city. When he saw them he rose to meet them and bowed low with his face to the ground. He said, 'I pray you, sirs, turn aside to my humble home, spend the night there and wash your feet; you can rise early and continue your journey.' 'No,' they answered, 'we will spend the night in the street.' But Lot was so insistent that they did turn aside and enter his house. He prepared a meal for them, baking unleavened cakes, and they ate them. Before they lay down to sleep, the men of Sodom, both young and old, surrounded the house—everyone without exception. They called to Lot and asked him where the men were who had entered his house that night. 'Bring them out,' they shouted, 'so that we can have intercourse with them.'   [Gen. 19:1–5]

Sodomy, unnatural sexual intercourse, gets its name from Sodom.

Lot went out into the doorway to them, closed the door behind him and said, 'No, my friends, do not be so wicked. Look, I have two daughters, both virgins; let me bring them out to you, and you can do what you like with them; but do not touch these men, because they have come under the shelter of my roof.' They said, 'Out of our way! This man has come and settled here as an alien, and does he now take it upon himself to judge us? We will treat you worse than them.'

The two men said to Lot, 'Have you anyone else here, sons-in-law, sons, or daughters, or any who belong to you in the city? Get them out of this place, because we are going to destroy it. The outcry against it has been so great that the Lord has sent us to destroy it.' So Lot went out and spoke to his intended sons-in-law. He said, 'Be quick and leave this place; the Lord is going to destroy the city.' But they did not take him seriously.

As soon as it was dawn, the angels urged Lot to go, saying, 'Be quick, take your wife and your two daughters who are here, or you will be swept away when the city is punished.' When he lingered, they took him by the hand, with his wife and his daughters, and, because the Lord had spared him, led him on until he was outside the city. When they had brought them out, they said, 'Flee for your lives; do not look back and do not stop anywhere in the Plain. Flee to the hills or you will be swept away.' And then the Lord rained down fire and brimstone from the skies on Sodom and Gomorrah. He overthrew those cities and destroyed all the Plain, with everyone living there and everything growing in the ground.   [Gen. 19:6–9a, 12–17, 24–25]

Modern archeology has identified Sodom and Gomorrah as the two cities which now lie buried in shallow water at the southern end of the Dead Sea. These cities, located on a geological fault at 1000 feet below sea level, were destroyed about this time by an earthquake and burned by inflammable natural gas (brimstone) vapors released in the earthquake. The destruction of these cities was a natural disaster widely known in the ancient world. The Hebrews interpreted the event as a sure sign of divine justice.

Lot readily accepted God's warning. He fled the city without looking back.

But Lot's wife, behind him, looked back, and she turned into a pillar of salt.   [Gen. 19:26]

Lot's wife showed, by looking back at Sodom, that she preferred the immorality of Sodom to obeying the will of God. We are told, puzzlingly, that she became a pillar of salt. This could mean either that she tarried in the city and was buried in the fine ash from the natural gas explosions, or, more symbolically, that she became morally as petrified and sterile as a cake of salt.

Next morning Abraham rose early and went to the place where he had stood in the presence of the Lord. He looked down towards Sodom and Gomorrah and all the wide extent of the Plain, and there he saw thick smoke rising high from the earth like the smoke of a lime-kiln. Thus, when God destroyed the cities of the Plain, he thought of Abraham and rescued Lot from the disaster, the overthrow of the cities where he had been living.   [Gen. 19:27–29]

ABRAHAM AND ISAAC

In fulfillment of the promise, Sarah gives birth to a son.

The Lord showed favour to Sarah as he had promised, and made good what he had said about her. She conceived and bore a son to Abraham for his old age, at the time which God had appointed. The son whom Sarah bore to him, Abraham named Isaac. When Isaac was eight days old Abraham circumcised him, as God had commanded.
                                                                      [Gen. 21:1–4]

For years, as they wandered, precariously searching each day for water and land, Abraham and Sarah had lived with the lonely sadness of having no descendant. It is not difficult to imagine the joy they felt at Isaac's birth.

Genesis, however, quickly shatters this joyful mood by re-counting next an event which occurs during Isaac's adolescence.

The time came when God put Abraham to the test. 'Abraham,' he called, and Abraham replied, 'Here I am.' God said, 'Take your son Isaac, your only son, whom you love, and go to the land of Moriah. There you shall offer him as a sacrifice on one of the hills which I will show you.'

[Gen. 22:1–2]

The sacrifice of children to win the favor of a god was the common practice of peoples throughout the Fertile Crescent. Abraham came now to believe that God required of him the sacrifice of what was most precious to him, his son Isaac. Abraham's faith in God had been tested over and over in the many years of wandering after God's call; now his faith undergoes the supreme test. Though God had given him a son and promised to bless his descendants, God seemed now to break his promise.

So Abraham rose early in the morning and saddled his ass, and he took with him two of his men and his son Isaac; and he split the firewood for the sacrifice, and set out for the place of which God had spoken. On the third day Abraham looked up and saw the place in the distance. He said to his men, 'Stay here with the ass while I and the boy go over there; and when we have worshipped we will come back to you.' So Abraham took the wood for the sacrifice and laid it on his son Isaac's shoulder; he himself carried the fire and the knife, and the two of them went on together. Isaac said to Abraham, 'Father,' and he answered, 'What is it, my son?' Isaac said, 'Here are the fire and the wood, but where is the young beast for the sacrifice?' Abraham answered, 'God will provide himself with a young beast for a sacrifice, my son.' And the two of them went on together and came to the place of which God had spoken. There Abraham built an altar and arranged the wood. He bound his son Isaac and laid him on the altar on top of the wood. Then he stretched out his hand and took the knife to kill his son; but the angel of the Lord called to him from heaven, 'Abraham, Abraham.' He answered, 'Here I am.' The angel of the Lord said, 'Do not raise your hand against the boy; do not touch him. Now I know that you are a God-fearing man. You have not withheld from me your son, your only son.' Abraham looked up, and there he saw a ram caught by its horns in a thicket. So he went and took the ram and offered it as a sacrifice instead of his son. Then the angel of the Lord called from heaven a second time to Abraham, 'This is the word of the Lord: By my own self I swear: inasmuch as you have done this and have not withheld your son, your only son, I will bless you abundantly and greatly multiply your descendants until they are as numerous as the stars in the sky and the grains of sand on the sea-shore. Your descendants shall possess the cities of their enemies. All nations on earth shall pray to be blessed as your descendants are blessed, and this because you have obeyed me.'   [Gen. 22:3–13, 15–18]

Put to the test, Abraham shows that, even though he could not understand God's ways, he nevertheless trusted God and was prepared to obey him even if it involved giving up what was most precious to him. Then as he was about to sacrifice his son, he realized, as clearly as if a messenger from heaven had proclaimed it, that God wanted not his son's death, but rather a demonstration of Abraham's trust.

We may have difficulty understanding how Abraham could have believed initially that God wanted him to offer his son as a sacrifice. (And, in fact, the Hebrews later became the first Middle Eastern people to forbid child sacrifice as contrary to God's will.) We should perhaps pause for a moment, however, to ponder the fact that no century has seen the lives of young men sacrificed on as great a scale as has the twentieth. With fervor and zeal fathers have proudly sent their sons to die sacrificially for what the fathers believed were worthwhile causes.

With this incident we conclude our study of the father of Israel. Abraham's greatness lay not in great charm, military skill, political shrewdness, or even leadership ability. He was a simple man of faith, outstandingly generous, and able to endure with patience endless trials and uncertainties in order to do what he believed was right. His life revealed what Israel discovered only after great hardship: that men's ultimate well being lies not in earthly power (money, weapons, influence) but in relationship with God.

Chapter 2

ISAAC AND JACOB

Abraham forbade his son Isaac to marry a Canaanite woman and found a suitable wife, Rebecca, for him from among his own people. To have allowed him (or others of the tribe) to marry outside the tribe would have meant the loss of tribal identity and the betrayal of the tribe's special calling.

Rebecca gave birth to twin sons. The older, Esau, was a hearty outdoors man, strong, hairy, a skillful hunter, quick-tempered and mercurial. He was his father Isaac's favorite. The younger twin, Jacob, was a quiet, pensive homebody, his mother's favorite. Hostility between the boys was natural. (Scholars believe the relationship of Jacob and Esau may reflect some of the tensions between the Hebrews and their near but different neighbors, the Edomites.)

One day Jacob prepared a broth and when Esau came in from the country, exhausted, he said to Jacob, 'I am exhausted; let me swallow some of that red broth': this is why he was called Edom ['Red']. Jacob said, 'Not till you sell me your rights as the first-born.' Esau replied, 'I am at death's door; what use is my birthright to me?' Jacob said, 'Not till you swear!'; so he swore an oath and sold his birthright to Jacob. Then Jacob gave Esau bread and the lentil broth, and he ate and drank and went away without more ado. Thus Esau showed how little he valued his birthright.   [Gen. 25:29–34]

The birthright was the position of honor which the eldest son held as head of the family; it also involved a double share in the inheritance. Esau was unstable and short-sighted, giving away his birthright for the momentary indulgence of a bowl of soup. A modern psychologist would evaluate Esau's action as an inability to postpone gratification. He clearly lacked the qualities necessary to assume the leadership role he was supposed to inherit from his father. The ambitious Jacob, on the other hand, ruthlessly took advantage not only of Esau but of their father Isaac.

When Isaac grew old and his eyes became so dim that he could not see, he called his elder son Esau and said to him, 'My son,' and he answered, 'Here I am.' Isaac said, 'Listen now: I am old and I do not know when I may die. Take your hunting gear, your quiver and your bow, and go out into the country and get me some venison. Then make me a savoury dish of the kind I like, and bring it to me to eat so that I may give you my blessing before I die.'　　　　　　[Gen. 27:1–4]

Before he dies the aged and blind Isaac prepares to give his blessing (an irrevocable will which passes on material possessions and spiritual strengths). Isaac's blindness has more than literal significance. Isaac played favorites, blinding himself to Esau's weakness, and was careless of what is precious, blind to the danger of theft.

Now Rebecca was listening as Isaac talked to his son Esau. When Esau went off into the country to find some venison and bring it home, she said to her son Jacob, 'I heard your father talking to your brother Esau, and he said, "Bring me some venison and make it into a savoury dish so that I may eat it and bless you in the presence of the Lord before I die." Listen to me, my son, and do what I tell you. Go to the flock and pick me out two fine young kids, and I will make them into a savoury dish for your father, of the kind he likes. Then take them in to your father, and he will eat them so that he may bless you before he dies.' Jacob said to his mother Rebecca, 'But my brother Esau is a hairy man, and my skin is smooth. Suppose my father feels me, he will know I am tricking him and I shall bring a curse upon myself instead of a blessing.' His mother answered him, 'Let the curse fall on me, my son, but do as I say; go and bring me the kids.' So Jacob fetched them and brought them to his mother, who made them into a savoury dish of the kind that his father liked. Then Rebecca took her elder son's clothes, Esau's best clothes which she kept by her in the house, and put them on her younger son Jacob. She put the goatskins on his hands and on the smooth nape of his neck; and she handed her son Jacob the savoury dish and the bread she had made. He came to his father and said, 'Father.' He answered, 'Yes, my son; who are you?' Jacob answered his father, 'I am Esau, your elder son. I have done as you told me. Come,

sit up and eat some of my venison, so that you may give me your blessing.' Isaac said to his son, 'What is this that you found so quickly?', and
Jacob answered, 'It is what the Lord your God put in my way.'

[Gen. 27:5–20]

Jacob not only lies to his father about who he is; he blasphe-
mously claims that *God* gave him the venison.

Isaac then said to Jacob, 'Come close and let me feel you, my son,
to see whether you are really my son Esau.' When Jacob came close to
his father, Isaac felt him and said, 'The voice is Jacob's voice, but the
hands are the hands of Esau.' He did not recognize him because his
hands were hairy like Esau's, and that is why he blessed him. He said,
'Are you really my son Esau?', and he answered, 'Yes.' Then Isaac said,
'Bring me some of your venison to eat, my son, so that I may give you
my blessing.' Then Jacob brought it to him, and he ate it; he brought
wine also, and he drank it. Then his father Isaac said to him, 'Come
near, my son, and kiss me.' So he came near and kissed him, and when
Isaac smelt the smell of his clothes he blessed him and said:

> 'Ah! The smell of my son is like the smell of open country
> blessed by the Lord.
> God give you dew from heaven
> and the richness of the earth,
> corn and new wine in plenty!
> Peoples shall serve you,
> nations bow down to you.
> Be lord over your brothers;
> may your mother's sons bow down to you.
> A curse upon those who curse you;
> a blessing on those who bless you!'

Isaac finished blessing Jacob; and Jacob had scarcely left his father
Isaac's presence, when his brother Esau came in from his hunting. He
too made a savoury dish and brought it to his father. He said, 'Come,
father, and eat some of my venison, so that you may give me your
blessing.' His father Isaac said, 'Who are you?' He said, 'I am Esau,
your elder son.' Then Isaac became greatly agitated and said, 'Then
who was it that hunted and brought me venison? I ate it all before you
came in and I blessed him, and the blessing will stand.' When Esau
heard what his father said, he gave a loud and bitter cry and said,
'Bless me too, father.' But Isaac said, 'Your brother came treacherously

and took away your blessing.' Esau said, 'He is rightly called Jacob. This is the second time he has supplanted me. He took away my right as the first-born and now he has taken away my blessing. Have you kept back any blessing for me?' Isaac answered, 'I have made him lord over you, and I have given him all his brothers as slaves. I have bestowed upon him corn and new wine for his sustenance. What is there left that I can do for you, my son?'

Esau bore a grudge against Jacob because of the blessing which his father had given him, and he said to himself, 'The time of mourning for my father will soon be here; then I will kill my brother Jacob.' When Rebecca was told what her elder son Esau was saying, she called her younger son Jacob, and she said to him, 'Esau your brother is threatening to kill you. Now, my son, listen to me. Slip away at once to my brother Laban in Harran. Stay with him for a while until your brother's anger cools. When it has subsided and he forgets what you have done to him, I will send and fetch you back. Why should I lose you both in one day?'   [Gen. 27:21–37, 41–45]

In this sad story of human weakness everyone loses. The blind Isaac cannot bless his favorite son. Esau is cheated by his brother's ambition and jealousy. The favorite-playing Rebecca is left alone as her son is forced to flee for his life. We must again note the Hebrews' remarkable candor: Jacob, destined to bear the patriarchal leadership, is shown to be a ruthless, conniving, despicable liar and deceiver, about as far removed from the ideally heroic and virtuous as it is possible to be.

JACOB IN EXILE

Leaving behind his dying father, his vengeful brother, and his mother, Jacob flees to his mother's family.

Jacob set out from Beersheba and went on his way towards Harran. He came to a certain place and stopped there for the night, because the sun had set; and, taking one of the stones there, he made it a pillow for his head and lay down to sleep. He dreamt that he saw a ladder, which rested on the ground with its top reaching to heaven, and angels of God were going up and down upon it. The Lord was standing beside him and said, 'I am the Lord, the God of your father Abraham and the God of Isaac. This land on which you are lying I will give to you and your descendants. They shall be countless as the dust upon the earth, and you shall spread far and wide, to north and south,

to east and west. All the families of the earth shall pray to be blessed
as you and your descendants are blessed. I will be with you, and I will
protect you wherever you go and will bring you back to this land; for
I will not leave you until I have done all that I have promised.'

[Gen. 28:10–15]

It is often in the wildernesses of life, when we are alone and
least expect it, that God becomes strikingly present. So it was
with Jacob the weary traveler. Though we have seen him only
as a self-centered and worldly, ambitious young man, in lonely
exile he becomes sensitive to the presence of God. Many years
later in exile and imprisonment the Jews looked back on this
story with great joy: God's love for Jacob continued even when
he was away from his home and when he had done nothing to
deserve that love. God renews to Jacob the promise he made to
Abraham and Isaac.

Jacob woke from his sleep and said, 'Truly the Lord is in this place,
and I did not know it.' Then he was afraid and said, 'How fearsome is
this place! This is no other than the house of God, this is the gate of
heaven.' Jacob rose early in the morning, took the stone on which he
had laid his head, set it up as a sacred pillar and poured oil on the top
of it. He named that place Beth-El; but the earlier name of the city was
Luz.
  Thereupon Jacob made his vow: 'If God will be with me, if he will
protect me on my journey and give me food to eat and clothes to wear,
and I come back safely to my father's house, then the Lord shall be my
God, and this stone which I have set up as a sacred pillar shall be a
house of God. And of all that thou givest me, I will without fail allot a
tenth part to thee.'   [Gen. 28:16–22]

Though deeply moved by his experience, Jacob's reaction is still
characteristically selfish. There is in his response no spontaneous
openness or gratitude. He bargains with God: *if* God does certain
things for him, *then* he will worship God and give him a cut of
his profits. Though his response is hardly that of a spiritual giant,
his offer to God of a tenth of his possessions is at least a small
step in directing his abilities toward something beyond his own
selfish ambitions.

Finally Jacob reaches the family of Laban, his mother's brother.

Jacob continued his journey and came to the land of the eastern tribes. There he saw a well in the open country and three flocks of sheep lying beside it, because the flocks were watered from that well. Over its mouth was a huge stone, and all the herdsmen used to gather there and roll it off the mouth of the well and water the flocks; then they would put it back in its place over the well. Jacob said to them, 'Where are you from, my friends?' 'We are from Harran', they replied. He asked them if they knew Laban the grandson of Nahor. They answered, 'Yes, we do.' 'Is he well?' Jacob asked; and they answered, 'Yes, he is well, and here is his daughter Rachel coming with the flock.' While he was talking to them, Rachel came up with her father's flock, for she was a shepherdess. When Jacob saw Rachel, the daughter of Laban his mother's brother, with Laban's flock, he stepped forward, rolled the stone off the mouth of the well and watered Laban's sheep. He kissed Rachel, and was moved to tears. He told her that he was her father's kinsman and Rebecca's son; so she ran and told her father. When Laban heard the news of his sister's son Jacob, he ran to meet him, embraced him, kissed him warmly and welcomed him to his home. Jacob told Laban everything, and Laban said, 'Yes, you are my own flesh and blood.' So Jacob stayed with him for a whole month.

Laban said to Jacob, 'Why should you work for me for nothing simply because you are my kinsman? Tell me what your wages ought to be.' Now Laban had two daughters: the elder was called Leah, and the younger Rachel. Leah was dull-eyed, but Rachel was graceful and beautiful. Jacob had fallen in love with Rachel and he said, 'I will work seven years for your younger daughter Rachel.' Laban replied, 'It is better that I should give her to you than to anyone else; stay with me.' So Jacob worked seven years for Rachel, and they seemed like a few days because he loved her. Then Jacob said to Laban, 'I have served my time. Give me my wife so that we may sleep together.' So Laban gathered all the men of the place together and gave a feast. In the evening he took his daughter Leah and brought her to Jacob, and Jacob slept with her. But when morning came, Jacob saw that it was Leah and said to Laban, 'What have you done to me? Did I not work for Rachel? Why have you deceived me?' Laban answered, 'In our country it is not right to give the younger sister in marriage before the elder. Go through with the seven days' feast for the elder, and the younger shall be given you in return for a further seven years' work.' Jacob agreed, and completed the seven days for Leah.

Then Laban gave Jacob his daughter Rachel as wife; and he gave his slave-girl Bilhah to serve his daughter Rachel. Jacob slept with Rachel also; he loved her rather than Leah, and he worked for Laban for a further seven years.   [Gen. 29:1–6, 9–23, 25–30]

As an oriental bride, Leah was heavily veiled. The deceiver Jacob now has the experience of being deceived.

Jacob remains with Laban's family for twenty years. Though his tender and abiding love for Rachel shows he is no longer purely selfish, he is still far from being a good man. Leah bears him son after son but he neglects her. By shrewd scheming and skillful management, the ambitious Jacob increases the size of his herds many times over, rousing Laban's sons to jealousy.

Jacob learnt that Laban's sons were saying, 'Jacob has taken everything that was our father's, and all his wealth has come from our father's property.' He also noticed that Laban was not so well disposed to him as he had once been. Then the Lord said to Jacob, 'Go back to the land of your fathers and to your kindred. I will be with you.' So Jacob sent to fetch Rachel and Leah to his flocks out in the country and said to them, 'I see that your father is not as well disposed to me as once he was; yet the God of my father has been with me. You know how I have served your father to the best of my power, but he has cheated me and changed my wages ten times over. Yet God did not let him do me any harm. If Laban said, "The spotted ones shall be your wages," then all the flock bore spotted young; and if he said, "The striped ones shall be your wages," then all the flock bore striped young.' Rachel and Leah answered him, 'We no longer have any part or lot in our father's house. Does he not look on us as foreigners, now that he has sold us and spent on himself the whole of the money paid for us? But all the wealth which God has saved from our father's clutches is ours and our children's. Now do everything that God has said.' Jacob at once set his sons and his wives on camels, and drove off all the herds and livestock which he had acquired in Paddan-aram, to go to his father Isaac in Canaan.

When Laban the Aramaean had gone to shear his sheep, Rachel stole her father's household gods, and Jacob deceived Laban, keeping his departure secret. So Jacob ran away with all that he had, crossed the River and made for the hill-country of Gilead. Three days later, when Laban heard that Jacob had run away, he took his kinsmen with him, pursued Jacob for seven days and caught up with him in the hill-country of Gilead. But God came to Laban in a dream by night and said to him, 'Be careful to say nothing to Jacob, either good or bad.'

When Laban overtook him, Jacob had pitched his tent in the hill-country of Gilead, and Laban pitched his in the company of his kinsmen in the same hill-country. Laban said to Jacob, 'What have you done? You have deceived me and carried off my daughters as though they were captives taken in war. Why did you slip away secretly without telling me? I would have set you on your way with songs and the music of tambourines and harps. You did not even let me kiss my daughters and their children. In this you were at fault. It is in my power to do you an injury, but yesterday the God of your father spoke to me; he told me to be careful to say nothing to you, either good or bad. I know that you went away because you were homesick and pining for your father's house, but why did you steal my gods?'

Jacob answered, 'I was afraid; I thought you would take your daughters from me by force. Whoever is found in possession of your gods shall die for it. Let our kinsmen here be witnesses: point out anything I have that is yours, and take it back.' Jacob did not know that Rachel had stolen the gods. So Laban went into Jacob's tent and Leah's tent and that of the two slave-girls, but he found nothing. When he came out of Leah's tent he went into Rachel's. Now she had taken the household gods and put them in the camel-bag and was sitting on them. Laban went through everything in the tent and found nothing. Rachel said to her father, 'Do not take it amiss, sir, that I cannot rise in your presence: the common lot of woman is upon me.' So for all his search Laban did not find his household gods.

Jacob was angry, and he expostulated with Laban, exclaiming, 'What have I done wrong? What is my offence, that you have come after me in hot pursuit and gone through all my possessions? Have you found anything belonging to your household? If so, set it here in front of my kinsmen and yours, and let them judge between the two of us. In all the twenty years I have been with you, your ewes and she-goats have never miscarried; I have not eaten the rams of your flocks; I have never brought to you the body of any animal mangled by wild beasts, but I bore the loss myself; you claimed compensation from me for anything stolen by day or by night. This was the way of it: by day the heat consumed me and the frost by night, and sleep deserted me. For twenty years I have been in your household. I worked for you fourteen years to win your two daughters and six years for your flocks, and you changed my wages ten times over. If the God of my father,

the God of Abraham and the Fear of Isaac, had not been with me,
you would have sent me away empty-handed. But God saw my labour
and my hardships, and last night he rebuked you.'

Laban answered Jacob, 'The daughters are my daughters, the children are my children, the flocks are my flocks; all that you see is mine.
But as for my daughters, what can I do today about them and the
children they have borne? Come now, we will make an agreement,
you and I, and let it stand as a witness between us. May the Lord
watch between you and me, when we are parted from each other's
sight. If you ill-treat my daughters or take other wives beside them
when no one is there to see, then God be witness between us.' Laban
said further to Jacob, 'Here is this cairn, and here the pillar which I
have set up between us. This cairn is witness and the pillar is witness: I
for my part will not pass beyond this cairn to your side, and you for
your part shall not pass beyond this cairn and this pillar to my side to
do an injury, otherwise the God of Abraham and the God of Nahor
will judge between us.' And Jacob swore this oath in the name of the
Fear of Isaac his father. He slaughtered an animal for sacrifice, there
in the hill-country, and summoned his kinsmen to the feast. So they
ate together and spent the night there.

Laban rose early in the morning, kissed his daughters and their child-
dren, blessed them and went home again. [Gen. 31:1–9, 14–44, 49–55]

Though the story of Jacob and Laban is a sorry recital of intra-
family haggling, deception, and cheating, it does end with reconciliation.

Wishing now to settle in Canaan, Jacob seeks to bring about
a reconciliation with his brother Esau. He sends his servants to
Esau to present his request with respect and humility.

Jacob sent messengers on ahead to his brother Esau to the district
of Seir in the Edomite country, and this is what he told them to say to
Esau, 'My lord, your servant Jacob says, I have been living with Laban
and have stayed there till now. I have oxen, asses, and sheep, and
male and female slaves, and I have sent to tell you this, my lord, so
that I may win your favour.' The messengers returned to Jacob and
said, 'We met your brother Esau already on the way to meet you with
four hundred men.'   [Gen. 32:3–6]

Jacob, filled with past guilt, hopes that his brother comes as a
friend, but fears he comes as an enemy to destroy him.

Jacob, much afraid and distressed, divided the people with him, as well as the sheep, cattle, and camels, into two companies, thinking that, if Esau should come upon one company and destroy it, the other company would survive. Jacob said, 'O God of my father Abraham, God of my father Isaac, O Lord at whose bidding I came back to my own country and to my kindred, and who didst promise me prosperity, I am not worthy of all the true and steadfast love which thou hast shown to me thy servant. When I crossed the Jordan, I had nothing but the staff in my hand; now I have two companies. Save me, I pray, from my brother Esau, for I am afraid that he may come and destroy me, sparing neither mother nor child. But thou didst say, I will prosper you and will make your descendants like the sand of the sea, which is beyond all counting.'   [Gen. 32:7–12]

Though Jacob sends wave after wave of presents ahead to appease his brother, he realizes human scheming alone won't deliver him. In mortal danger he turns to God, showing a deepened awareness of himself: "I am not worthy of all the true and steadfast love which thou hast shown me."

During the night Jacob rose, took his two wives, his two slave-girls, and his eleven sons, and crossed the ford of Jabbok. He took them and sent them across the gorge with all that he had. So Jacob was left alone, and a man wrestled with him there till daybreak. When the man saw that he could not throw Jacob, he struck him in the hollow of his thigh, so that Jacob's hip was dislocated as they wrestled. The man said, 'Let me go, for day is breaking,' but Jacob replied, 'I will not let you go unless you bless me.' He said to Jacob, 'What is your name?', and he answered, 'Jacob.' The man said, 'Your name shall no longer be Jacob, but Israel, because you strove with God and with men, and prevailed.' Jacob said, 'Tell me, I pray, your name.' He replied, 'Why do you ask my name?', but he gave him his blessing there. Jacob called the place Peniel, 'because', he said, 'I have seen God face to face and my life is spared.'   [Gen. 32:22–30]

What took place during the lonely night at the river crossing is unclear. What is clear is that Jacob, after years of trial and exile, filled with guilt about the past and anxiety about the future, tossed and turned anxiously in his sleep and appears to have come to grips with who he is and what he values. As a result of this self-searching struggle he becomes, in a sense, a new person.

Symbolically he wins a new name, Israel ("he struggles with God"), and a blessing as he meets the trial of the new day.

The story draws to a dramatic and poignant close:

> Jacob raised his eyes and saw Esau coming towards him with four hundred men; so he divided the children between Leah and Rachel and the two slave-girls. He put the slave-girls with their children in front, Leah with her children next, and Rachel with Joseph last. He then went on ahead of them, bowing low to the ground seven times as he approached his brother. Esau ran to meet him and embraced him; he threw his arms round him and kissed him, and they wept. [Gen. 33:1–4]

Though we know Esau to have been short-sighted, foolish, and quick to anger, we now see him equally quick to forgive and to forget. With spontaneous affection he runs to embrace the fearful Jacob.

> Esau said, 'What was all that company of yours that I met?' And he answered, 'It was meant to win favour with you, my lord.' Esau answered, 'I have more than enough. Keep what is yours, my brother.' But Jacob said, 'On no account: if I have won your favour, then, I pray, accept this gift from me; for, you see, I come into your presence as into that of a god, and you receive me favourably. Accept this gift which I bring you; for God has been gracious to me, and I have all I want.' So he urged him, and he accepted it.   [Gen. 33:8–11]

Chapter 3

JOSEPH

Jacob (now called Israel) settled in Canaan with his whole family. Of all his children, Jacob's favorite was Joseph, his eleventh son, but his first son by Rachel. Joseph was therefore spoiled; the elegant coat which his father gave him indicates that, alone of the sons, he did not have to work.

When Joseph was a boy of seventeen, he used to accompany his brothers, the sons of Bilhah and Zilpah, his father's wives, when they were in charge of the flock; and he brought their father a bad report of them. Now Israel loved Joseph more than any other of his sons, because he was a child of his old age, and he made him a long, sleeved robe. When his brothers saw that their father loved him more than any of them, they hated him and could not say a kind word to him. Joseph had a dream; and when he told it to his brothers, they hated him still more. He said to them, 'Listen to this dream I have had. We were in the field binding sheaves, and my sheaf rose on end and stood upright, and your sheaves gathered round and bowed low before my sheaf.' His brothers answered him, 'Do you think you will one day be a king and lord it over us?' and they hated him still more because of his dreams and what he said. He had another dream, which he told to his father and his brothers. He said, 'Listen: I have had another dream. The sun and moon and eleven stars were bowing down to me.' When he told it to his father and his brothers his father took him to task: 'What is this dream of yours?' he said. 'Must we come and bow low to the ground before you, I and your mother and your brothers?' His brothers were jealous of him, but his father did not forget. [Gen. 37:2b–11]

Psychologists tell us that dreams often express a wish. The young Joseph's dreams reveal him as an egotist who thought he was superior to his brothers.

Rebelling against their arrogant tattletale brother and their father's favoritism, the brothers determine to rid the family of Joseph. With supreme irony, Jacob—the man who betrayed his brother and deceived his father—is betrayed and deceived by his own sons.

Joseph's brothers went to mind their father's flocks in Shechem. Israel said to him, 'Your brothers are minding the flocks in Shechem; come, I will send you to them,' and he said, 'I am ready.' He said to him, 'Go and see if all is well with your brothers and the sheep, and bring me back word.'

So Joseph followed his brothers and he found them in Dothan. They saw him in the distance, and before he reached them, they plotted to kill him. They said to each other, 'Here comes that dreamer. Now is our chance; let us kill him and throw him into one of these pits and say that a wild beast has devoured him. Then we shall see what will come of his dreams.' When Reuben heard, he came to his rescue, urging them not to take his life. 'Let us have no bloodshed,' he said. 'Throw him into this pit in the wilderness, but do him no bodily harm.' He meant to save him from them so as to restore him to his father. When Joseph came up to his brothers, they stripped him of the long, sleeved robe which he was wearing, took him and threw him into the pit. The pit was empty and had no water in it.

Then they sat down to eat some food and, looking up, they saw an Ishmaelite caravan coming in from Gilead on the way down to Egypt, with camels carrying gum tragacanth and balm and myrrh. Judah said to his brothers, 'What shall we gain by killing our brother and concealing his death? Why not sell him to the Ishmaelites? Let us do him no harm, for he is our brother, our own flesh and blood'; and his brothers agreed with him. Meanwhile some Midianite merchants passed by and drew Joseph up out of the pit. They sold him for twenty pieces of silver to the Ishmaelites, and they brought Joseph to Egypt. When Reuben went back to the pit, Joseph was not there. He rent his clothes and went back to his brothers and said, 'The boy is not there. Where can I go?'

Joseph's brothers took his robe, killed a goat and dipped it in the goat's blood. Then they tore the robe, the long, sleeved robe, brought it to their father and said, 'Look what we have found. Do you recognize it? Is this your son's robe or not?' Jacob did recognize it, and he replied, 'It is my son's robe. A wild beast has devoured him. Joseph has been torn to pieces.' Jacob rent his clothes, put on sackcloth and mourned his son for a long time. His sons and daughters all tried to comfort him, but he refused to be comforted. He said, 'I will go to my grave mourning for my son.' Thus Joseph's father wept for him. Meanwhile the Midianites had sold Joseph in Egypt to Potiphar, one of Pharaoh's eunuchs, the captain of the guard. [Gen. 37:12–14, 17b–36]

JOSEPH IN EGYPT

In disaster some people give up in despair. "God was with Joseph," however. Though his fall from favorite son to slave was great, he made the best of a bad situation and created a worthwhile new life.

The Lord was with Joseph and he prospered. He lived in the house of his Egyptian master, who saw that the Lord was with him and was giving him success in all that he undertook. Thus Joseph found favour with his master, and he became his personal servant. Indeed, his master put him in charge of his household and entrusted him with all that he had. From the time that he put him in charge of his household and all his property, the Lord blessed the Egyptian's household for Joseph's sake. The blessing of the Lord was on all that was his in house and field. He left everything he possessed in Joseph's care, and concerned himself with nothing but the food he ate.

Now Joseph was handsome and good-looking, and a time came when his master's wife took notice of him and said, 'Come and lie with me.' But he refused and said to her, 'Think of my master. He does not know as much as I do about his own house, and he has entrusted me with all he has. He has given me authority in this house second only to his own, and has withheld nothing from me except you, because you are his wife. How can I do anything so wicked, and sin against God?' She kept asking Joseph day after day, but he refused to lie with her and be in her company. One day he came into the house as usual to do his work, when none of the men of the household were there indoors. She caught him by his cloak, saying, 'Come and lie with me,' but he left the cloak in her hands and ran out of the house. When she saw that he had left his cloak in her hands and had run out of the house, she called out to the men of the household, 'Look at this! My husband has brought in a Hebrew to make a mockery of us. He came in here to lie with me, but I gave a loud scream. When he heard me scream and call out, he left his cloak in my hand and ran off.' She kept his cloak with her until his master came home, and then she repeated her tale. She said, 'That Hebrew slave whom you brought in to make a mockery of me, has been here with me. But when I screamed for help and called out, he left his cloak in my hands and ran off.' When Joseph's master heard his wife's story of what his slave had done to her, he was furious. He took Joseph and put him in the Round Tower, where the king's prisoners were kept; and there he stayed in the Round Tower.   [Gen. 39:2–20]

As a boy Joseph had been arrogant and self-centered, yet favor was showered upon him. Now, by an ironic twist, Joseph does what is right and is punished. Angry at Joseph's moral strength (which shows up her own weakness) and embittered by this handsome man's rejection of her, Potiphar's wife gets her revenge. Once again Joseph falls from a high position to a low one.

But, again, "the Lord was with Joseph," and again Joseph makes the best of a bad situation. His imprisonment turns out to be a blessing in disguise.

But the Lord was with Joseph and kept faith with him, so that he won the favour of the governor of the Round Tower. He put Joseph in charge of all the prisoners in the tower and of all their work. He ceased to concern himself with anything entrusted to Joseph, because the Lord was with Joseph and gave him success in everything.

It happened later that the king's butler and his baker offended their master the king of Egypt. Pharaoh was angry with these two eunuchs, the chief butler and the chief baker, and he put them in custody in the house of the captain of the guard, in the Round Tower where Joseph was imprisoned. The captain of the guard appointed Joseph as their attendant, and he waited on them. One night, when they had been in prison for some time, they both had dreams, each needing its own interpretation—the king of Egypt's butler and his baker who were imprisoned in the Round Tower. When Joseph came to them in the morning, he saw that they looked dejected. So he asked these eunuchs, who were in custody with him in his master's house, why they were so downcast that day. They replied, 'We have each had a dream and there is no one to interpret it for us.' Joseph said to them, 'Does not interpretation belong to God? Tell me your dreams.' So the chief butler told Joseph his dream: 'In my dream', he said, 'there was a vine in front of me. On the vine there were three branches, and as soon as it budded, it blossomed and its clusters ripened into grapes.

Now I had Pharaoh's cup in my hand, and I plucked the grapes, crushed them into Pharaoh's cup and put the cup into Pharaoh's hand.' Joseph said to him, 'This is the interpretation. The three branches are three days: within three days Pharaoh will raise you and restore you to your post, and then you will put the cup into Pharaoh's hands as you used to do when you were his butler. But when things go well with you, if you think of me, keep faith with me and bring my case to Pharaoh's notice and help me to get out of this house. By force I was carried off from the land of the Hebrews, and I have done nothing here to deserve being put in this dungeon.'

When the chief baker saw that Joseph had given a favourable interpretation, he said to him, 'I too had a dream, and in my dream there were three baskets of white bread on my head. In the top basket there was every kind of food which the baker prepares for Pharaoh, and the birds were eating out of the top basket on my head.' Joseph answered, 'This is the interpretation. The three baskets are three days: within three days Pharaoh will raise you and hang you up on a tree, and the birds of the air will eat your flesh.'

The third day was Pharaoh's birthday and he gave a feast for all his servants. He raised the chief butler and the chief baker in the presence of his court. He restored the chief butler to his post, and the butler put the cup into Pharaoh's hand; but he hanged the chief baker. All went as Joseph had said in interpreting the dreams for them. Even so the chief butler did not remember Joseph, but forgot him.

Nearly two years later Pharaoh had a dream: he was standing by the Nile, and there came up from the river seven cows, sleek and fat, and they grazed on the reeds. After them seven other cows came up from the river, gaunt and lean, and stood on the river bank beside the first cows. The cows that were gaunt and lean devoured the cows that were sleek and fat. Then Pharaoh woke up. He fell asleep again and had a second dream: he saw seven ears of corn, full and ripe, growing on one stalk. Growing up after them were seven other ears, thin and shrivelled by the east wind. The thin ears swallowed up the ears that were full and ripe. Then Pharaoh woke up and knew that it was a dream. When morning came, Pharaoh was troubled in mind; so he summoned all the magicians and sages of Egypt. He told them his dreams, but there was no one who could interpret them for him. Then Pharaoh's chief butler spoke up and said, 'It is time for me to recall my faults. Once Pharaoh was angry with his servants, and he imprisoned me and the chief baker in the house of the captain of the guard. One night we both had dreams, each needing its own interpretation. We had with us a young Hebrew, a slave of the captain of the guard, and we told him our dreams and he interpreted them for us, giving each man's dream its own interpretation. Each dream came true as it had been interpreted to us: I was restored to my position, and he was hanged.'

Pharaoh thereupon sent for Joseph, and they hurriedly brought him out of the dungeon. He shaved and changed his clothes, and came in to Pharaoh.   [Gen. 39:21–41:14]

Joseph's kindness to the dejected butler two years previously now pays him dividends as he is brought to the Pharaoh's attention.

Pharaoh said to him, 'I have had a dream, and no one can interpret it to me. I have heard it said that you can understand and interpret dreams.' Joseph answered, 'Not I, but God, will answer for Pharaoh's welfare.'   [Gen. 41:15–16]

This is not the sort of remark we would have anticipated from the Joseph we first met as an arrogant adolescent. Humbled by his suffering, he attributes whatever insights and qualities he has to God.

Then Pharaoh said to Joseph, 'In my dream I was standing on the bank of the Nile, and there came up from the river seven cows, fat and sleek, and they grazed on the reeds. After them seven other cows came up that were poor, very gaunt and lean; I have never seen such gaunt creatures in all Egypt. These lean, gaunt cows devoured the first cows, the fat ones. They were swallowed up, but no one could have guessed that they were in the bellies of the others, which looked as gaunt as before. Then I woke up. After I had fallen asleep again, I saw in a dream seven ears of corn, full and ripe, growing on one stalk. Growing up after them were seven other ears, shrivelled, thin, and blighted by the east wind. The thin ears swallowed up the seven ripe ears. When I told all this to the magicians, no one could explain it to me.'

Joseph said to Pharaoh, 'Pharaoh's dreams are one dream. God has told Pharaoh what he is going to do. The seven good cows are seven years, and the seven good ears of corn are seven years. It is all one dream. The seven lean and gaunt cows that came up after them are seven years, and the empty ears of corn blighted by the east wind will be seven years of famine. It is as I have said to Pharaoh: God has let Pharaoh see what he is going to do. There are to be seven years of great plenty throughout the land. After them will come seven years of famine; all the years of plenty in Egypt will be forgotten, and the famine will ruin the country. The good years will not be remembered in the land because of the famine that follows; for it will be very severe. The doubling of Pharaoh's dream means that God is already resolved to do this, and he will very soon put it into effect. Pharaoh should now look for a shrewd and intelligent man, and put him in charge of the country. This is what Pharaoh should do: appoint controllers over the land, and take one fifth of the produce of Egypt during the seven years of plenty. They should collect all this food produced in the good years that are coming and put the corn under Pharaoh's control in store in the cities, and keep it under guard. This food will be a reserve for the country against the seven years of famine which will come upon Egypt. Thus the country will not be devastated by the famine.'

The plan pleased Pharaoh and all his courtiers, and he said to them, 'Can we find a man like this man, one who has the spirit of a god in him?' He said to Joseph, 'Since a god has made all this known to you, there is no one so shrewd and intelligent as you. You shall be in charge of my household, and all my people will depend on your every word. Only my royal throne shall make me greater than you.' Pharaoh said to Joseph, 'I hereby give you authority over the whole land of Egypt.' He took off his signet-ring and put it on Joseph's finger, he had him dressed in fine linen, and hung a gold chain round his neck. He mounted him in his viceroy's chariot and men cried 'Make way!' before him. Thus Pharaoh made him ruler over all Egypt and said to him, 'I am the Pharaoh. Without your consent no man shall lift hand or foot throughout Egypt.'

Joseph was thirty years old when he entered the service of Pharaoh king of Egypt. When he took his leave of the king, he made a tour of inspection through the country. During the seven years of plenty there were abundant harvests, and Joseph gathered all the food produced in Egypt during those years and stored it in the cities, putting in each the food from the surrounding country. He stored the grain in huge quantities; it was like the sand of the sea, so much that he stopped measuring: it was beyond all measure.

When the seven years of plenty in Egypt came to an end, seven years of famine began, as Joseph had foretold. There was famine in every country, but throughout Egypt there was bread. So when the famine spread through all Egypt, the people appealed to Pharaoh for bread, and he ordered them to go to Joseph and do as he told them. In every region there was famine, and Joseph opened all the granaries and sold corn to the Egyptians, for the famine was severe. The whole world came to Egypt to buy corn from Joseph, so severe was the famine everywhere.   [Gen. 41:17–44, 46–49, 53–57]

Joseph is now the second most powerful man in Egypt, occupying the role of Prime Minister. Ancient history records a number of remarkable incidents in which slaves reached similar pinnacles of power. Many scholars believe Joseph held power in Egypt about 1680 B.C. under the Hyksos dynasty. Foreigners themselves, the Hyksos would have seen no difficulty in putting a non-Egyptian in power.

JOSEPH AND HIS BROTHERS

Joseph exercised power unselfishly and honestly for the good of all. When famine spread throughout the Fertile Crescent, Egypt alone was prepared. From all over the Near East came tribes seeking food. Among them were Joseph's brothers from Canaan.

When Jacob saw that there was corn in Egypt, he said to his sons, 'Why do you stand staring at each other? I have heard that there is corn in Egypt. Go down and buy some so that we may keep ourselves alive and not starve.' So Joseph's brothers, ten of them, went down to buy grain from Egypt, but Jacob did not let Joseph's brother Benjamin go with them, for fear that he might come to harm.

So the sons of Israel came down with everyone else to buy corn, because of the famine in Canaan. Now Joseph was governor of all Egypt, and it was he who sold the corn to all the people of the land. Joseph's brothers came and bowed to the ground before him, and when he saw his brothers, he recognized them but pretended not to know them and spoke harshly to them. 'Where do you come from?' he asked. 'From Canaan,' they answered, 'to buy food.' Although Joseph had recognized his brothers, they did not recognize him. He remembered also the dreams he had had about them; so he said to them, 'You are spies; you have come to spy out the weak points in our defences.' They answered, 'No, sir: your servants have come to buy food. We are all sons of one man. Your humble servants are honest men, we are not spies.' 'No,' he insisted, 'it is to spy out our weaknesses that you have come.' They answered him, 'Sir, there are twelve of us, all brothers, sons of one man in Canaan. The youngest is still with our father, and one has disappeared.'   [Gen. 42:1–13]

Jacob and Rachel, after Joseph's supposed death, had a twelfth and last son, Benjamin. Though Joseph bears his brothers no malice, he engages in a bit of sadism in frightening them.

But Joseph said again to them, 'No, as I said before, you are spies. This is how you shall be put to the proof: unless your youngest brother comes here, by the life of Pharaoh, you shall not leave this place. Send one of your number to bring your brother; the rest will be kept in prison. Thus your story will be tested, and we shall see whether you are telling the truth. If not, then, by the life of Pharaoh, you must be spies.' So he kept them in prison for three days.

On the third day Joseph said to the brothers, 'Do what I say and your lives will be spared; for I am a God-fearing man: If you are honest men, your brother there shall be kept in prison, and the rest of you shall take corn for your hungry households and bring your youngest brother to me; thus your words will be proved true, and you will not die.'

They said to one another, 'No doubt we deserve to be punished because of our brother, whose suffering we saw; for when he pleaded with us we refused to listen. That is why these sufferings have come upon us.'   [Gen. 42:14–21]

Joseph's demands concerning their (now) youngest brother remind them of their treatment of Joseph when he was their youngest brother. They freely confess their guilt and shame to one another, and regard the fix they are now in as just punishment for their evil deed.

But Reuben said, 'Did I not tell you not to do the boy a wrong? But you would not listen, and his blood is on our heads, and we must pay.' They did not know that Joseph understood, because he had used an interpreter. Joseph turned away from them and wept. Then, turning back, he played a trick on them. First he took Simeon and bound him before their eyes; then he gave orders to fill their bags with grain, to return each man's silver, putting it in his sack, and to give them supplies for the journey. All this was done; and they loaded the corn on to their asses and went away. When they stopped for the night, one of them opened his sack to give fodder to his ass, and there he saw his silver at the top of the pack. He said to his brothers, 'My silver has been returned to me, and here it is in my pack.' Bewildered and trembling, they said to each other, 'What is this that God has done to us?'   [Gen. 42:22–28]

The silver is the money they had paid to Joseph for the grain. They see this also as a divine punishment for what they had done to Joseph years earlier.

When they came to their father Jacob in Canaan, they told him all that had happened to them. They said, 'The man who is lord of the country spoke harshly to us and made out that we were spies. We said to him, "We are honest men, we are not spies. There are twelve of us, all brothers, sons of one father. One has disappeared, and the youngest is with our father in Canaan." This man, the lord of the country, said to us, "This is how I shall find out if you are honest men. Leave one of your brothers with me, take food for your hungry households and go. Bring your youngest brother to me, and I shall know that you are not spies, but honest men. Then I will restore your brother to you, and you can move about the country freely." ' But on emptying their sacks, each of them found his silver inside, and when they and their father saw the bundles of silver, they were afraid. Their father Jacob said to them, 'You have robbed me of my children. Joseph has disappeared; Simeon has disappeared; and now you are taking Benjamin. Everything is against me.' Reuben said to his father, 'You may kill both my sons if I do not bring him back to you. Put him in my charge, and I shall bring him back.' But Jacob said, 'My son shall not go with you, for his brother is dead and he alone is left. If he comes to any harm on the journey, you will bring down my grey hairs in sorrow to the grave.'

The famine was still severe in the country. When they had used up the corn they had brought from Egypt, their father said to them, 'Go back and buy a little more corn for us to eat.' But Judah replied, 'The man plainly warned us that we must not go into his presence unless our brother was with us.' Israel said, 'Why have you treated me so badly? Why did you tell the man that you had yet another brother?' They answered, 'He questioned us closely about ourselves and our family: "Is your father still alive?" he asked, "Have you a brother?", and we answered his questions. How could we possibly know that he would tell us to bring our brother to Egypt?' Judah said to his father Israel, 'Send the boy with me; then we can start at once. By doing this we shall save our lives, ours, yours, and our dependants,' and none of us will starve. I will go surety for him and you may hold me responsible. If I do not bring him back and restore him to you, you shall hold me guilty all my life. If we had not wasted all this time, by now we could have gone back twice over.'

Their father Israel said to them, 'If it must be so, then do this: take in your baggage, as a gift for the man, some of the produce for which our country is famous: a little balsam, a little honey, gum tragacanth, myrrh, pistachio nuts, and almonds. Take double the amount of silver and restore what was returned to you in your packs; perhaps it was a mistake. Take your brother with you and go straight back to the man. May God Almighty make him kindly disposed to you, and may he send back the one whom you left behind, and Benjamin too. As for me, if I am bereaved, then I am bereaved.' So they took the gift and double the amount of silver, and with Benjamin they started at once for Egypt, where they presented themselves to Joseph.

When Joseph saw Benjamin with them, he said to his steward, 'Bring these men indoors, kill a beast and make dinner ready, for they will eat with me at noon.' He did as Joseph told him and brought the men into the house. When they came in they were afraid, for they thought, 'We have been brought in here because of that affair of the silver which was replaced in our packs the first time. He means to trump up some charge against us and victimize us, seize our asses and make us his slaves.' So they approached Joseph's steward and spoke to him at the door of the house. They said, 'Please listen, my lord. After our first visit to buy food, when we reached the place where we were to spend the night, we opened our packs and each of us found his silver in full weight at the top of his pack. We have brought it back with us, and have added other silver to buy food. We do not know who put the silver in our packs.' He answered, 'Set your minds at rest; do not be afraid. It was your God, the God of your father, who hid treasure for you in your packs. I did receive the silver.' Then he brought Simeon out to them.

The steward brought them into Joseph's house and gave them water to wash their feet, and provided fodder for their asses. They had their gifts ready when Joseph arrived at noon, for they had heard that they were to eat there. When Joseph came into the house, they presented him with the gifts which they had brought, bowing to the ground before him. He asked them how they were and said, 'Is your father well, the old man of whom you spoke? Is he still alive?' They answered, 'Yes, my lord, our father is still alive and well.' And they bowed low and prostrated themselves. Joseph looked and saw his own mother's son, his brother Benjamin, and asked, 'Is this your youngest brother, of whom you told me?', and to Benjamin he said, 'May God be gracious to you, my son!' Joseph was overcome; his feelings for his brother mastered him, and he was near to tears. So he went into the inner room and wept. Then he washed his face and came out; and, holding back his feelings, he ordered the meal to be served. They served him by himself, and the brothers by themselves, and the Egyptians who were at dinner were also served separately; for Egyptians hold it an abomination to eat with Hebrews. The brothers were seated in his presence, the eldest first according to his age and so on down to the youngest: they looked at one another in astonishment. Joseph sent them each a portion from what was before him, but Benjamin's was five times larger than any of the other portions. Thus they drank with him and all grew merry.

Joseph gave his steward this order: 'Fill the men's packs with as much food as they can carry and put each man's silver at the top of his pack. And put my goblet, my silver goblet, at the top of the youngest brother's pack with the silver for the corn.' He did as Joseph said. At daybreak the brothers were allowed to take their asses and go on their journey; but before they had gone very far from the city, Joseph said to his steward, 'Go after those men at once, and when you catch up with them, say, "Why have you repaid good with evil? Why have you stolen the silver goblet? It is the one from which my lord drinks, and which he uses for divination. You have done a wicked thing." ' When he caught up with them, he repeated all this to them, but they replied, 'My lord, how can you say such things? No, sir, God forbid that we should do any such thing! You remember the silver we found at the top of our packs? We brought it back to you from Canaan. Why should we steal silver or gold from your master's house? If any one of us is found with the goblet, he shall die; and, what is more, my lord, we will all become your slaves.' He said, 'Very well, then; I accept what you say. The man in whose possession it is found shall be my slave, but the rest of you shall go free.' Each man quickly lowered his pack to the ground and opened it. The steward searched them, beginning with the eldest and finishing with the youngest, and the goblet was found in Benjamin's pack.

At this they rent their clothes; then each man loaded his ass and they returned to the city. Joseph was still in the house when Judah and his brothers came in. They threw themselves on the ground before him, and Joseph said, 'What have you done? You might have known that a man like myself would practise divination.' Judah said, 'What shall we say, my lord? What can we say to prove our innocence? God has found out our sin.'   [Gen. 42:29–43:3; 43:6–44:16a]

Judah does not plead the brothers' innocence; he nobly accepts the mysterious fact that an ancient evil (their selling of Joseph) has caught up with them.

'Here we are, my lord, ready to be made your slaves, we ourselves as well as the one who was found with the goblet.' Joseph answered, 'God forbid that I should do such a thing! The one who was found with the goblet shall become my slave, but the rest of you can go home to your father in peace.'

Then Judah went up to him and said, 'Please listen, my lord. Let me say a word to your lordship, I beg. Do not be angry with me, for you are as great as Pharaoh. You, my lord, asked us whether we had a father or a brother. We answered, "We have an aged father, and he has a young son born in his old age; this boy's full brother is dead and he alone is left of his mother's children, he alone, and his father loves him." Your lordship answered, "Bring him down to me so that I may set eyes on him." We told you, my lord, that the boy could not leave his father, and that his father would die if he left him. But you answered, "Unless your youngest brother comes here with you, you shall not enter my presence again." We went back to your servant our father, and told him what your lordship had said. When our father told us to go and buy food, we answered, "We cannot go down; for without our youngest brother we cannot enter the man's presence; but if our brother is with us, we will go." Our father, my lord, then said to us, "You know that my wife bore me two sons. One left me, and I said, 'He must have been torn to pieces.' I have not seen him to this day. If you take this one from me as well, and he comes to any harm, then you will bring down my grey hairs in trouble to the grave." Now, my lord, when I return to my father without the boy—and remember, his life is bound up with the boy's—what will happen is this: he will see that the boy is not with us and will die, and your servants will have brought down our father's grey hairs in sorrow to the grave. Indeed, my lord, it was I who went

surety for the boy to my father. I said, "If I do not bring him back
to you, then you shall hold me guilty all my life." Now, my lord,
let me remain in place of the boy as your lordship's slave, and let
him go with his brothers. How can I return to my father without the
boy? I could not bear to see the misery which my father would suffer.'
[Gen. 44:16b–34]

The brothers' offering of themselves in place of their brother
Benjamin shows Joseph that their hearts have changed and that
they love their father and brother deeply.

Joseph could no longer control his feelings in front of his attendants,
and he called out, 'Let everyone leave my presence.' So there was nobody present when Joseph made himself known to his brothers, but
so loudly did he weep that the Egyptians and Pharaoh's household
heard him. Joseph said to his brothers, 'I am Joseph; can my father
be still alive?' His brothers were so dumbfounded at finding themselves
face to face with Joseph that they could not answer. Then Joseph
said to his brothers, 'Come closer,' and so they came close. He said,
'I am your brother Joseph whom you sold into Egypt. Now do not be
distressed or take it amiss that you sold me into slavery here; it was
God who sent me ahead of you to save men's lives. For there have
now been two years of famine in the country, and there will be another five years with neither ploughing nor harvest. God sent me ahead
of you to ensure that you will have descendants on earth, and to
preserve you all, a great band of survivors. So it was not you who sent
me here, but God, and he has made me a father to Pharaoh, and lord
over all his household and ruler of all Egypt.   [Gen. 45:1–8]

Though Joseph, in the many terrible sufferings he endured, must
have felt that life was absurd and unjust, he nevertheless carried
on in faith. Now, having grown through his sufferings, and having
been in a position in Egypt to save his brothers' lives, he sees
meaning in all his previous sufferings and a divine purpose
behind all events.

'Make haste and go back to my father and give him this message from
his son Joseph: "God has made me lord of all Egypt. Come down to
me; do not delay." ' . . . Then he threw his arms round his brother
Benjamin and wept, and Benjamin too embraced him weeping. He
kissed all his brothers and wept over them, and afterwards his brothers
talked with him. . . . Thus they went up from Egypt and came to their

father Jacob in Canaan. There they gave him the news that Joseph was still alive and that he was ruler of all Egypt. He was stunned and could not believe it, but they told him all that Joseph had said; and when he saw the wagons which Joseph had sent to take him away, his spirit revived. Israel said, 'It is enough. Joseph my son is still alive; I will go and see him before I die.'   [Gen. 45:9, 14–15, 25–28]

After seventeen years in Egypt, Jacob blessed his descendants and died.

When their father was dead Joseph's brothers were afraid and said, 'What if Joseph should bear a grudge against us and pay us out for all the harm that we did to him?' They therefore approached Joseph with these words: 'In his last words to us before he died, your father gave us this message for you: "I ask you to forgive your brothers' crime and wickedness; I know they did you harm." So now forgive our crime, we beg; for we are servants of your father's God.' When they said this to him, Joseph wept. His brothers also wept and prostrated themselves before him; they said, 'You see, we are your slaves.' But Joseph said to them, 'Do not be afraid. Am I in the place of God? You meant to do me harm; but God meant to bring good out of it by preserving the lives of many people, as we see today. Do not be afraid. I will provide for you and your dependants.' Thus he comforted them and set their minds at rest.   [Gen. 50:15–21]

Joseph's statement perfectly summarizes Israel's understanding of reality. Midst all the inexplicable events of human life, God's love remains steadfast. Though Israel might be faithless, God's love is forever poured out. "Fear not, you meant evil against me, but God meant it for good."

Chapter 4

MOSES

In about 1580 B.C., not long after Joseph's death, the Egyptians drove out the Hyksos, the foreigners who had ruled Egypt in Joseph's time, and "a new king ascended the throne of Egypt, one who knew nothing of Joseph." Though they had enjoyed favor during the Hyksos' rule of Egypt, the Hebrews were suspected and persecuted as a foreign minority group when the Egyptians regained control of the country. The great ancient civilizations were heavily dependent on slave labor for public works (canals and roads) and for private household service. The Israelites who remained in Egypt were soon enslaved. The Egyptians were the greatest builders of the ancient world and needed a vast slave population to undertake construction of the mammoth temples, palaces, and pyramid-tombs they wanted to build. Naturally, they encouraged the Hebrews to have many children: the more Hebrews the more slaves.

The Book of Exodus opens in the reign of Pharaoh Seti I (about 1309–1290 B.C.). By this time the Hebrew population had grown so large that the Egyptians undertook to limit it to less than one-third of the Egyptian in order to prevent a slave uprising. Pharaoh said to his people:

'These Israelites have become too many and too strong for us. We must take precautions to see that they do not increase any further; or we shall find that, if war breaks out, they will join the enemy and fight against us, and they will become masters of the country.' So they were made to work in gangs with officers set over them, to break their spirit with heavy labour. This is how Pharaoh's store-cities, Pithom and Rameses, were built. But the more harshly they were treated, the more their numbers increased beyond all bounds, until the Egyptians came to loathe the sight of them. So they treated their Israelite slaves with ruthless severity, and made life bitter for them with cruel servitude, setting them to work on clay and brick-making, and all sorts of work in the fields. In short they made ruthless use of them as slaves in every kind of hard labour.

Pharaoh then ordered all his people to throw every new-born Hebrew boy into the Nile, but to let the girls live.

A descendant of Levi married a Levite woman who conceived and bore a son. When she saw what a fine child he was, she hid him for three months, but she could conceal him no longer. So she got a rush basket for him, made it watertight with clay and tar, laid him in it, and put it among the reeds by the bank of the Nile. The child's sister took her stand at a distance to see what would happen to him. Pharaoh's daughter came down to bathe in the river, while her ladies-in-waiting walked along the bank. She noticed the basket among the reeds and sent her slave-girl for it. She took it from her and when she opened it, she saw the child. It was crying, and she was filled with pity for it. 'Why,' she said, 'it is a little Hebrew boy.' Thereupon the sister said to Pharaoh's daughter, 'Shall I go and fetch one of the Hebrew women as a wet-nurse to suckle the child for you?' Pharaoh's daughter told her to go; so the girl went and called the baby's mother. Then Pharaoh's daughter said to her, 'Here is the child, suckle him for me, and I will pay you for it myself.' So the woman took the child and suckled him. When the child was old enough, she brought him to Pharaoh's daughter, who adopted him and called him Moses, 'because,' she said, 'I drew him out of the water.' [Ex. 1:9–14; 1:22–2:10]

Though born of Hebrew parents, Moses grew up in the Pharaoh's court with all the personal and educational advantages of the most privileged class of Egyptian society. One day—we are not told how—he discovered the secret of his birth. No doubt suddenly, for the first time, he became aware of the oppression of the Hebrews. Soon afterward, in a flash of outrage, he threw away all his advantages as an Egyptian courtier and cast his lot with his downtrodden people.

One day when Moses was grown up, he went out to his own kinsmen and saw them at their heavy labour. He saw an Egyptian strike one of his fellow-Hebrews. He looked this way and that, and, seeing there was no one about, he struck the Egyptian down and hid his body in the sand. When he went out next day, two Hebrews were fighting together. He asked the man who was in the wrong, 'Why are you striking him?' 'Who set you up as an officer and judge over

us?' the man replied. 'Do you mean to murder me as you murdered
the Egyptian?' Moses was alarmed. 'The thing must have become
known,' he said to himself. When Pharaoh heard of it, he tried to
put Moses to death, but Moses made good his escape and settled in
the land of Midian.   [Ex. 2:11–15]

Midian is an area at the southeastern tip of the Sinai Desert
peninsula. Moses married into the family of Jethro, the Midianite
leader, and remained there many years working as a shepherd
for his father-in-law.

Scholars believe that Moses' understanding of the God of his
forefathers was enriched and deepened here, possibly through
Jethro's influence. While among the Midianites, Moses had an
awesome experience of God's presence. We associate significant
experiences with places. We recall where we were when we heard
that President Kennedy had been shot or where we were when
men first landed on the moon. Moses associated his vivid experience of God—a moment in which all his random thoughts
and wrestlings seemed to fall into place—with the sight of a
burning bush. Some desert shrubs produce a gas which burns
for brief periods but does not consume the plant itself. This may
have been what Moses saw. Or perhaps the brilliant red desert
sunset may have produced in the bush the effect of fire. Whatever the explanation, at this spot Moses became afire with new
insight into the nature of reality.

Moses was minding the flock of his father-in-law Jethro, priest of
Midian. He led the flock along the side of the wilderness and came
to Horeb, the mountain of God. There the angel of the Lord appeared
to him in the flame of a burning bush. Moses noticed that, although
the bush was on fire, it was not being burnt up; so he said to himself,
'I must go across to see this wonderful sight. Why does not the bush
burn away?' When the Lord saw that Moses had turned aside to look,
he called to him out of the bush, 'Moses, Moses.' And Moses answered,
'Yes, I am here.' God said, 'Come no nearer; take off your sandals;
the place where you are standing is holy ground.' Then he said, 'I
am the God of your forefathers, the God of Abraham, the God of
Isaac, the God of Jacob.' Moses covered his face, for he was afraid to
gaze on God.

The Lord said, 'I have indeed seen the misery of my people in Egypt.
I have heard their outcry against their slave-masters. I have taken

heed of their sufferings, and have come down to rescue them from the power of Egypt, and to bring them up out of that country into a fine, broad land; it is a land flowing with milk and honey, the home of Canaanites, Hittites, Amorites, Perizzites, Hivites, and Jebusites. The outcry of the Israelites has now reached me; yes, I have seen the brutality of the Egyptians towards them. Come now; I will send you to Pharaoh and you shall bring my people Israel out of Egypt.' 'But who am I,' Moses said to God, 'that I should go to Pharaoh, and that I should bring the Israelites out of Egypt?' God answered, 'I am with you. This shall be the proof that it is I who have sent you: when you have brought the people out of Egypt, you shall all worship God here on this mountain.'

Then Moses said to God, 'If I go to the Israelites and tell them that the God of their forefathers has sent me to them, and they ask me his name, what shall I say?' God answered, 'I AM; that is who I am. Tell them that I AM has sent you to them.' And God said further, 'You must tell the Israelites this, that it is Yahweh the God of their forefathers, the God of Abraham, the God of Isaac, the God of Jacob, who has sent you to them. This is my name for ever; this is my title in every generation.'   [Ex. 3:1–15]

A name meant a great deal to the Israelites. A name was said to express a person's character (e.g., Israel, "he who wrestles with God"). Therefore Moses was asking God, "What are you like?" Moses goes away with two insights into the nature of God. The first name for God is a puzzling phrase which has caused endless scholarly debate. Its meaning remains a mystery. Our English version translates the phrase, "I am; that is who I am." Some feel that the phrase is emphasizing that God is Being Itself, vibrant existing Reality which cannot be controlled. Others point out the active and creative aspects of the Hebrew verb "to be," and feel the phrase means "He who causes things to be (or to happen)." Still others see the name as a rebuke to Moses for his arrogance in trying to categorize or label the God of the universe in a word, and they translate the phrase, "I am who I am," i.e., "you cannot pigeon-hole me." The other name for God comes from the Hebrew letters YHWH, pronounced "Yahweh," though traditionally spelled in English "Jehovah." This is an equally puzzling word which also has to do with being and becoming. The Hebrews came to feel that these names were too sacred for them to utter, and in reading scripture they always said "Adonai" or "Lᴏʀᴅ" instead of the divine name whenever it occurred. Our translation follows that practice. That this is no new God—but rather a new manifestation of his people's God—is made clear by the final name for God given here: "the God of Abraham, of Isaac, and of Jacob."

The dialogue between Moses and God at the burning bush is a pictorial transcript of what was going on inside Moses' mind. Out of his mental confusion, out of his groping for the answers to life's problems as he tended his sheep through many silent hours, came now a clear insight into reality as well as a sense of what he should do with his life. He became aware of the presence in his own life of the God who had been known by his ancestors. This God now calls Moses to a dangerous leadership role, but also promises: "I am with you."

Moses makes all sorts of excuses: "The people won't believe me when I tell them," and "I am a poor speaker." We all shy away from a responsibility that promises to be costly or perilous. Moses, however, finally accepts the obligation and returns to Egypt. The quickness with which his people accept him as leader attests to the enormous forcefulness of his personality.

A different pharaoh now ruled Egypt, Rameses II (1290–1224 ʙ.ᴄ.). Moses, now leader and spokesman of the Hebrew slave minority, and Aaron, his right-hand man, go to the king with a modest request: that the Hebrews be allowed to take a day off to go into the desert to celebrate a religious festival.

After this, Moses and Aaron came to Pharaoh and said, 'These are the words of the Lord the God of Israel: "Let my people go so that they may keep my pilgrim-feast in the wilderness." ' 'Who is the Lord,' asked Pharaoh, 'that I should obey him and let Israel go? I care nothing for the Lord: and I tell you I will not let Israel go.' They replied, 'It has happened that the God of the Hebrews met us. So let us go three days' journey into the wilderness to offer sacrifice to the Lord our God, or else he will attack us with pestilence or sword.' But the king of Egypt said, 'Moses and Aaron, what do you mean by distracting the people from their work? Back to your labours!'

That very day Pharaoh ordered the people's overseers and their foremen not to supply the people with the straw used in making bricks, as they had done hitherto. 'Let them go and collect their own straw, but see that they produce the same tally of bricks as before. On no account reduce it. They are a lazy people, and that is why they are clamouring to go and offer sacrifice to their god. Keep the men hard at work; let them attend to that and take no notice of a pack of lies.' The overseers and foremen went out and said to the people, 'Pharaoh's orders are that no more straw is to be supplied. Go and get it for yourselves wherever you can find it; but there will be no reduction in your daily task.' So the people scattered all over Egypt to gather stubble for straw, while the overseers kept urging them on, bidding them complete, day after day, the same quantity as when straw was supplied. Then the Israelite foremen were flogged because they were held responsible by Pharaoh's overseers, who asked them, 'Why did you not complete the usual number of bricks yesterday or today?' So the foremen came and appealed to Pharaoh: 'Why do you treat your servants like this?' they said. 'We are given no straw, yet they keep on telling us to make bricks. Here are we being flogged, but it is your people's fault.' But Pharaoh replied, 'You are lazy, you are lazy. That is why you talk about going to offer sacrifice to the Lord. Now go; get on with your work. You will be given no straw, but you must produce the tally of bricks.' When they were told that they must not let the daily tally of bricks fall short, the Israelite foremen saw that they were in trouble. As they came out from Pharaoh's presence they found Moses and Aaron waiting to meet them, and said, 'May this bring the Lord's judgement down upon you: you have made us stink in the nostrils of Pharaoh and his subjects; you have put a sword in their hands to kill us.'

Moses went back to the Lord, and said, 'Why, O Lord, hast thou brought misfortune on this people? And why didst thou ever send me? Since I first went to Pharaoh to speak in thy name he has heaped misfortune on thy people, and thou hast done nothing at all to rescue them.' The Lord answered, 'Now you shall see what I will do to Pharaoh. In the end Pharaoh will let them go with a strong hand, nay, will drive them from his country with an outstretched arm.' [Ex. 5:1–4; 5:6–6:1]

God reminds Moses of his promise, "I am with you." Though earthly power seems to block all that Moses is striving for, appearances are deceptive. The Hebrews were not a philosophical people, but we might express their faith this way in philosophical terms: God's purpose ultimately prevails; to be on his side is always to win in the end.

As is frequently the case with oppressed peoples, the more the Hebrews' moderate requests were denied, the greater became their demands. Moses now approaches Pharaoh and asks that his people be permitted to leave Egypt altogether.

There then follows a series of natural disasters ("plagues") which afflict the Egyptians. Moses is quick to associate these disasters with Egypt's oppression of the Israelites. He assures the pharaoh that, will he but promise to let the Israelites go, his troubles will cease. All the plagues are natural disasters which we know occur in the Nile valley. The Nile rises rapidly in the late spring and rubbish is swept into it. This decays, smells, and, along with red dirt from the Abyssinian mountains, discolors the river ("turns the river into blood") and makes it unfit for drinking. In early summer the river recedes and the tadpoles become frogs which occasionally breed in unaccountably vast numbers and become a problem. Since the river cannot support that many frogs, they die and decay and breed flies and gnats (whose breeding is also encouraged by excess water remaining in small pools). These can afflict cattle and men with disease: cattle with murrain and men with a skin disease ("boils") which is irritated by the area's red dust. Hailstones sometimes fall in the Nile in January. Locusts are still well known, even in the western world. Sandstorms can blot out the sun, causing darkness. Moses and the Israelites took this unusual concurrence of disasters as a sign that God was with them, and that, if necessary, he would beat the pharaoh into submission. Later generations, retelling these stories with the benefit of knowing their outcome, naturally perceived them as the direct intervention of God and added elements of wonder and magic to them.

The encounters between the pharaoh and Moses fall into a pattern. Moses goes to the pharaoh in the midst of each disaster and demands, "These are the words of the Lord the God of the Hebrews, 'Let my people go in order to worship me.'" Pharaoh is persuaded by the seriousness of the situation and gives in: "Pray to the Lord to take the frogs [or whatever the plague happens to be] away from me and my people, and I will let you go to sacrifice to the Lord." When the plague is over, however, Pharaoh's heart again hardens, he regrets his concession to the Israelites and reneges: "but when Pharaoh found that he was given relief he became obdurate."

After the ninth plague is finished, Pharaoh adds a final threat to Moses: "Take care you do not see my face again, for on the day you do, you die." The stage is now set for the tenth and final plague, the death of the first-born sons of Egypt. This ghastly event is probably based on an outbreak of one of the many periodic fatal epidemics which until the late Middle Ages could kill over half a population in a given area. The Israelites tended to see in all natural events the direct involvement of God. They therefore perceived this final plague to be God's judgment on the Egyptians. Later in their history they came to feel God was given neither to anger nor partisanship, but at this point they saw him as actively causing the disaster.

The situation now reaches the crisis point. Yahweh addresses Moses:

'I shall pass through the land of Egypt and kill every first-born of man and beast. Thus will I execute judgement, I the Lord, against all the gods of Egypt. And as for you, the blood will be a sign on the houses in which you are: when I see the blood I will pass over you; the mortal blow shall not touch you, when I strike the land of Egypt.'

Moses summoned all the elders of Israel and said to them, 'Go at once and get sheep for your families and slaughter the Passover. Then take a bunch of marjoram, dip it in the blood in the basin and smear some blood from the basin on the lintel and the two door-posts. Nobody may go out through the door of his house till morning. The Lord will go through Egypt and strike it, but when he sees the blood on the lintel and the two door-posts, he will pass over that door and will not let the destroyer enter your houses to strike you. You shall keep this as a rule for you and your children for all time. When you enter the land which the Lord will give you as he promised, you shall observe this rite. Then, when your children ask you, "What is the meaning of this rite?" you shall say, "It is the Lord's Passover, for he passed over the houses of the Israelites in Egypt when he struck the Egyptians but spared our houses." ' The people bowed down and prostrated themselves.

The Israelites went and did all that the Lord had commanded Moses and Aaron; and by midnight the Lord had struck down every first-born in Egypt, from the first-born of Pharaoh on his throne to the first-born of the captive in the dungeon, and the first-born of cattle. Before night was over Pharaoh rose, he and all his courtiers and all the

Egyptians, and a great cry of anguish went up, because not a house in Egypt was without its dead. Pharaoh summoned Moses and Aaron while it was still night and said, 'Up with you! Be off, and leave my people, you and your Israelites. Go and worship the Lord, as you ask; take your sheep and cattle, and go; and ask God's blessing on me also.' The Egyptians urged on the people and hurried them out of the country, 'or else,' they said, 'we shall all be dead.' The people picked up their dough before it was leavened, wrapped their kneading-troughs in their cloaks, and slung them on their shoulders.

[Ex. 12:12–13, 21–34]

Ever since this night on which their houses were "passed over" by death, the Jews have celebrated the event annually in the Feast of the Passover.

Chapter 5

THE EXODUS

The Exodus—the Hebrews' safe escape from slavery in Egypt to freedom, in about 1280 B.C.—is the central event of Israel's history. In that event, the Hebrews believed, Yahweh revealed forever both that he was the Lord of the universe whose power utterly surpassed that of the strongest earthly powers, and that he was a God of absolute goodness whose passionate and steadfast love surrounded those who were faithful to him. Forever after, therefore, the Israelites referred to Yahweh as the one "who brought us forth out of the land of Egypt."

As they depart, the Israelites do not head directly to Canaan because to do so would lead them into an Egyptian army encampment.

The Israelites set out from Rameses on the way to Succoth, about six hundred thousand men on foot, not counting dependants. And with them too went a large company of every kind, and cattle in great numbers, both flocks and herds.　　　　　　　　　　[Ex. 12:37–38]

The figure of 600,000 men (implying a total of two or three million people) is a wild exaggeration, like most of the figures ancient historians give us. (There are many instances, even in our own time, of war protesters standing in a crowd of 25,000 and honestly estimating the number of fellow protesters at a million.) Compiling this written account hundreds of years later, the writers only knew that to the people involved the crowd of escaping slaves seemed immense. Some scholars interpret the Hebrew words as indicating that 600 *families* were involved in the Exodus. Probably no more than 2000 Israelites in all left Egypt.

The dough they had brought from Egypt they baked into unleavened cakes, because there was no leaven; for they had been driven out of Egypt and allowed no time even to get food ready for themselves.

They set out from Succoth and encamped at Etham on the edge of the wilderness. And all the time the Lord went before them, by day a pillar of cloud to guide them on their journey, by night a pillar of fire to give them light, so that they could travel night and day. The pillar of cloud never left its place in front of the people by day, nor the pillar of fire by night.   [Ex. 12:39; 13:20–22]

Still today the Bedouins carry braziers (pots of burning coals which smoke) before them as they move from place to place. These smoke during the day and the burning coals are visible at night. This may explain "the pillar of cloud by day and the pillar of fire by night." Yet we should beware of taking the narrative too literally; we frequently use literal terms ("he has fire in his eyes" or "my memory is cloudy") to express non-literal truths; the Israelites frequently used the symbols of fire (as at the burning bush) and cloud (as we shall shortly see on Mt. Sinai) to express God's power and transcendence. At any rate, the Israelites believed God was present with them leading them to freedom.

When the king of Egypt was told that the Israelites had slipped away, he and his courtiers changed their minds completely, and said, 'What have we done? We have let our Israelite slaves go free!' So Pharaoh put horses to his chariot, and took his troops with him. The Egyptians, all Pharaoh's chariots and horses, cavalry and infantry, pursued them and overtook them encamped beside the sea by Pi-hahiroth to the east of Baal-zephon. Pharaoh was almost upon them when the Israelites looked up and saw the Egyptians close behind. In their terror they clamoured to the Lord for help and said to Moses, 'Were there no graves in Egypt, that you should have brought us here to die in the wilderness? See what you have done to us by bringing us out of Egypt! Is not this just what we meant when we said in Egypt, "Leave us alone; let us be slaves to the Egyptians"? We would rather be slaves to the Egyptians than die here in the wilderness.'
                      [Ex. 14:5–6, 9–12]

At the first sign of trouble this unruly mob of former slaves panics. Slavery in Egypt now seems preferable to the uncertainties of life in the desert. Slavery has its good points: material and mental security. Freedom has its risks. Moses, however, retains his confidence in God and rebukes the timidity of his fellow Israelites:

'Have no fear,' Moses answered; 'stand firm and see the deliverance that the Lord will bring you this day; for as sure as you see the Egyptians now, you will never see them again. The Lord will fight for you; so hold your peace.' [Ex. 14:13–14]

CROSSING THE SEA OF REEDS

The Hebrews arrived in their flight at the Sea of Reeds, the narrow marshy body of water at the upper end of the lakes north of the Red Sea. (Near modern El Kantara [see map].) Modern observers have noted that this area is usually flooded, but that a strong wind can free it almost completely of water. Providentially the wind enables the Hebrew horde, on foot and without heavy baggage, to cross the marsh. The Egyptians, laden with armor and conveyed by heavy chariots, are bogged down and swamped as the water returns.

Then Moses stretched out his hand over the sea, and the Lord drove the sea away all night with a strong east wind and turned the sea-bed into dry land. The waters were torn apart, and the Israelites went through the sea on the dry ground, while the waters made a wall for them to right and to left. The Egyptians went in pursuit of them far into the sea, all Pharaoh's horse, his chariots, and his cavalry. In the morning watch the Lord looked down on the Egyptian army through the pillar of fire and cloud, and he threw them into a panic. He clogged their chariot wheels and made them lumber along heavily, so that the Egyptians said, 'It is the Lord fighting for Israel against Egypt; let us flee.' Then the Lord said to Moses, 'Stretch out your hand over the sea, and let the water flow back over the Egyptians, their chariots and their cavalry.' So Moses stretched out his hand over the sea, and at daybreak the water returned to its accustomed place; but the Egyptians were in flight as it advanced, and the Lord swept them out into the sea. The water flowed back and covered all Pharaoh's army, the chariots and the cavalry, which had pressed the pursuit into the sea. Not one man was left alive. Meanwhile the Israelites had passed along the dry ground through the sea, with the water making a wall for them to right and to left. That day the Lord saved Israel from the power of Egypt, and the Israelites saw the Egyptians lying dead on the sea-shore. When Israel saw the great power which the Lord had put forth against Egypt, all the people feared the Lord, and they put their faith in him and in Moses his servant. [Ex. 14:21–31]

B. D. Napier has written:

"Israel rehearsed, retold, reenacted, and relived this most significant single moment of her past. We ought to understand, of any such incomprehensible moment of time, that the participants themselves would be unable to answer the question, 'Exactly what happened?' The pursued were an ill-organized, virtually unarmed, and now panic-ridden column of walking men, women, children, flocks, bearing such conglomerate and awkward possessions as could not or would not be left behind. The pursuers, in whatever numbers, were a compact, disciplined, swiftly maneuverable unit, equipped with the world's finest weapons and faced now only with the relatively easy assignment of turning back this clumsy herd of helpless fugitives. How many in the Moses group, facing such odds, anticipated any better outcome than frustration, return to Egypt, and the imposition of brutally punitive measures? How many indeed feared death at the hands of Pharaoh's lusty charioteers, now fast closing the gap . . . ? The item which is clearly incontrovertible is that suddenly the pursued found themselves without pursuer. The chase was a chase no more. The hunter had abandoned the hunt. We would assume that this impossible piece of news passed from the rear of the pathetically slow, ragged, fleeing column toward the front, moved along by incredulous voices." [1]

Incredulity became belief. The Israelites were now free. They have forever regarded their escape as a divine deliverance, a ratification of God's past promise to Abraham, and the greatest of all proofs of God's protection of and concern for them in the present and future.

Egyptian records make no mention of this event which was so centrally important to the Israelites. This is not difficult to understand. The escape of a small group of slaves would probably not have been of sufficient interest or importance to the Egyptians for them to have taken the trouble to chip it into a stone monument where posterity could read it. We also know that when the Egyptians lost a battle they pretended it had not occurred and made no record of it.

PROBLEMS IN THE WILDERNESS

Masses of people are apt to be fickle. The Israelite exiles were no exception. The later Jews writing about their ancestors at the time of the Exodus made no effort to whitewash them. When the Egyptians were pursuing them before the Reed Sea crossing, many of the Israelites cried out in fear, "Let us go back and serve the Egyptians." Now, shortly after their miraculous escape, they forget about their providential deliverance and fall to complaining about conditions in the wilderness and to reflecting on their slavery in Egypt as "the good old days." No sooner are they free than they complain about freedom.

At Marah, a desert oasis where they stop, the water is so bitter that it is undrinkable.

For three days they travelled through the wilderness without finding water. They came to Marah, but could not drink the Marah water because it was bitter; that is why the place was called Marah. The people complained to Moses and asked, 'What are we to drink?' Moses cried to the Lord, and the Lord showed him a log which he threw into the water, and then the water became sweet.   [Ex. 15:22b–25a]

Moses' faith in God made him confident that there *were* answers to the problems which his people did little but complain about. Rather than despairing, he searched until he found a solution: the leaf or bark of a tree (probably barberry) which sweetened the taste of the water.

Next the Israelites fell to complaining about the scarcity of food in the desert. Again they longed for the good old days.

The Israelites complained to Moses and Aaron in the wilderness and said, 'If only we had died at the Lord's hand in Egypt, where we sat round the fleshpots and had plenty of bread to eat! But you have brought us out into this wilderness to let this whole assembly starve to death.' The Lord said to Moses, 'I will rain down bread from heaven for you. Each day the people shall go out and gather a day's supply, so that I can put them to the test and see whether they will follow my instructions or not. But on the sixth day, when they prepare what they bring in, it shall be twice as much as they have gathered on other days.'

The Lord spoke to Moses and said, 'I have heard the complaints of the Israelites. Say to them, "Between dusk and dark you will have flesh to eat and in the morning bread in plenty. You shall know that I the Lord am your God." '

That evening a flock of quails flew in and settled all over the camp, and in the morning a fall of dew lay all around it. When the dew was gone, there in the wilderness, fine flakes appeared, fine as hoar-frost on the ground. When the Israelites saw it, they said to one an-other, 'What is that?', because they did not know what it was. Moses said to them, 'That is the bread which the Lord has given you to eat. This is the command the Lord has given: "Each of you is to gather as much as he can eat: let every man take an omer a head for every person in his tent." '

Israel called the food manna; it was white, like coriander seed, and it tasted like a wafer made with honey.   [Ex. 16:2–5, 11–16, 31]

Quail are known to migrate from Europe through this area and often to rest or die here exhausted from the lengthy journey. They are therefore easy to catch. Manna is a common desert species of tamarisk which exudes a sweet juice from its trunk. This falls to the ground and forms small edible pellets.[2]

At the next stage of their journey, they are again without water. They focus their complaining on Moses. As leader, he is the natural scapegoat:

They encamped at Rephidim, where there was no water for the peo-ple to drink, and a dispute arose between them and Moses. When they said, 'Give us water to drink,' Moses said, 'Why do you dispute with me? Why do you challenge the Lord?' There the people became so thirsty that they raised an outcry against Moses: 'Why have you brought us out of Egypt with our children and our herds to let us all die of thirst?' Moses cried to the Lord, 'What shall I do with these people? In a moment they will be stoning me.' The Lord answered, 'Go forward ahead of the people; take with you some of the elders of Israel and the staff with which you struck the Nile, and go. You will find me waiting for you there, by a rock in Horeb. Strike the rock; water will pour out of it, and the people shall drink.' Moses did this in the sight of the elders of Israel. He named the place Massah and Meribah, because the Israelites had disputed with him and challenged the Lord with their question, 'Is the Lord in our midst or not?'   [Ex. 17:1b–7]

This last question reveals the natural tendency to use God for one's own purposes. The Hebrews think God should somehow spare them from all human discomforts and sufferings, and they reject him the minute he seems not to accommodate their every need. Again Moses' confidence in God makes him sure a solution can be found. He forms a search party and discovers a spring.

Though he was a man of courageous faith and iron will, Moses was also humble: he could take criticism and advice. Almost single-handedly Moses had controlled and led the unruly mob on their journey. The Israelites now reach Jethro's land and encamp at the foot of Mt. Sinai (or Mt. Horeb) in the southern part of the Sinai desert peninsula. Exhausted by continually having to settle disputes, Moses accepts his father-in-law's advice to delegate authority.

Jethro, Moses' father-in-law, now came to him with his sons and his wife, to the wilderness where he was encamped at the mountain of God. Moses was told, 'Here is Jethro, your father-in-law, coming to you with your wife and her two sons.' Moses went out to meet his father-in-law, bowed low to him and kissed him, and they greeted one another. When they came into the tent Moses told him all that the Lord had done to Pharaoh and to Egypt for Israel's sake, and about all their hardships on the journey, and how the Lord had saved them. Jethro rejoiced at all the good the Lord had done for Israel in saving them from the power of Egypt. He said, 'Blessed be the Lord who has saved you from the power of Egypt and of Pharaoh. Now I know that the Lord is the greatest of all gods, because he has delivered the people from the power of the Egyptians who dealt so arrogantly with them.' Jethro, Moses' father-in-law, brought a whole-offering and sacrifices for God; and Aaron and all the elders of Israel came and shared the meal with Jethro in the presence of God.

The next day Moses took his seat to settle disputes among the people, and they were standing round him from morning till evening. When Jethro saw all that he was doing for the people, he said, 'What are you doing for all these people? Why do you sit alone with all of them standing round you from morning till evening?' 'The people come to me,' Moses answered, 'to seek God's guidance. Whenever there is a dispute among them, they come to me, and I decide between man and man. I declare the statutes and laws of God.' But his father-in-law said to Moses, 'This is not the best way to do it. You will only wear yourself out and wear out all the people who are here. The task is too heavy for you; you cannot do it by yourself. Now listen to me: take my advice, and God be with you. It is for you to be the people's representative before God, and bring their disputes to him. You must instruct them in the statutes and laws, and teach them how they must behave and what they must do. But you must yourself search for capable, God-fearing men among all the people, honest and incorruptible men, and appoint them over the people as officers over units of a thousand, of a hundred, of fifty or of ten. They shall sit as a permanent court for the people; they must refer difficult cases to you but decide simple cases themselves. In this way your burden will be lightened, and they will share it with you. If you do this, God will give you strength, and you will be able to go on. And, moreover, this whole people will here and now regain peace and harmony.' Moses listened to his father-in-law and did all he had suggested.   [Ex. 18:5–24]

Throughout this period of deprivation and hardship the Israelites were tested. The weak and uncommitted fell by the wayside and gradually the unwieldy mob of refugees was welded into a tough and unified people.

Chapter 6

MOUNT SINAI

The Hebrews are now encamped at the foot of Mount Sinai, the sacred mountain oasis where as a young man Moses had so vividly experienced God's presence in the burning bush. They have moved symbolically from the wilderness desert, from fruitlessness, dryness, and barrenness, to the mountain, to refreshment, exaltation, a mountaintop experience.

At Mount Sinai the Israelites pause to reflect on what has happened to them. Here they come to see clearly and to acknowledge explicitly the passionate, steadfast love which God has demonstrated toward them again and again. Here the motley crew of refugees realizes its exalted calling to be the Lord's own community, specially chosen to reveal Yahweh's love to all men. And here they begin to see how their grateful acceptance of God's love and their response to that love involves them in certain attitudes and actions.

Moses, ascending the mountain to reflect alone, is overwhelmed by the awareness of all that God has done for his people: his steadfast love in the past and present, his promise for the future.

Moses went up the mountain of God, and the Lord called to him from the mountain and said, 'Speak thus to the house of Jacob, and tell this to the sons of Israel: You have seen with your own eyes what I did to Egypt, and how I have carried you on eagles' wings and brought you here to me. If only you will now listen to me and keep my covenant, then out of all peoples you shall become my special possession; for the whole earth is mine. You shall be my kingdom of priests, my holy nation. These are the words you shall speak to the Israelites.' [Ex. 19:3–6]

Descending the mountain, Moses shares his insights with his people and tells them to prepare themselves formally to recognize God's loving presence among them.

Moses came and summoned the elders of the people and set before them all these commands which the Lord had laid upon him. The people all answered together, 'Whatever the Lord has said we will do.' Moses brought this answer back to the Lord. The Lord said to Moses, 'I am now coming to you in a thick cloud, so that I may speak to you in the hearing of the people, and their faith in you may never fail.' Moses told the Lord what the people had said, and the Lord said to him, 'Go to the people and hallow them today and tomorrow and make them wash their clothes. They must be ready by the third day, because on the third day the Lord will descend upon Mount Sinai in the sight of all the people. You must put barriers round the mountain and say, "Take care not to go up the mountain or even to touch the edge of it." 'Moses came down from the mountain to the people. He hallowed them and they washed their clothes. He said to the people, 'Be ready by the third day; do not go near a woman.'
[Ex. 19:7–12, 14–15]

Unlike some modern people who perceive God as a genial pal who operates on their own level, the Israelites realized that the God of the universe was to be approached thoughtfully and seriously.

When they later tried to recount their experience at Mount Sinai, the Israelites found words inadequate. Like us, they used hyperbolic and picturesque imagery to try to convey the significance of what happened.

On the third day, when morning came, there were peals of thunder and flashes of lightning, dense cloud on the mountain and a loud trumpet blast; the people in the camp were all terrified.

Moses brought the people out from the camp to meet God, and they took their stand at the foot of the mountain. Mount Sinai was all smoking because the Lord had come down upon it in fire; the smoke went up like the smoke of a kiln; all the people were terrified, and the sound of the trumpet grew ever louder. Whenever Moses spoke, God answered him in a peal of thunder.   [Ex. 19:16–19]

Bernhard W. Anderson has remarked, "It is significant that Israel adopted religious metaphors not from the quiet rhythms and beauties of nature, but from the violent storm that shakes the earth, overwhelming man with awareness of the transcendence and holiness of God and a sense of the frailty and precariousness of human life." [3]

THE TEN COMMANDMENTS

The extraordinary realization of the Israelites at Sinai was that this utterly transcendent God loved them and had chosen them to be his own.

Moses perceived the relationship between God and men to be a covenant. Undoubtedly Moses was aware of the contractual agreement which the Hittite kings made with their vassals, and this influenced his understanding of the relationship of Yahweh and Israel. A Hittite king initiated a covenant with his vassals by declaring his position and his rights; then he stipulated the conditions by which he would offer his vassals protection: they must agree to live peacefully with his other vassals and to serve no other king. Note how the Ten Commandments (the obligations of the Israelites) are preceded by a similar declaration of God's position and rights:

The Lord came down upon the top of Mount Sinai and summoned Moses to the mountain-top, and Moses went up.

God spoke, and these were his words:

I am the Lord your God who brought you out of Egypt, out of the land of slavery.   [Ex. 19:20; 20:1–2]

God's principal offering to Israel is not laws, but himself. Transcending the universe is a God of purpose. He has freely chosen Israel to carry out his purpose: "I am the Lord *your* God." Without their deserving it he has poured out his love for them: "who brought you out of Egypt, out of the land of slavery." This is the central revelation of Judaism. All else flows from this.

The Commandments which follow indicate something of the lifestyle that must result if Israel accepts God's ardent transforming love.

You shall have no other god to set against me.

You shall not make a carved image for yourself nor the likeness of anything in the heavens above, or on the earth below, or in the waters under the earth.

You shall not bow down to them or worship them; for I, the Lord your God, am a jealous god. I punish the children for the sins of the fathers to the third and fourth generations of those who hate me. But I keep faith with thousands, with those who love me and keep my commandments.   [Ex. 20:3–6]

For Israel nothing must be more important than God. Israel's chief goal must not be prosperity or security. "You shall have no other god to set against me." God is far above nature. Though he involves himself in human events, in his totality he is infinitely beyond our understanding and control. To make a physical representation of him is to deny that he is transcendent. We may cringe at Israel's anthropopathic description of God as "jealous." But that is a word which suitably expresses God's love and his insistence that Israel may not toy with his love or dabble at being his people. They must either accept him alone and fully, or reject him. The God of Israel is not a cozy God to be played with. He loves and saves his people, but he is also the ultimate arbiter of justice in the universe. The somber reality is that those who deliberately ignore or make light of the opportunities he offers bring unhappiness not only on themselves but even on their children. Unfortunately children do suffer for the selfishness of their parents.

You shall not make wrong use of the name of the Lord your God; the Lord will not leave unpunished the man who misuses his name.
[Ex. 20:7]

This commandment has nothing to do with what is popularly known as "swearing." It is directed against two evils. To the Jews a name was very important. A name and the person named were regarded as inseparable. What is forbidden here is the glib or frivolous use of religion. God loves us and seeks our response and commitment. To go through the motions of worship, to utter his name, and then to live as if we had little or no commitment: that is the vain use of God's name. The other forbidden evil is the use of God's name for magical cursings and blessings. Real religion is not magic. Magic tries to manipulate God for one's own purposes. The religious man seeks to do God's will.

Remember to keep the sabbath day holy. You have six days to labour and do all your work. But the seventh day is a sabbath of the Lord your God; that day you shall not do any work, you, your son or your daughter, your slave or your slave-girl, your cattle or the alien within your gates; for in six days the Lord made heaven and earth,

the sea, and all that is in them, and on the seventh day he rested. Therefore the Lord blessed the sabbath day and declared it holy.

[Ex. 20:8–11]

At Sinai the Israelites came to realize the danger of losing perspective. They realized the human tendency to become immersed in and obsessed with the "things" of this world. One of their responses to God's love, then, was deliberately to set aside one day of the week from work. On this day they were to reflect with joy upon the love which the Lord of all Creation had shown them in the past and to think about the implications of his love in the present. To do so would enable them to return to the regular affairs of life renewed by a fresh perspective.

Honour your father and your mother, that you may live long in the land which the Lord your God is giving you. [Ex. 20:12]

Most of us have been taught that this commandment is directed toward young children, who should respect and obey their parents. The commandment, however, is directed toward adults. Israel is called to realize that all human lives are sacred, including the lives of the aged. That society in which the majority cannot respect (i.e., *honor*, not necessarily *enjoy* and *like*) those who are different (in age, in viewpoint, in usefulness) will be a short-lived society.

Our acceptance of and response to God's love for us involves us in an attitude toward others which precludes a whole variety of acts which are destructive of human relationships.

You shall not commit murder.
You shall not commit adultery.
You shall not steal.
You shall not give false evidence against your neighbour.

[Ex. 20:13–16]

The final commandment deals not with an outward act but with the source of external acts, man's mind or imagination. It goes, in other words, to the heart of the matter. The Talmud states that "he who violates the last commandment violates them all."

You shall not covet your neighbour's house; you shall not covet your neighbour's wife, his slave, his slave-girl, his ox, his ass, or anything that belongs to him. [Ex. 20:17]

Andrew M. Greeley writes: "Covetousness is a symptom that a man has not really put his trust in Yahweh, he still puts his trust in himself. . . . He is restless and dissatisfied with what he has and wants what someone else has because he believes that he can find security in his possessions. The one who has truly given his heart over to the covenant knows that security can come only from Yahweh. . . . The Yahwist does not covet because he does not need his neighbor's wife or goods for his own well being and happiness." [4]

Moses came and told the people all the words of the Lord, all his laws. The whole people answered with one voice and said, 'We will do all that the Lord has told us.' [Ex. 24:3]

After the people's acceptance of God's offer of love and protection and all that that entailed in attitude and behavior, the covenant was sealed, as was the custom, by a sacrifice and covenant meal.

Moses wrote down all the words of the Lord. He rose early in the morning and built an altar at the foot of the mountain, and put up twelve sacred pillars, one for each of the twelve tribes of Israel. He then sent the young men of Israel and they sacrificed bulls to the Lord as whole-offerings and shared-offerings. Moses took half the blood and put it in basins and the other half he flung against the altar. Then he took the book of the covenant and read it aloud for all the people to hear. They said, 'We will obey, and do all that the Lord has said.' Moses then took the blood and flung it over the people, saying, 'This is the blood of the covenant which the Lord has made with you on the terms of this book.'

Moses went up with Aaron, Nadab and Abihu, and seventy of the elders of Israel. They stayed there before God; they ate and they drank. [Ex. 24:4–9a, 11b]

As a visible reminder (but not an image) of God's presence among the people, Moses felt the desirability of having a sanctuary (a holy place). This was to be a portable tent in the midst of the Hebrew camp. Inside would be placed the Ark of the Covenant, a wooden box which was to remind the Israelites of God's presence. According to various traditions, the Ark may have contained the tablets on which the Ten Commandments were inscribed, or some rocks from Mount Sinai where God had been so vividly present, or a jar of manna from the wilderness. There are indications that originally it was not a box but a portable throne on which the invisible Yahweh was seated.

THE GOLDEN CALF

Leaving the people at the foot of the mountain, Moses ascends alone to ponder the implications of the Covenant. Men quickly fall into the worship of *things*—success, pleasure, material possessions—and the chosen people, though fresh from sealing the Covenant, lapsed swiftly into idolatry in Moses' absence. Whatever may have been God's reason for choosing Israel, it was certainly not because the Israelites were especially good or deserving.

When the people saw that Moses was so long in coming down from the mountain, they confronted Aaron and said to him, 'Come, make us gods to go ahead of us. As for this fellow Moses, who brought us up from Egypt, we do not know what has become of him.' Aaron answered them, 'Strip the gold rings from the ears of your wives and daughters, and bring them to me.' So all the people stripped themselves of their gold earrings and brought them to Aaron. He took them out of their hands, cast the metal in a mould, and made it into the image of a bull-calf. 'These,' he said, 'are your gods, O Israel, that brought you up from Egypt.' Then Aaron was afraid and built an altar in front of it and issued this proclamation, 'Tomorrow there is to be a pilgrim-feast to the Lord.' Next day the people rose early, offered whole-offerings, and brought shared-offerings. After this they sat down to eat and drink and then gave themselves up to revelry.
[Ex. 32:1–6]

The Israelites were probably familiar with the Egyptian worship of Apis, a god who was represented as a bull, or with the Canaanite practice of worshiping bulls as symbols of fertility.

Moses turned and went down the mountain with the two tablets of the Tokens in his hands, inscribed on both sides; on the front and on the back they were inscribed. The tablets were the handiwork of

God, and the writing was God's writing, engraved on the tablets. Joshua, hearing the uproar the people were making, said to Moses, 'Listen! There is fighting in the camp.' Moses replied,

> 'This is not the clamour of warriors,
>   nor the clamour of a defeated people;
>   it is the sound of singing that I hear.'

As he approached the camp, Moses saw the bull-calf and the dancing, and he was angry; he flung the tablets down, and they were shattered to pieces at the foot of the mountain.   [Ex. 32:15–19]

Israel's actions, in effect, shatter and destroy its covenant relationship with God.

> Then he took the calf they had made and burnt it; he ground it to powder, sprinkled it on water, and made the Israelites drink it.
>   [Ex. 32:20]

Moses' aim was not merely vengeance. He believed that some concrete penitential action was desirable in order to make a lasting impression on the people. Moses could easily have said "Forget it" or vented his anger and gone on. He wisely provided a physical means by which the people could express and work out their repentance.

Moses' deepest disappointment and anger was reserved for Aaron, his right-hand man.

> He demanded of Aaron, 'What did this people do to you that you should have brought such great guilt upon them?' Aaron replied, 'Do not be angry, sir. The people were deeply troubled; that you well know. And they said to me, "Make us gods to go ahead of us, because, as for this fellow Moses, who brought us up from Egypt, we do not know what has become of him." So I said to them, "Those of you who have any gold, strip it off." They gave it me, I threw it in the fire, and out came this bull-calf.'   [Ex. 32:21–24]

Aaron's weak disclaimer of responsibility ranks among the most deceitful excuses of all time.

Moses makes no effort to conceal his outrage at the people. He rebukes them angrily and punishes them sternly. Underneath, however, his abiding love for his people remains. His love and aspirations for his people make his disappointment in them all the more bitter.

The next day Moses said to the people, 'You have committed a great sin. I shall now go up to the Lord; perhaps I may be able to secure pardon for your sin.' So Moses returned to the Lord and said, 'O hear me! This people has committed a great sin: they have made themselves gods of gold. If thou wilt forgive them, forgive. But if not, blot out my name, I pray, from thy book which thou hast written." The Lord answered Moses, 'It is the man who has sinned against me that I will blot out from my book. But go now, lead the people to the place which I have told you of. My angel shall go ahead of you, but a day will come when I shall punish them for their sin.' And the Lord smote the people for worshipping the bull-calf which Aaron had made.

[Ex. 32:30–35]

God forgives the Israelites and renews his promise to them, but concludes with the stern words, "I will visit their sin upon them." This statement utters, albeit in a strikingly anthropopathic way, a profound truth: though evil can be forgiven, the *consequences* of evil cannot be eliminated.

The Lord orders Moses to "lead the people on to the land I have promised." Moses takes up the journey with humility and prayer: "May the Lord go in our company. However stubborn a people we are, forgive our iniquity and our sin and take us as thy own possession." However, despite the Exodus, the testing in the wilderness, and the Mount Sinai experience, the Israelites are still too undisciplined and weak-hearted to enter the promised land of Canaan.

The Lord spoke to Moses and said, 'Send men out to explore the land of Canaan which I am giving to the Israelites, from each of their fathers' tribes send one man, and let him be a man of high rank.' . . .

When Moses sent them to explore the land of Canaan, he said to them, 'Make your way up by the Negeb, and go on into the hill-country. See what the land is like, and whether the people who live there are strong or weak, few or many. See whether it is easy or difficult country in which they live, and whether the cities in which they live are weakly defended or well fortified; is the land fertile or barren, and does it grow trees or not? Go boldly in and take some of its fruit.' It was the season when the first grapes were ripe.

After forty days they returned from exploring the country, and came back to Moses and Aaron and the whole community of Israelites at Kadesh in the wilderness of Paran. They made their report to them

and to the whole community, and showed them the fruit of the country. And this was the story they told Moses: 'We made our way into
the land to which you sent us. It is flowing with milk and honey, and
here is the fruit it grows; but its inhabitants are sturdy, and the cities
are very strongly fortified.

Then Caleb called for silence before Moses and said, 'Let us go up
at once and occupy the country; we are well able to conquer it.' But
the men who had gone with him said, 'No, we cannot attack these
people; they are stronger than we are.' Thus their report to the
Israelites about the land which they had explored was discouraging:
'The country we explored,' they said, 'will swallow up any who go to
live in it. All the people we saw there are men of gigantic size. When
we set eyes on the Nephilim (the sons of Anak belong to the Nephilim)
we felt no bigger than grasshoppers; and that is how we looked to
them.'   [Num. 13:1–2, 17–20, 25–28a, 30–33]

The inhabitants of Canaan seem like giants to the faint-hearted
Israelites who look upon themselves as weak grasshoppers. Lack-
ing courage and confidence, they look back on the "good old
days" and again fall into complaining.

Then the whole Israelite community cried out in dismay; all night
long they wept. One and all they made complaints against Moses
and Aaron: 'If only we had died in Egypt or in the wilderness!' they
said. 'Far happier if we had! Why should the Lord bring us to this
land, to die in battle and leave our wives and our dependants to become the spoils of war? To go back to Egypt would be better than
this.' And they began to talk of choosing someone to lead them back.
                                                          [Num. 14:1–4]

However, year after year, as the generation of former slaves
died and the uncommitted fell away, the community of Israel
became a tougher, free-hearted people who looked not to the
security of the past but to the promise of the future. After many
years the Israelites moved up to the border of Canaan. At Mount
Nebo, overlooking the promised land, after commissioning Joshua
to lead the people, the aged Moses died. Israel's preparation was
now complete.

Chapter 7

THE PROMISED LAND

The long-awaited time has now arrived. Toughened and unified by its experiences in the desert, the former slave rabble is now ready to enter the promised land "flowing with milk and honey" (a description only a people used to the desert could give to a land as poor in resources as Canaan).

After the death of Moses the servant of the Lord, the Lord said to Joshua son of Nun, his assistant, 'My servant Moses is dead; now it is for you to cross the Jordan, you and this whole people of Israel, to the land which I am giving them. Every place where you set foot is yours: I have given it to you, as I promised Moses. From the desert and the Lebanon to the great river, the river Euphrates, and across all the Hittite country westwards to the Great Sea, all this shall be your land. No one will ever be able to stand against you: as I was with Moses, so will I be with you; I will not fail you or forsake you. Be strong, be resolute; it is you who are to put this people in possession of the land which I swore to give to their fathers. Only be strong and resolute; observe diligently all the law which my servant Moses has given you. You must not turn from it to right or left, if you would prosper wherever you go.' [Josh 1:1–7]

God's promise of land and protection is not an act of indulgence. It is a provisional promise. If Israel is faithful to its covenant with God, if it shows by its lifestyle that it is truly God's people, then it cannot fail.

Since the invasion will be no picnic, Israel is encouraged a second time:

'This is my command: be strong, be resolute; do not be fearful or dismayed, for the Lord your God is with you wherever you go.' Then Joshua told the officers to pass through the camp and give this order to the people: 'Get food ready to take with you; for within three days you will be crossing the Jordan to occupy the country which the Lord your God is giving you to possess.' [Josh. 1:9–11]

After scouting the enemy and attending to the necessary preparations, Israel camps at the edge of the Jordan River.

Joshua then said to the people, 'Hallow yourselves, for tomorrow the Lord will do a great miracle among you.' To the priests he said, 'Lift up the Ark of the Covenant and pass in front of the people.' So they lifted up the Ark of the Covenant and went in front of the people. Then the Lord said to Joshua, 'Today I will begin to make you stand high in the eyes of all Israel, and they shall know that I will be with you as I was with Moses. Give orders to the priests who carry the Ark of the Covenant, and tell them that when they come to the edge of the waters of the Jordan, they are to take their stand in the river.'

Then Joshua said to the Israelites, 'Come here and listen to the words of the Lord your God. By this you shall know that the living God is among you and that he will drive out before you the Canaanites, the Hittites, the Hivites, the Perizzites, the Girgashites, the Amorites, and the Jebusites: the Ark of the Covenant of the Lord, the lord of all the earth, is to cross the Jordan at your head. Choose twelve men from the tribes of Israel, one man from each tribe. When the priests carrying the Ark of the Lord, the lord of all the earth, set foot in the waters of the Jordan, then the waters of the Jordan will be cut off; the water coming down from upstream will stand piled up like a bank.' So the people set out from their tents to cross the Jordan, with the priests in front of them carrying the Ark of the Covenant. [Josh. 3:5–14]

The Jordan River lies along a geological fault; as a result landslides occasionally block its flow for short periods of time. (In this century two such blockages have occurred, in 1909 and 1927.) As the Israelites come to the river, their crossing is facilitated by such a blockage. Though this occurrence is, of course, "natural," the Israelites viewed its timing as more than accidental.

Now the Jordan is in full flood in all its reaches throughout the time of harvest. When the priests reached the Jordan and dipped their feet in the water at the edge, the water coming down from upstream was brought to a standstill; it piled up like a bank for a long way back, as far as Adam, a town near Zarethan. The waters coming down to the Sea of the Arabah, the Dead Sea, were completely cut off, and the people crossed over opposite Jericho. The priests carrying the Ark of the Covenant of the Lord stood firm on the dry bed in the middle of the Jordan; and all Israel passed over on dry ground until the whole nation had crossed the river. [Josh. 3:15–17]

After setting up a stone memorial to remind future generations of the safe crossing into Canaan, Joshua is at once confronted with two problems: the natural poverty of Canaan (poor soil, low rainfall) and the hostility of the Canaanites, who regarded the land as theirs. The people of Canaan naturally viewed the Israelites with alarm, since the land was barely able to support the people already there.

Israel's first great obstacle after crossing the Jordan was the fortified Canaanite town of Jericho. Rather than proceed against it immediately, Joshua with keen psychological insight pauses so that the Hebrew community can consolidate, reaffirm its unity and its distinctive calling, and prepare for what lies ahead.

When all the Amorite kings to the west of the Jordan and all the Canaanite kings by the sea-coast heard that the Lord had dried up the waters before the advance of the Israelites until they had crossed, their courage melted away and there was no more spirit left in them for fear of the Israelites.

At that time the Lord said to Joshua, 'Make knives of flint, seat yourself, and make Israel a circumcised people again.' Joshua thereupon made knives of flint and circumcised the Israelites at Gibeath haaraloth. This is why Joshua circumcised them: all the males who came out of Egypt, all the fighting men, had died in the wilderness on the journey from Egypt. The people who came out of Egypt had all been circumcised, but not those who had been born in the wilderness during the journey. When the circumcision of the whole nation was complete, they stayed where they were in camp until they had recovered. [Josh. 5:1–5, 8]

Circumcision, the symbolic act by which a male is initiated into the Covenant community, is the distinctive badge of Israel's identity. At the Passover the community celebrates the Exodus, vividly recalling God's loving protection of them in the past.

The Israelites encamped in Gilgal, and at sunset on the fourteenth day of the month they kept the Passover in the lowlands of Jericho.

On the day after the Passover, they ate their unleavened cakes and parched grain, and that day it was the produce of the country. It was from that day, when they first ate the produce of the country, that the manna ceased. The Israelites received no more manna; and that year they ate what had grown in the land of Canaan.

[Josh. 5:10–12]

JOSHUA AND THE BATTLE FOR CANAAN

Now that the community is prepared, Joshua sets out for Jericho. His scouts had told him that the Canaanites were terrified of this mob of invaders, and that the people of the countryside had retired behind Jericho's walls. Ascertaining correctly the fearful and paranoid mentality of people who build walls around themselves, Joshua embarks on a war of nerves.

Jericho was bolted and barred against the Israelites; no one went out, no one came in. The Lord said to Joshua, 'Look, I have delivered Jericho and her king into your hands. You shall march round the city with all your fighting men, making the circuit of it once, for six days running. Seven priests shall go in front of the Ark carrying seven trumpets made from rams' horns. On the seventh day you shall march round the city seven times and the priests shall blow their trumpets. At the blast of the rams' horns, when you hear the trumpet sound, the whole army shall raise a great shout; the wall of the city will collapse and the army shall advance, every man straight ahead.' So Joshua son of Nun summoned the priests and gave them their orders: 'Take up the Ark of the Covenant; let seven priests with seven trumpets of ram's horn go in front of the Ark of the Lord.' Then he said to the army, 'March on and make the circuit of the city, and let the men drafted from the two and a half tribes go in front of the Ark of the Lord.' When Joshua had spoken to the army, the seven priests carrying the seven trumpets of ram's horn before the Lord passed on and blew the trumpets, with the Ark of the Covenant of the Lord following them. The drafted men marched in front of the priests who blew the trumpets, and the rearguard followed the Ark, the trumpets sounding as they marched. But Joshua ordered the army not to shout, or to raise their voices or utter a word, till the day came when he would tell them to shout; then they were to give a loud shout. Thus he caused the Ark of the Lord to go round the city, making the circuit of it once, and then they went back to the camp and spent the night there.

Joshua rose early in the morning and the priests took up the Ark of the Lord. The seven priests carrying the seven trumpets of ram's horn went marching in front of the Ark of the Lord, blowing the trumpets as they went, with the drafted men in front of them and the rearguard following the Ark of the Lord, the trumpets sounding as they marched. They marched round the city once on the second day and returned to the camp; this they did for six days.   [Josh. 6:1–14]

One can imagine the tensions aroused in the people of Jericho as this procession, in solemn silence broken only by the piercing blasts of the horns, circuited the town, dramatically reminding those inside of their isolation.

But on the seventh day they rose at dawn and marched seven times round the city in the same way; that was the only day on which they marched round seven times. The seventh time the priests blew the trumpets and Joshua said to the army, 'Shout! The Lord has given you the city.' So they blew the trumpets, and when the army heard the trumpet sound, they raised a great shout, and down fell the walls. The army advanced on the city, every man straight ahead, and took it. Thus the Lord was with Joshua, and his fame spread throughout the country.   [Josh. 6:15–16, 20, 27]

With a spine-chilling roar, no doubt even more blood-curdling than the infamous "rebel yell" of the American Civil War, the Israelites enter the city. Psychologically exhausted and terrified, Jericho collapses—her ability to defend herself destroyed.

Before attacking Jericho the Israelites had put it under "ban." They swore an oath that, if victorious, they would take no spoils for themselves, but would offer the city and its people entirely to God.

The city shall be under solemn ban: everything in it belongs to the Lord. No one is to be spared except the prostitute Rahab and everyone who is with her in the house, because she hid the men whom we sent. And you must beware of coveting anything that is forbidden under the ban; you must take none of it for yourselves; this would put the Israelite camp itself under the ban and bring trouble on it. All the silver and gold, all the vessels of copper and iron, shall be holy; they belong to the Lord and they must go into the Lord's treasury.
[Josh. 6:17–19]

When they captured Jericho, therefore, they remained true to their oath.

Under the ban they destroyed everything in the city; they put everyone to the sword, men and women, young and old, and also cattle, sheep, and asses.   [Josh. 6:21]

Israel used "the ban" (such as that on Jericho) only rarely, unlike other ancient peoples who used it regularly. But that does not prevent us from being appalled by the idea that God could ever be pleased by such a holocaust. As centuries passed, in fact, the Israelites' understanding of God deepened and they ceased to use the "ban" as a tactic. Before we cast too many stones at the Israelites, we might do well to remember our nation's acceptance of the destruction of Hiroshima, Nagasaki, and Dresden, all sacrificed for what was believed to be a "righteous" cause. We may well pause to consider how far mankind has progressed since Jericho.

Though the Israelites enjoyed great success at first and established control of the highlands near the Jordan River, they soon bogged down. After fifty years (roughly 1250 to 1200 b.c.) they still had not succeeded in gaining control of the inland plains from the Canaanites. Their success remained confined to the hill country.

We tend to think of Israel at this time as a united nation. In reality it was a confederation of twelve quite independent tribes. Included in the tribes were descendants of Israelites who had not gone to Egypt with Jacob's twelve sons. These Israelites, who had remained in Canaan, had not of course shared with the twelve tribes (descendants of Joseph's sons) the great experiences of the Exodus and Mt. Sinai. They had therefore not been included in the Covenant.

The twelve tribes customarily gathered at a central place once a year for a family reunion. As time passed those who had been present at the Exodus and at Mt. Sinai died. Their children, born in Canaan, took their places, joined by the Canaanite Jews who had never gone to Egypt. In order to include in the Covenant those not at Mt. Sinai, and to give opportunity for recommitment to those who were there, the tribes gathered each year to recall, by vivid retelling and reenactment, the great events of their family's past, and to commit themselves afresh to the Covenant.

Though they met later at Shiloh, in Joshua's time they gathered at Shechem.

Joshua assembled all the tribes of Israel at Shechem. He summoned the elders of Israel, the heads of families, the judges and officers; and they presented themselves before God. Joshua then said this to all the people: 'This is the word of the Lord the God of Israel: "Long ago your forefathers lived beside the Euphrates, and they worshipped other gods. I took your father Abraham from beside the Euphrates and led him through the length and breadth of Canaan. I gave him many descendants: I gave him Isaac, and to Isaac I gave Jacob and Esau. I put Esau in possession of the hill-country of Seir, but Jacob and his sons went down to Egypt. I sent Moses and Aaron, and I struck the Egyptians with plagues—you know well what I did among them— and after that I brought you out; I brought your fathers out of Egypt and you came to the Red Sea. The Egyptians sent their chariots and cavalry to pursue your fathers to the sea. But when they appealed to the Lord, he put a screen of darkness between you and the Egyptians, and brought the sea down on them and it covered them; you saw for yourselves what I did to Egypt. For a long time you lived in the wilderness. Then you crossed the Jordan and came to Jericho. The citizens of Jericho fought against you, but I delivered them into your hands. I spread panic before you, and it was this, not your sword or your bow, that drove out the two kings of the Amorites. I gave you land on which you had not laboured, cities which you had never built; you have lived in those cities and you eat the produce of vineyards and olive-groves which you did not plant." '

[Josh. 24:1–7, 11–13, abridged]

'Hold the Lord in awe then, and worship him in loyalty and truth. Banish the gods whom your fathers worshipped beside the Euphrates and in Egypt, and worship the Lord. But if it does not please you to worship the Lord, choose here and now whom you will worship: the gods whom your forefathers worshipped beside the Euphrates, or the gods of the Amorites in whose land you are living. But I and my family, we will worship the Lord.' The people answered, 'God forbid that we should forsake the Lord to worship other gods, for it was the Lord our God who brought us and our fathers up from Egypt, that land of slavery; it was he who displayed those great signs before our eyes and guarded us on all our wanderings among the many peoples through whose lands we passed. The Lord drove out before us the Amorites and all the peoples who lived in that country. We too will worship the Lord; he is our God.' He said to them, 'Then here and now banish the foreign gods that are among you, and turn your hearts to the Lord the God of Israel.' The people said to Joshua, 'The Lord our God we will worship and his voice we will obey.' So Joshua made a covenant that day with the people; he drew up a statute and an ordinance for them in Shechem and wrote its terms in the book of the law of God. He took a great stone and set it up there under the terebinth in the sanctuary of the Lord, and said to all the people, 'This stone is a witness against us; for it has heard all the words which the Lord has spoken to us. If you renounce your God, it shall be a witness against you.' Then Joshua dismissed the people, each man to his patrimony. [Josh. 24:14–18, 23–28]

THE CONFLICT OF CULTURES

No sooner was Joshua dead, however, than many of the Israelites defected from this pledge. Canaanite civilization was highly developed. In striking contrast to the uncultured nomadic Israelites, the Canaanites were skillful artists and successful merchants, and lived in fortified cities with good municipal facilities such as drainage. While the Israelites knew little of agriculture, the Canaanites were experienced, successful farmers. While Israel was a simple society in which each individual was roughly equal to every other, Canaanite society was considerably structured. Each of the Canaanite cities was ruled by a king and aristocracy who lived in luxury, supported by servants and by small farmers who worked the fields outside the city.

The Canaanites worshiped gods called *baals* (agricultural deities associated with land) and their female counterparts, the *baalaths*. The Canaanites believed that fertility (in crops, cattle, and children) came from intercourse between the baals and baalaths. The Canaanites engaged in intercourse in temple orgies, believing that by doing so they would suggest to the baals and their consorts that they have intercourse and thereby bring fertility. As the Israelites settled down to farming, Yahweh, their historical God, now seemed irrelevant to their new needs in Canaan. Though Yahweh had acted decisively in history, the Israelites did not associate him with nature or agriculture. Desiring good crops, many turned to baal worship, intermarried into Canaanite families, and abandoned the faith of their fathers.

ISRAEL UNDER THE JUDGES

The twelve tribes lived in tent villages scattered through the hill country. Separate and disorganized, they came together only for their annual reunion and in the face of enemy attack. Emergencies tended to produce leaders: a powerful person in one of the tribes would become the rallying point of whatever tribes were under attack. The leaders who emerged were called "judges," a broad term which, in Hebrew, means one who vindicates the peoples' rights. After the emergency had passed, the judge, as a man of stature, often undertook to settle disputes among people of the various tribes.

One prominent judge was Gideon, who united the Israelites against the Midianites and inaugurated a puritanical campaign to root out baal worship among his own people.

The judge best known to us is Samson. Shortly after Joshua's death (about 1200 B.C.), the Israelites were confronted by a new enemy, the Philistines. These people came from the Mediterranean island of Crete and worked their way up the coast of Palestine into the hill country where they encountered the Israelites. The Philistines struck terror in the hearts of the various peoples of Canaan: they were large, strong, fierce fighters, equipped with iron weapons. They quickly gained control of the trade routes along the coast. In danger, the threatened Israelite tribes called on Samson, a member of the Danite tribe.

From his birth (to a woman previously regarded as unable to conceive) onward, Samson proved himself an extraordinary character. A person of legendary strength, he is reputed to have torn an attacking lion to bits with his bare hands and to have fought thirty Philistines simultaneously and killed them all. He married a Philistine woman but left her in a rage without consummating the marriage, letting loose three hundred foxes with burning torches tied to their tails to destroy her father's fields. Though he is described as "filled with God's spirit" as the leader of the Israelites, his understanding of God's ethical demands was primitive. At best he had an eye-for-an-eye sense of justice, while at worst he was ruthless and vengeful. The Book of Judges no doubt embellishes an already good story in recording Samson's extraordinary feats. In one encounter he alone is alleged to have killed a thousand men with the jawbone of an ass. At Gaza he carted off the massive gates to the city when the Philistines tried to capture him. But like many powerful men who forget they are human, he was trapped and nearly destroyed by a weakness in his character.

After this Samson fell in love with a woman named Delilah, who lived in the valley of Sorek. The lords of the Philistines went up country to see her and said, 'Coax him and find out what gives him his great strength, and how we can master him, bind him and so hold him captive; then we will each give you eleven hundred pieces of silver.' So Delilah said to Samson, 'Tell me what gives you your great strength, and how you can be bound and held captive.' Samson replied, 'If they bind me with seven fresh bowstrings not yet dry, then I shall become as weak as any other man.' So the lords of the Philistines brought her seven fresh bowstrings not yet dry, and she bound him with them. She had men already hidden in the inner room, and she cried, 'The Philistines are upon you, Samson!' But he snapped the bowstrings as a strand of tow snaps when it feels the fire, and his strength was not tamed. Delilah said to Samson, 'I see you have made a fool of me and told me lies. Tell me this time how you can be bound.' He said to her, 'If you bind me tightly with new ropes that have never been used, then I shall become as weak as any other man.' So Delilah took new ropes and bound him with them. Then she cried, 'The Philistines are upon you, Samson!', while the men waited hidden in the inner room. He snapped the ropes off his arms like pack-thread. Delilah said to him, 'You are still making a fool of me and have told me lies. Tell me: how can you be bound?' He said, 'Take the seven loose locks of my hair and weave them into the warp, and then drive them tight with the beater; and I shall become as weak as any other man.' So she lulled him to sleep, wove the seven loose locks of his hair into the warp, and drove them tight with the beater, and cried, 'The Philistines are upon you, Samson!' He woke from sleep and pulled away the warp and the loom with it. She said to him, 'How can you say you love me when you do not confide in me? This is the third time you have made a fool of me and have not told me what gives you your great strength.' She so pestered him with these words day after day, pressing him hard and wearying him to death, that he told her his secret. 'No razor has touched my head,' he said, 'because I am a Nazirite, consecrated to God from the day of my birth. If my head were shaved, then my strength would leave

me, and I should become as weak as any other man.' Delilah saw
that he had told her his secret; so she sent to the lords of the Philistines
and said, 'Come up at once, he has told me his secret.' So the lords
of the Philistines came up and brought the money with them. She
lulled him to sleep on her knees, summoned a man and he shaved
the seven locks of his hair for her. She began to take him captive and
his strength left him. The Philistines seized him, gouged out his eyes
and brought him down to Gaza. There they bound him with fetters of
bronze, and he was set to grinding corn in the prison.

[Judg. 16:4–19, 21]

The Israelites saw Samson's downfall as a warning: even the
strongest of men is weak, and the man who does not know his
human frailties courts disaster. One mistake, the result of one
small weakness, can cancel out all a man's strengths. A man
speeds in a car, thinking he can get away with it (perhaps he
has before) and is killed. Those who write about Samson also
felt his story had a clear moral: he who abandons the service of
God and man for self-indulgence is brought to ruin.

But the story does not end in disaster. Humiliated and doomed
to servitude, the now blinded Samson ironically "sees" the truth
about his arrogant reliance on his own supposedly invincible
strength.

But his hair, after it had been shaved, began to grow again.

The lords of the Philistines assembled together to offer a great sacrifice to their god Dagon and to rejoice before him. They said, 'Our
god has delivered Samson our enemy into our hands.' The people,
when they saw him, praised their god, chanting·

Our god has delivered our enemy into our hands,
the scourge of our land who piled it with our dead.

When they grew merry, they said, 'Call Samson, and let him fight to
make sport for us.' So they summoned Samson from prison and he
made sport before them all. They stood him between the pillars, and
Samson said to the boy who held his hand, 'Put me where I can feel
the pillars which support the temple, so that I may lean against them.'
The temple was full of men and women, and all the lords of the
Philistines were there, and there were about three thousand men and
women on the roof watching Samson as he fought. Samson called on
the Lord and said, 'Remember me, O Lord God, remember me: give

me strength only this once, O God, and let me at one stroke be
avenged on the Philistines for my two eyes.'   [Judg. 16:22–28]

Samson no longer relies on his own strength, but on God. He
asks no permanent endowment of strength, but strength only for
this occasion, to undertake what he believes to be a righteous
act.

He put his arms round the two central pillars which supported the
temple, his right arm round one and his left round the other, and
braced himself and said, 'Let me die with the Philistines.' Then Samson
leaned forward with all his might, and the temple fell on the lords
and on all the people who were in it.   [Judg. 16:29–30a]

It is sometimes only by disaster and humiliation that a man comes
to act nobly. Nothing in Samson's life speaks so highly of him as
does his sacrificial death, accomplished with characteristic dramatic flare: "Let me die with the Philistines!"

ISRAEL BECOMES A MONARCHY

Despite all the efforts of the tribes, the Philistine menace continued to grow. By 1050 B.C. the invaders had destroyed the
tribes' national shrine at Shiloh and captured the Ark of the Covenant. Samuel was now judge, an elder statesman greatly respected
by all the tribes. The people more and more vociferously demanded that Samuel appoint a king who could unite and organize the tribes and drive the Philistines away. Samuel reminded them that Yahweh was Israel's king and that the remedy
they proposed for Israel's problems (an earthly king) might well
be worse than the disease (disunity) they sought to cure.

'This will be the sort of king who will govern you', he said. 'He will
take your sons and make them serve in his chariots and with his
cavalry, and will make them run before his chariot. Some he will appoint officers over units of a thousand and units of fifty. Others will
plough his fields and reap his harvest; others again will make weapons
of war and equipment for mounted troops. He will take your daughters
for perfumers, cooks, and confectioners, and will seize the best of
your cornfields, vineyards, and olive-yards, and give them to his
lackeys. He will take a tenth of your grain and your vintage to give
to his eunuchs and lackeys. Your slaves, both men and women, and
the best of your cattle and your asses he will seize and put to his

own use. He will take a tenth of your flocks, and you yourselves will become his slaves. When that day comes, you will cry out against the king whom you have chosen; but it will be too late, the Lord will not answer you.' The people refused to listen to Samuel; 'No,' they said, 'we will have a king over us; then we shall be like other nations, with a king to govern us, to lead us out to war and fight our battles.' So Samuel, when he had heard what the people said, told the Lord; and he answered, 'Take them at their word and appoint them a king.' Samuel then dismissed all the men of Israel to their homes.

[1 Sam. 8:11–22]

Though this account of Samuel's speech is probably colored by the bitterness of a latter-day editor who had experienced the excesses of the Israelite monarchy, it also reflects the genuine doubts which many Israelites, including Samuel, had about the desirability of having a king. Not only had the Israelites long acknowledged that their only king was Yahweh, but their experience in the desert and in Canaan had made them a democratic society in which each man counted equally and in which even leaders were only first among equals.

However, Samuel gives in to popular demand. His choice for king falls on a man of striking appearance.

There was a man from the district of Benjamin, whose name was Kish. He was a man of substance, and had a son named Saul, a young man in his prime; there was no better man among the Israelites than he. He was a head taller than any of his fellows.

One day some asses belonging to Saul's father Kish had strayed, so he said to his son Saul, 'Take one of the servants with you, and go and look for the asses.' They crossed the hill-country of Ephraim and went through the district of Shalisha but did not find them; they passed through the district of Shaalim but they were not there; they passed through the district of Benjamin but again did not find them. When they had entered the district of Zuph, Saul said to the servant with him, 'Come, we ought to turn back, or my father will stop thinking about the asses and begin to worry about us.' The servant answered, 'There is a man of God in the city here, who has a great reputation, because everything he says comes true.' So they went up to the city, and just as they were going in, there was Samuel coming towards them on his way up to the shrine.

Now the day before Saul came, the Lord had disclosed his intention to Samuel in these words: 'At this same time tomorrow I will send you a man from the land of Benjamin. Anoint him prince over my people Israel, and then he shall deliver my people from the Philistines. I have seen the sufferings of my people and their cry has reached my ears.' The moment Saul appeared the Lord said to Samuel, 'Here is the man of whom I spoke to you. This man shall rule my people.' Saul came up to Samuel in the gateway and said, 'Would you tell me where the seer lives?' Samuel replied, 'I am the seer. Go on ahead of me to the hill-shrine and you shall eat with me today; in the morning I will set you on your way, after telling you what you have on your mind. Trouble yourself no more about the asses lost three days ago, for they have been found. But what is it that all Israel is wanting? It is you and your ancestral house.'

Samuel took a flask of oil and poured it over Saul's head, and he kissed him and said, 'The Lord anoints you prince over his people Israel; you shall rule the people of the Lord and deliver them from the enemies round about them. You shall have a sign that the Lord has anointed you prince to govern his inheritance: when you reach the Hill of God, where the Philistine governor resides, you will meet a company of prophets coming down from the hill-shrine, led by lute, harp, fife, and drum, and filled with prophetic rapture. Then the spirit of the Lord will suddenly take possession of you, and you too will be rapt like a prophet and become another man.

As Saul turned to leave Samuel, God gave him a new heart.

[1 Sam. 9:1a, 2–6a, 14–20; 10:1, 5–6, 9]

Even as Saul leaves, he begins to become a new man. Samuel has made it clear that kingship is not a personal honor, but a sacred responsibility. Many people remarked on what a changed man Truman was after he was suddenly thrust into the presidency upon Roosevelt's death. In Saul's case, also, the job appears to have "made the man."

Saul's first test came when the Ammonites attacked the Israelite city of Jabesh. Unaided by their fellow Israelites, the city fathers lamented their doom.

When Saul heard this, the spirit of God suddenly seized him. In his anger he took a pair of oxen and cut them in pieces, and sent messengers with the pieces all through Israel to proclaim that the same would be done to the oxen of any man who did not follow Saul and Samuel into battle.   [1 Sam. 11:6–7a]

This brilliant symbolic act galvanized the Israelites.

The fear of the Lord fell upon the people and they came out, to a man.

[1 Sam. 11:7b]

Victory for Israel followed swiftly, and in joyful celebration Saul was proclaimed king by all the people.

Chapter 8

SAUL AND DAVID

In many respects Saul was more the last of the judges than the first of the kings. With great forcefulness he unified the tribes for military purposes, but he was not interested in extending his power over other areas of Israelite life. Under Saul there was no attempt to disrupt the tribal organization. No centralized bureaucracy, no taxes, no military draft, no legal system existed on a national basis. Saul himself continued to live as a simple soldier in his modest home at Gibeah. There was about him nothing of the oriental potentate. He remained throughout his life readily accessible to his people. He was not a great intellect or skillful administrator. Saul was a soldier and he viewed his duty as king to be primarily military: to rid Israel of the Philistine menace. His simple soldier's faith is perhaps best expressed by his son Jonathan, on the eve of battle: "Now we will visit the post of those uncircumcised rascals. Perhaps the Lord will take a hand in it, and if he will, nothing can stop him. He can bring us safe through, whether we are few or many." (1 Sam. 14:6)

However, only the strongest of men can resist being corrupted in a position of absolute authority. And Saul was not the strongest of men. Corruption emerges in a man in little ways at first. Impatience is an early sign. One day, instead of waiting for Samuel to offer the sacrificial prayers (a duty strictly set aside for him), Saul impatiently rode roughshod over the delicate checks and balances of Israelite society and offered the prayers himself.

By the time of war against the Amalekites Saul had become a thief and a liar. The Amalekites had tried to wipe out the Israelite tribes altogether. Their goal was the extermination of every Israelite man, woman, and child. Their atrocities against Israel were infamous. The Israelite tribes had therefore determined to conduct a holy war against the Amalekites. They purified themselves (refusing intercourse) and committed themselves to take no spoils if they won, but rather to offer all the people and possessions they captured to Yahweh as a sacrifice. This they believed was God's will.

Samuel said to Saul, 'The Lord sent me to anoint you king over his people Israel. Now listen to the voice of the Lord. This is the very word of the Lord of Hosts: "I am resolved to punish the Amalekites for what they did to Israel, how they attacked them on their way up from Egypt." Go now and fall upon the Amalekites and destroy them, and put their property under ban. Spare no one; put them all to death, men and women, children and babes in arms, herds and flocks, camels and asses.'   [1 Sam. 15:1-3]

We recoil in horror (and perhaps indulge ourselves in condescension) at Israel's primitive understanding of God. Yet in no century have more innocent people been indiscriminately slaughtered in ostensibly righteous causes than in our own. Holy wars of total obliteration were common to all ancient Middle Eastern peoples. In the next few hundred years Israel was to become distinctive among these peoples for eliminating such wars as unethical.

Then Saul cut the Amalekites to pieces, all the way from Havilah to Shur on the borders of Egypt. Agag the king of the Amalekites he took alive, but he destroyed all the people, putting them to the sword. Saul and his army spared Agag and the best of the sheep and cattle, the fat beasts and the lambs and everything worth keeping; they were unwilling to destroy them, but anything that was useless and of no value they destroyed.   [1 Sam. 15:7-9]

Saul decides to spare the best of the Amalekites' cattle in order to keep them for himself.

Then the word of the Lord came to Samuel: 'I repent of having made Saul king, for he has turned his back on me and has not obeyed my commands.' Samuel was angry; all night he cried aloud to the Lord. Early next morning he went to meet Saul, but was told that he had gone to Carmel; Saul had set up a monument for himself there, and had then turned and gone down to Gilgal. There Samuel found him, and Saul greeted him with the words, 'The Lord's blessing upon you! I have obeyed the Lord's commands.'   [1 Sam. 15:10-13]

Saul lies, claiming to have carried out his instructions.

But Samuel said, 'What then is this bleating of sheep in my ears? Why do I hear the lowing of cattle?' Saul answered, 'The people have taken them from the Amalekites. These are what they spared, the best of the sheep and cattle, to sacrifice to the Lord your God. The rest we completely destroyed.'   [1 Sam. 15:14–15]

Caught red-handed, Saul tries to cover his selfishness with a cloak of righteousness.

So Samuel went on, 'Time was when you thought little of yourself, but now you are head of the tribes of Israel, and the Lord has anointed you king over Israel. The Lord sent you with strict instruction to destroy that wicked nation, the Amalekites; you were to fight against them until you had wiped them out. Why then did you not obey the Lord? Why did you pounce upon the spoil and do what was wrong in the eyes of the Lord?

Because you have rejected the word of the Lord,
the Lord has rejected you as king.'   [1 Sam. 15:17–19, 23b]

DAVID AND GOLIATH

Having dealt with the Amalekites, Saul was forced to turn his attention to the Philistines who again attacked the Israelites.

The Philistines collected their forces for war and massed at Socoh in Judah. Saul and the Israelites also massed, and drew up their lines facing the Philistines, the Philistines occupying a position on one hill and the Israelites on another, with a valley between them.
                        [1 Sam. 17:1–3, abridged]

The two armies were ranged against each other on opposite hillsides of a valley. The army which attacked had to go down into the valley and cross a river, exposing itself to great danger from the opposing forces which were on advantageously higher ground. Each side naturally hoped the other would withdraw. In the war of nerves which ensued the Philistines succeeded in demoralizing the Israelites:

A champion came out from the Philistine camp, a man named Goliath, from Gath; he was over nine feet in height. He had a bronze helmet on his head, and he wore plate-armour of bronze, weighing five thousand shekels. On his legs were bronze greaves, and one of his weapons was a dagger of bronze. The shaft of his spear was like a weaver's beam, and its head, which was of iron, weighed six hundred shekels; and his shield-bearer marched ahead of him. The champion stood and shouted to the ranks of Israel, 'Why do you come out to do battle, you slaves of Saul? I am the Philistine champion; choose your man to meet me. If he can kill me in fair fight, we will become your slaves; but if I prove too strong for him and kill him, you shall be our slaves and serve us. Here and now I defy the ranks of Israel. Give me a man,' said the Philistine, 'and we will fight it out.' When Saul and the Israelites heard what the Philistine said, they were shaken and dismayed.   [1 Sam. 17:4–11]

At this desperate moment our attention is drawn to an unlikely figure—a "handsome, ruddy-cheeked, bright-eyed" shepherd boy: David, Son of Jesse of Bethlehem. Though he was probably just old enough to be a soldier, as the youngest son he had to remain at home tending the sheep while his older brothers were away at war.

The shepherd's life is lonely and dangerous. We know David was a sensitive child who loved music, played the harp, and sang with unusual skill. In the days and nights of solitude in the fields under the sun and stars he reflected on the meaning of life. He faced an endless stream of dangers (wild animals, cliffs, thieves) alone. He knew and cared for each of his sheep, and they recognized him as their protector. It was natural for him, therefore, to view his relationship to the Lord of the universe in terms of his experience as a shepherd.

The Lord is my shepherd; I shall want nothing
He makes me lie down in green pastures,
and leads me beside the waters of peace;
he renews life within me,
and for his name's sake guides me in the right path.
Even though I walk through a valley dark as death
I fear no evil, for thou art with me,
thy staff and thy crook are my comfort.   [Ps. 23:1–4]

He was not at all noticed by the world. A mere shepherd boy, he seemed destined to be among the nameless, faceless millions who cast not even a shadow on history.

Morning and evening for forty days the Philistine came forward and took up his position. Then one day Jesse said to his son David,

'Take your brothers an ephah of this parched grain and these ten loaves of bread, and run with them to the camp. These ten cream-cheeses are for you to take to the commanding officer. See if your brothers are well and bring back some token from them.' Saul and the brothers and all the Israelites were in the Vale of Elah, fighting the Philistines. Early next morning David left someone in charge of the sheep, set out on his errand and went as Jesse had told him. He reached the lines just as the army was going out to take up position and was raising the war-cry. The Israelites and the Philistines drew up their ranks opposite each other. David left his things in charge of the quartermaster, ran to the line and went up to his brothers to greet them. While he was talking to them the Philistine champion, Goliath, came out from the Philistine ranks and issued his challenge in the same words as before; and David heard him. When the Israelites saw the man they ran from him in fear. 'Look at this man who comes out day after day to defy Israel,' they said. 'The king is to give a rich reward to the man who kills him; he will give him his daughter in marriage too and will exempt his family from service due in Israel.' Then David turned to his neighbours and said, 'What is to be done for the man who kills this Philistine and wipes out our disgrace? And who is he, an uncircumcised Philistine, to defy the army of the living God?'   [1 Sam. 17:16–27]

Here—in breathtakingly simple terms—is Israel's faith. Even the most powerful earthly forces cannot stand against God. Every Israelite present had time and again recalled in worship God's deliverance of Israel at the Exodus and in the wilderness. But, in the dangers of this situation, God seemed remote. Belief in God was a pleasant tradition, a community custom, not a factor in present circumstances. David's statement is therefore all the more stunning: "And who is he to defy the army of the *living* God?"

His brothers were not impressed. The last thing they wanted was to be embarrassed in front of their fellow soldiers by their ranting brother.

His elder brother Eliab overheard David talking with the men and grew angry. 'What are you doing here?' he asked. 'And who have you left to look after those few sheep in the wilderness? I know you, you impudent young rascal; you have only come to see the fighting.'
                                                    [1 Sam. 17:28]

Others, however, *were* impressed by the intensity and sincerity of this striking boy.

What David had said was overheard and reported to Saul, who sent for him. David said to him, 'Do not lose heart, sir. I will go and fight this Philistine.' Saul answered, 'You cannot go and fight with this Philistine; you are only a lad, and he has been a fighting man all his life.' David said to Saul, 'Sir, I am my father's shepherd; when a lion or bear comes and carries off a sheep from the flock, I go after it and attack it and rescue the victim from its jaws. Then if it turns on me, I seize it by the beard and batter it to death. Lions I have killed and bears, and this uncircumcised Philistine will fare no better than they; he has defied the army of the living God. The Lord who saved me from the lion and the bear will save me from this Philistine.'

[1 Sam. 17:31–37]

David was no cocky fool. He offers *experience* as his qualification. As a shepherd he had fought lions (the Syrian lion is smaller than the African) and bears which, like Goliath, attacked a weak and innocent flock. He is certain that the same Lord—the living God—who enabled him to protect his flock will enable him to defeat Goliath.

Saul, the great warrior, knows the situation is hopeless. But, pressed by the eager youth, he gives his permission and a despairing blessing: "Go then, and the Lord go with you."

He put his own tunic on David, placed a bronze helmet on his head and gave him a coat of mail to wear; he then fastened his sword on David over his tunic. But David hesitated, because he had not tried them, and said to Saul, 'I cannot go with these, because I have not tried them.' So he took them off. Then he picked up his stick, chose five smooth stones from the brook and put them in a shepherd's bag which served as his pouch. He walked out to meet the Philistine with his sling in his hand.

The Philistine came on towards David, with his shield-bearer marching ahead; and he looked David up and down and had nothing but contempt for this handsome lad with his ruddy cheeks and bright eyes. He said to David, 'Am I a dog that you come out against me with sticks?' And he swore at him in the name of his god. 'Come on,' he said, 'and I will give your flesh to the birds and the beasts.' David answered, 'You have come against me with sword and spear and dagger, but I have come against you in the name of the Lord of Hosts, the God of the army of Israel which you have defied. The Lord will put you into my power this day; I will kill you and cut your head off and leave your carcass and the carcasses of the Philistines to the birds and the wild beasts; all the world shall know that there is a God in Israel. All those who are gathered here shall see that the Lord saves neither by sword nor spear; the battle is the Lord's, and he will put you all into our power.'

When the Philistine began moving towards him again, David ran quickly to engage him. He put his hand into his bag, took out a stone, slung it, and struck the Philistine on the forehead. The stone sank into his forehead, and he fell flat on his face on the ground. So David proved the victor with his sling and stone; he struck Goliath down and gave him a mortal wound, though he had no sword. Then he ran to the Philistine and stood over him, and grasping his sword, he drew it out of the scabbard, dispatched him and cut off his head. The Philistines, when they saw that their hero was dead, turned and ran.   [1 Sam. 17:38b–51]

In the face of the giant problems of life (war, poverty, personal difficulties) we are tempted to overlook the small talents we have and say, "What can *I* do?" Though a mere boy, too small even to wear the armor offered him by Saul, David employed what talents he had with bold confidence that the living God would use them to overcome evil with good.

DAVID IN SAUL'S HOUSEHOLD

Saul had said to Abner his commander-in-chief, when he saw David going out against the Philistine, 'That boy there, Abner, whose son is he?' 'By your life, your majesty,' said Abner, 'I do not know.' The king said to Abner, 'Go and find out whose son the lad is.' When David came back after killing the Philistine, Abner took him and presented him to Saul with the Philistine's head still in his hand. Saul asked him, 'Whose son are you, young man?', and David answered, 'I am the son of your servant Jesse of Bethlehem.'   [1 Sam. 17:55–58]

David and Saul's son Jonathan seem to have formed an immediate friendship, and David is taken into Saul's family.

That same day, when Saul had finished talking with David, he kept him and would not let him return any more to his father's house,

for he saw that Jonathan had given his heart to David and had grown
to love him as himself. So Jonathan and David made a solemn compact because each loved the other as dearly as himself. And Jonathan
stripped off the cloak he was wearing and his tunic, and gave them
to David, together with his sword, his bow, and his belt.

[1 Sam. 18:1–4]

Jonathan had himself been—though to a lesser degree—the
fair-haired boy of Israel. Though scarcely older than David, he
had distinguished himself in battle and was loved and admired
by his father's soldiers. We might expect, therefore, that Jonathan
would have felt a jealous anger at this instant hero who was suddenly Israel's idol. Jonathan, however, was one of those rare individuals who knows no envy and who is able to witness the
triumphs of others without any competitive feeling that, in some
sense, his own accomplishments are thereby reduced. Both Jonathan and David were brilliant, intense, deep, and sensitive youths.
Their friendship was instinctive and complete, never clouded by
competition or jealousy.

David succeeded so well in every venture on which Saul sent him
that he was given a command in the army, and his promotion pleased
the ordinary people, and even pleased Saul's officers.

At the home-coming of the army when David returned from the
slaughter of the Philistines, the women came out from all the cities of
Israel to look on, and the dancers came out to meet King Saul with
tambourines, singing, and dancing. The women as they made merry
sang to one another:

Saul made havoc among thousands
but David among tens of thousands.

Saul was furious, and the words rankled. He said, 'They have given
David tens of thousands and me only thousands; what more can they
do but make him king?' From that day forward Saul kept a jealous
eye on David.   [1 Sam. 18:5–9]

Samuel's denunciation and rejection of Saul, with all the attendant guilt feelings, and the terrible strain of the seemingly
endless war with the Philistines, took a heavy toll on the king.
The tremendous popularity of David—obviously surpassing his
own—made Saul murderously jealous. Depressed and paranoid,

he brooded that David was somehow a threat to him. First he
appointed him to an army command.

David led his men into action, and succeeded in everything that he
undertook, because the Lord was with him. When Saul saw how successful he was, he was more afraid of him than ever; all Israel and
Judah loved him because he took the field at their head.

[1 Sam. 18:14–16]

Then Saul promised David his daughter Michal if David could
bring him the foreskins of a hundred Philistines. Hopeful that
David would be killed in battle trying to get the foreskins,
Saul's despair increased all the more when David returned with
not one hundred but two hundred Philistine foreskins.

Poisoned and consumed by jealous hatred, the pathetically
deranged king now undertakes to kill David himself.

Saul spoke to Jonathan his son and all his household about killing
David. But Jonathan was devoted to David and told him that his
father Saul was looking for an opportunity to kill him. 'Be on your
guard tomorrow morning,' he said; 'conceal yourself, and remain in
hiding.' Jonathan spoke up for David to his father Saul and said to
him, 'Sir, do not wrong your servant David; he has not wronged you;
his conduct towards you has been beyond reproach.' Saul listened to
Jonathan and swore solemnly by the Lord that David should not be
put to death. So Jonathan called David and told him all this; then
he brought him to Saul, and he was in attendance on the king as
before.

An evil spirit from the Lord came upon Saul as he was sitting in
the house with his spear in his hand; and David was playing the
harp. Saul tried to pin David to the wall with the spear, but he
avoided the king's thrust so that Saul drove the spear into the wall.
David escaped and got safely away. That night Saul sent servants to
keep watch on David's house, intending to kill him in the morning,
but David's wife Michal warned him to get away that night, 'or tomorrow,' she said, 'you will be a dead man.' She let David down
through a window and he slipped away and escaped. Michal took
their household gods and put them on the bed; at its head she laid
a goat's-hair rug and covered it all with a cloak. When the men
arrived to arrest David she told them he was ill. Saul sent them back
to see David for themselves. 'Bring him to me, bed and all,' he said,

'and I will kill him.' When they came, there were the household gods on the bed and the goat's-hair rug at its head. Then Saul said to Michal, 'Why have you played this trick on me and let my enemy get safe away?' And Michal answered, 'He said to me, "Help me to escape or I will kill you." '

Meanwhile David made good his escape and came to Samuel at Ramah, and told him how Saul had treated him. Then he and Samuel went to Naioth and stayed there. Saul was told that David was there, and he sent a party of men to seize him. [1 Sam. 19:1–2, 4, 6–7, 9–19]

With exquiste irony the story next focuses on the deep and loving friendship between Saul's son and David.

Then David made his escape from Naioth in Ramah and came to Jonathan. 'What have I done?' he asked. 'What is my offence? What does your father think I have done wrong, that he seeks my life?' Jonathan answered him, 'God forbid! There is no thought of putting you to death. I am sure my father will not do anything whatever without telling me. Why should my father hide such a thing from me? I cannot believe it!' David said, 'I am ready to swear to it: your father has said to himself, "Jonathan must not know this or he will resent it," because he knows that you have a high regard for me. As the Lord lives, your life upon it, there is only a step between me and death.'
[1 Sam. 20:1–3]

Jonathan was the sort of person who found it hard to believe evil of any man. But the intense sincerity of his beloved friend convinces him that he should investigate.

So they went together into the fields, and Jonathan said to David, 'I promise you, David, in the sight of the Lord the God of Israel, this time tomorrow I will sound my father for the third time and, if he is well disposed to you, I will send and let you know. If my father means mischief, the Lord do the same to me and more, if I do not let you know and get you safely away. Jonathan pledged himself afresh to David because of his love for him, for he loved him as himself. Then he said to him, 'Tomorrow is the new moon, and you will be missed when your place is empty. So go down at nightfall for the third time to the place where you hid on the evening of the feast and stay by the mound there. Then I will shoot three arrows towards it, as though I were aiming at a mark. Then I will send my boy to find the arrows. If I say to him, "Look, the arrows are on this side of you, pick them up," then you can come out of hiding. You will be quite safe, I swear it; for there will be nothing amiss. But if I say to the lad, "Look, the arrows are on the other side of you, further on," then the Lord has said that you must go; the Lord stand witness between us for ever to the pledges we have exchanged.'

So David hid in the fields. The new moon came, the dinner was prepared, and the king sat down to eat. Saul took his customary seat by the wall, and Abner sat beside him; Jonathan too was present, but David's place was empty. That day Saul said nothing, for he thought that David was absent by some chance, perhaps because he was ritually unclean. But on the second day, the day after the new moon, David's place was still empty, and Saul said to his son Jonathan, 'Why has not the son of Jesse come to the feast, either yesterday or today?' Jonathan answered Saul, 'David asked permission to go to Bethlehem. He asked my leave and said, "Our family is holding a sacrifice in the town and my brother himself has ordered me to be there. Now, if you have any regard for me, let me slip away to see my brothers." That is why he has not come to dine with the king.' Saul was angry with Jonathan, 'You son of a crooked and unfaithful mother! You have made friends with the son of Jesse only to bring shame on yourself and dishonour on your mother; I see how it will be. As long as Jesse's son remains alive on earth, neither you nor your crown will be safe. Send at once and fetch him; he deserves to die.' Jonathan answered his father, 'Deserves to die! Why? What has he done?' At that, Saul picked up his spear and threatened to kill him; and he knew that his father was bent on David's death. Jonathan left the table in a rage and ate nothing on the second day of the festival; for he was indignant on David's behalf because his father had humiliated him.

Next morning, Jonathan went out into the fields to meet David at the appointed time, taking a young boy with him. He said to the boy, 'Run and find the arrows; I am going to shoot.' The boy ran on, and he shot the arrows over his head. When the boy reached the place where Jonathan's arrows had fallen, Jonathan called out after him, 'Look, the arrows are beyond you. Hurry! No time to lose! Make haste!' The boy gathered up the arrows and brought them to his master; but only Jonathan and David knew what this meant; the boy knew nothing. Jonathan handed his weapons to the boy and told him to take them back to the city. When the boy had gone, David got up from behind the mound and bowed humbly three times. Then they kissed one another and shed tears together, until David's grief was even greater than Jonathan's. Jonathan said to David, 'Go in safety; we have pledged each other in the name of the Lord who is witness for ever between you and me and between your descendants and mine.'

[1 Sam. 20:12–13, 17–42]

DAVID IN EXILE

Hungry, unarmed, and alone, David stops briefly, in his flight from Saul's house, at the shrine at Nob. By inventing a story David waylays the priests' suspicions, commits them to tell no one he has been there, and gets food and armor for himself.

David made his way to the priest Ahimelech at Nob, who hurried out to meet him and said, 'Why have you come alone and no one with you?' David answered Ahimelech, 'I am under orders from the king: I was to let no one know about the mission on which he was sending me or what these orders were. When I took leave of my men I told them to meet me in such and such a place. Now, what have you got by you? Let me have five loaves, or as many as you can find.' The priest answered David, 'I have no ordinary bread available. There is only the sacred bread; but have the young men kept themselves from women?' David answered the priest, 'Women have been denied us hitherto, when I have been on campaign, even an ordinary campaign, and the young men's bodies have remained holy; and how much more will they be holy today?' So, as there was no other bread there, the priest gave him the sacred bread, the Bread of the Presence, which had just been taken from the presence of the Lord to be replaced by freshly baked bread on the day that the old was removed. One of Saul's servants happened to be there that day, detained before the Lord; his name was Doeg the Edomite, and he was the strongest of all Saul's herdsmen. David said to Ahimelech, 'Have you a spear or sword here at hand? I have no sword or other weapon with me, because the king's business was urgent.' The priest answered, 'There is the sword of Goliath the Philistine whom you slew in the Vale of Elah; it is wrapped up in a cloak behind the ephod. If you wish to take that, take it; there is no other weapon here.' David said, 'There is no sword like it; give it to me.'   [1 Sam. 21:1b–9]

Continuing his journey, David comes to Gath where he is taken into custody by the soldiers of Achish, the king of Gath. Again by cunning and deception he escapes.

That day, David went on his way, eluding Saul, and came to Achish king of Gath. The servants of Achish said to him, 'Surely this is David, the king of his country, the man of whom they sang as they danced:

> Saul made havoc among thousands
> but David among tens of thousands.'

These words were not lost on David, and he became very much afraid of Achish king of Gath. So he altered his behaviour in public and acted like a lunatic in front of them all, scrabbling on the double doors of the city gate and dribbling down his beard. Achish said to his servants, 'The man is mad! Why bring him to me? Am I short of madmen that you bring this one to plague me? Must I have this fellow in my house?'   [1 Sam. 21:10–15]

Finally at Adullam in the south, David is joined by family and friends. He also attaches to himself a growing band of malcontent soldiers. "Men in any kind of distress or in debt or with a grievance gathered about him, about 400 in number, and he became their chief."

One of the most revealing stories about David concerns three men who

went down towards the beginning of harvest to join David at the cave of Adullam, while a band of Philistines was encamped in the Vale of Rephaim. At that time David was in the stronghold and a Philistine garrison held Bethlehem. One day a longing came over David, and he exclaimed, 'If only I could have a drink of water from the well by the gate of Bethlehem!' At this the heroic three made their way through the Philistine lines and drew water from the well by the gate of Bethlehem and brought it to David. But David refused to drink it; he poured it out to the Lord and said, 'God forbid that I should do such a thing! Can I drink the blood of these men who risked their lives for it?' So he would not drink it.   [2 Sam. 23:13–17]

Meanwhile, Saul's passion to murder David was such that when he heard of David's encounter with the priests at Nob, he had all the priests and their families hacked to death. Pursued by Saul, David was forced to establish friendly relations with the Philistines. They were only too happy to encourage internal divisions in Israel, and gave him a small southern town as his base of operations. Fortunately the Philistine general did not trust David enough to enroll him directly in the battle against Saul.

When Saul returned from the pursuit of the Philistines, he learnt that David was in the wilderness of En-gedi. So he took three thousand men picked from the whole of Israel and went in search of David and his men to the east of the Rocks of the Wild Goats. There beside the road were some sheepfolds, and near by was a cave, at the far end of which David and his men were sitting concealed. Saul came to the cave and went in to relieve himself.   [1 Sam. 24:1–3]

As the unsuspecting Saul squats to relieve himself, David's men urge him to kill the king:

His men said to David, 'The day has come: the Lord has put your enemy into your hands, as he promised he would, and you may do what you please with him.' David said to his men, 'God forbid that I should harm my master, the Lord's anointed, or lift a finger against him; he is the Lord's anointed.' So David reproved his men severely and would not let them attack Saul. He himself got up stealthily and cut off a piece of Saul's cloak; but when he had cut it off, his conscience smote him. Saul rose, left the cave and went on his way; whereupon David also came out of the cave and called after Saul, 'My lord the king!' When Saul looked round, David prostrated himself in obeisance and said to him, 'Why do you listen when they say that David is out to do you harm? Today you can see for yourself that the Lord put you into my power in the cave; I had a mind to kill you, but no, I spared your life and said, "I cannot lift a finger against my master, for he is the Lord's anointed." Look, my dear lord, look at this piece of your cloak in my hand. I cut it off, but I did not kill you; this will show you that I have no thought of violence or treachery against you, and that I have done you no wrong; yet you are resolved to take my life. May the Lord judge between us! but though he may take vengeance on you for my sake, I will never lift my hand against you; "One wrong begets another," as the old saying goes, yet I will never lift my hand against you. Who has the king of Israel come out against? What are you pursuing? A dead dog, a mere flea. The Lord will be judge and decide between us; let him look into my cause, he will plead for me and will acquit me.'   [1 Sam. 24:4–15]

Later David was given another opportunity to slay Saul as he slept, and again he refused to do so. Quoting the ancient proverb that one wrong begets another, he rejected violence as a solution. David's attitude was one of respect and propriety. Saul the king was anointed by God; God would decide the fates of both Saul and David. There was no need for David to take matters into his own hands, to do anything rash or extreme.

In the meantime, the astute and canny David set about strengthening his own position by establishing a power base in his home district of Judah. First, he married a rich Judean widow by the name of Abigail. Then he made efforts to ingratiate himself with the men of Judah by helping them fight off their enemies, though he took great pains to delude the Philistines into thinking he was hated by his own people.

THE DEATH OF SAUL AND JONATHAN

The Philistines were now poised to mount a massive attack on Saul's army. Haunted by Samuel's rejection of him, threatened by David's increasing popularity and strength, the pathetically distraught Saul sought some way to consult Yahweh about what he should do. There was, however, no one to turn to: Samuel was now dead, Saul had wiped out the priests at Nob, and the court prophets were unable to help. Though in his early days Saul had tried to rid Israel of necromancers (spiritualists who allegedly consult the dead), in desperation he now turns superstitiously to just such a medium, the witch at Endor.

Saul put on different clothes and went in disguise with two of his men. He came to the woman by night and said, 'Tell me my fortunes by consulting the dead, and call up the man I name to you.' But the woman answered, 'Surely you know what Saul has done, how he has made away with those who call up ghosts and spirits; why do you press me to do what will lead to my death?' Saul swore her an oath: 'As the Lord lives, no harm shall come to you for this.' The woman asked whom she should call up, and Saul answered, 'Samuel.' When the woman saw Samuel appear, she shrieked and said to Saul, 'Why have you deceived me? You are Saul!' The king said to her, 'Do not be afraid. What do you see?' The woman answered, 'I see a ghostly form coming up from the earth.' 'What is it like?' he asked; she answered, 'Like an old man coming up, wrapped in a cloak.' Then Saul knew it was Samuel, and he bowed low with his face to the ground, and prostrated himself. Samuel said to Saul, 'Why have you disturbed me and brought me up?' Saul answered, 'I am in great trouble; the Philistines are pressing me and God has turned away; he no longer answers me through prophets or through dreams, and I have summoned you to tell me what I should do.' Samuel said, 'Why do you ask me, now that the Lord has turned from you and become your adversary? He has done what he foretold through me. He has torn the kingdom from your hand and given it to another man, to David. For the same reason the Lord will let your people Israel fall into the hands of the Philistines and, what is more, tomorrow you and your sons shall be with me. Yes, indeed, the Lord will give the Israelite army into the hands of the Philistines.' Saul was overcome and fell his full length to the ground, terrified by Samuel's words. He had no strength left, for he had eaten nothing all day and all night.

[1 Sam. 28:8–17, 19–20]

We note that Saul did not see Samuel, but only heard his distant voice. Mediums are often skillful ventriloquists. The message of doom may have been placed by the witch in Samuel's mouth as a way of getting even with Saul for his earlier persecution of mediums. The most likely explanation, however, is that the distraught Saul, in the face of impending doom, experienced an hallucination which was the result of long and guilty brooding over his disobedience of God's will.

As predicted, doom came in the ensuing battle of Mount Gilboa.

The Philistines fought a battle against Israel, and the men of Israel were routed, leaving their dead on Mount Gilboa. The Philistines hotly pursued Saul and his sons and killed the three sons, Jonathan, Abinadab and Malchishua. The battle went hard for Saul, for some archers came upon him and he was wounded in the belly by the archers. So he said to his armour-bearer, 'Draw your sword and run me through, so that these uncircumcised brutes may not come and taunt me and make sport of me.' But the armour-bearer refused, he dared not; whereupon Saul took his own sword and fell on it. When the armour-bearer saw that Saul was dead, he too fell on his sword and died with him. Thus they all died together on that day, Saul, his three sons, and his armour-bearer, as well as his men. And all the Israelites in the district of the Vale and of the Jordan, when they saw that the other Israelites had fled and that Saul and his sons had perished, fled likewise, abandoning their cities, and the Philistines went in and occupied them.

Next day, when the Philistines came to strip the slain, they found Saul and his three sons lying dead on Mount Gilboa. They cut off his head and stripped him of his weapons; then they sent messengers through the length and breadth of their land to take the good news to idols and people alike. They deposited his armour in the temple of Ashtoreth and nailed his body on the wall of Beth-shan.

[1 Sam. 31:1–10]

Tragic as this tale of Saul's defeat and suicide is, it ends with a beautiful act of human bravery. In gratitude for Saul's deliverance of their city many years earlier, the men of Jabesh-gilead risked their lives to rescue the decapitated and impaled body of Saul from public disgrace.

When the inhabitants of Jabesh-gilead heard what the Philistines had done to Saul, the bravest of them journeyed together all night long and recovered the bodies of Saul and his sons from the wall of Beth-shan; they brought them back to Jebesh and anointed them there with spices.   [1 Sam. 31:11–12]

David was heartbroken when a messenger brought him the news. His eulogy of Saul's bravery and Jonathan's devotion to his father (even though Jonathan knew his father's faults) is one of the noblest treasures of all literature. Though he knew Saul's weaknesses and had experienced his hatred, David did not allow Saul's faults to obscure his greatness.

> O prince of Israel, laid low in death!
> How are the men of war fallen!   [2 Sam. 1:19]

With shame and anguish, David imagines the exaltation and gloating of the Philistines over their victory:

> Tell it not in Gath,
> proclaim it not in the streets of Ashkelon,
> lest the Philistine women rejoice,
> lest the daughters of the uncircumcised exult.
> Hills of Gilboa, let no dew or rain fall on you,
> no showers on the uplands!

For there the shields of the warriors lie tarnished,
and the shield of Saul, no longer bright with oil.

[2 Sam. 1:20–21]

Warriors' shields were oiled to make enemies' weapons slide
off them. Saul's shield now lies dry and weather-beaten.

Delightful and dearly loved were Saul and Jonathan;
in life, in death, they were not parted.
They were swifter than eagles,
stronger than lions.
Weep for Saul, O daughters of Israel!
who clothed you in scarlet and rich embroideries,
who spangled your dress with jewels of gold.
How are the men of war fallen, fallen on the field!
O Jonathan, laid low in death!
I grieve for you, Jonathan my brother;
dear and delightful you were to me;
your love for me was wonderful,
surpassing the love of women.
Fallen, fallen are the men of war;
and their armour left on the field.   [2 Sam. 1:23–27]

Chapter 9

DAVID THE KING

After Saul's death (in 1000 B.C.) the tribe of Judah proclaimed David king. The other tribes—those in the North—pledged loyalty to Saul's son Ishbosheth. The young Ishbosheth lacked both the experience and the talent to be an effective king and was only a front for Saul's general Abner. David's power base (Judah) was so insignificant that he had to remain, in appearance at least, a vassal to the Philistines. Though his forces skirmished with those of Ishbosheth, David had no intention of trying to force himself on the northern tribes as king. With the same wise patience which he had shown in Saul's reign, David waited seven years until, inevitably, Ishbosheth and Abner quarreled. Then, with lightning speed, the situation changed. Abner came to David and, in return for a favored position in David's court, pledged that he would win over to David all the northern tribes.

No sooner had David and Abner come to an agreement than Joab, David's nephew and general, murdered Abner. The ostensible reason Joab killed Abner was to avenge the death of his brother whom Abner had killed in battle. The real reason, however, was Joab's jealous fear that Abner would now take his place as David's right-hand man in military affairs. At about the same time two men, seeking David's favor, murdered Ishbosheth in his sleep. Though these murders conveniently removed the principal forces opposing David's control of Israel, there is no evidence that David was in any way involved in them and he condemned the killers with fervor.

Now all the tribes of Israel came to David at Hebron and said to him, 'We are your own flesh and blood. In the past, while Saul was still king over us, you led the forces of Israel to war and you brought them home again. And the Lord said to you, "You shall be shepherd of my people Israel; you shall be their prince." '   [2 Sam. 5:1–2]

The tribes acknowledged that David was chosen by God to be their king, but they nevertheless obtained a covenant from him. Israel's king was not an absolute ruler. The covenant spelt out his obligations to his people and his duty to consult the tribal leaders on state affairs.

All the elders of Israel came to the king at Hebron; there David made a covenant with them before the Lord, and they anointed David king over Israel. David came to the throne at the age of thirty and reigned for forty years. [2 Sam. 5:3–4]

JERUSALEM — THE CITY OF DAVID

David's principal aim was to reconcile the northern and southern tribes and to weld them into a unified nation. His first step was to secure as his capital a city which was unconnected with either the northern or southern tribes. Such a city was Jerusalem, the city-state of a people known as the Jebusites. It lay between the northern and southern tribes 2400 feet above sea level on a hill surrounded by valleys. Its position made it a nearly impregnable fortress. In about 993 B.C. David seized it from the over-confident Jebusites and made it the capital of all Israel.

The Jebusites had a sophisticated governmental organization centered on a powerful king whose duties were both religious and political. Under Saul, whose interests were largely military, the Israelite tribes had never been unified except in making war. David, however, had a different idea of kingship, and found the Jebusites' government a convenient model for his own nation.

David's seizure of Jerusalem was a brilliant maneuver. It provided him with a national capital which was centrally located on neutral ground between the two principal factions of the nation. Its strategic location and natural impregnability provided Israel with a virtually unconquerable national stronghold. Its governmental traditions provided a model for Israel as it changed from a loose confederation of tribes to a unified nation.

Israel's most pressing problem was the continuing Philistine threat. With extraordinary dispatch the united Israelites under David's spirited leadership crushed the Philistines in a series of battles. At the battle of Gath they ended the Philistine menace once and for all.

David now undertook the consolidation of Israel. Gradually limiting the autonomy of the tribes, David centralized most aspects of Israelite life under his control at Jerusalem. A national administration was established, taxes were for the first time collected on a nationwide basis, and justice was dispensed by a central judiciary in the capital. A civil service, modeled after Egypt's, was needed to handle these responsibilities. As a result an elitist, cultured, urbane upper class arose in Israel. And the old egalitarianism of tribal life, in which all men (even leaders) were equal, died out. The armed forces were unified under Joab. Forced labor was used to fortify Jerusalem and to erect huge public buildings.

JERUSALEM — ZION, CITY OF GOD

Most striking of all, David made Jerusalem the religious center of Israel. After defeating the Philistines, David recovered from them the Ark of the Covenant. The Ark, along with the personnel and rites connected with the old tribal confederation shrines of Shechem and Shiloh, was now brought by David to Jerusalem. Midst exultant songs and shouts of joy, the Ark entered through the gates of the city:

> Lift up your heads, you gates,
> lift yourselves up, you everlasting doors,
> that the king of glory may come in.
> Who is the king of glory?
> The Lord strong and mighty,
> the Lord mighty in battle.
> Lift up your heads, you gates,
> lift them up, you everlasting doors,
> that the king of glory may come in.
> Who then is the king of glory?
> The king of glory is the Lord of Hosts.   [Ps. 24:7–10]

Attired not as king but in the simplest linen garments of a priest, David was overcome with ecstasy and danced with wild abandon before the Ark.

> David, wearing a linen ephod, danced without restraint before the Lord. He and all the Israelites brought up the Ark of the Lord with shouting and blowing of trumpets.   [2 Sam. 6:14–15]

The Ark was then placed in a tent reminiscent of that which covered it in the Sinai wilderness wanderings.

When they had brought in the Ark of the Lord, they put it in its place inside the tent that David had pitched for it, and David offered whole-offerings and shared-offerings before the Lord. After David had completed these sacrifices, he blessed the people in the name of the Lord of Hosts and gave food to all the people, a flat loaf of bread, a portion of meat, and a cake of raisins, to every man and woman in the whole gathering of the Israelites.   [2 Sam. 6:17–19a]

Jerusalem was now not only "the city of David" but "Zion, city of God." Even conservatives who had been offended by David's abolition of tribal rights were caught up in this great act of national rededication to God which David had brought about.

In the golden age of David—as in most times of peace and prosperity—culture flourished. David himself was the principal moving force behind the development of Israel's music and literature, most of which was religious in orientation. A gifted musician, he founded a guild of musicians and a music school. His own reflective poems and songs are the basis of the collection of prayers and hymns which we know today as the Psalms.

David had established a priesthood to nourish the religious life of the people and to lead them in worship. He had long cherished the dream of building a great temple to house the Ark.

As soon as the king was established in his house and the Lord had given him security from his enemies on all sides, he said to Nathan the prophet, 'Here I live in a house of cedar, while the Ark of God is housed in curtains.' Nathan answered the king, 'Very well, do whatever you have in mind, for the Lord is with you.'   [2 Sam. 7:1–3]

Having slept on their conversation, Nathan wakes up realizing he has thoughtlessly approved an action which is wrong.

But that night the word of the Lord came to Nathan: 'Go and say to David my servant, "This is the word of the Lord: Are you the man to build me a house to dwell in? Down to this day I have never dwelt in a house since I brought Israel up from Egypt; I made my journey in a tent and a tabernacle. Wherever I journeyed with Israel, did I ever ask any of the judges whom I appointed shepherds of my people Israel why they had not built me a house of cedar?" '[2 Sam. 7:4–7]

"God needs no house to dwell in, but rather sets his presence in the midst of his people wherever they are. . . . God's true dwelling place is the people he is shaping. . . ." [5]

It is not for David to give Yahweh a house! Yahweh promises to give David a house (a heritage) which will last forever:

'Then say this to my servant David: "This is the word of the Lord of Hosts: I took you from the pastures, and from following the sheep, to be prince over my people Israel. I have been with you wherever you have gone, and have destroyed all the enemies in your path. I will make you a great name among the great ones of the earth. I will assign a place for my people Israel; there I will plant them, and they shall dwell in their own land. They shall be disturbed no more, never again shall wicked men oppress them as they did in the past, ever since the time when I appointed judges over Israel my people; and I will give you peace from all your enemies. The Lord has told you that he would build up your royal house. When your life ends and you rest with your forefathers, I will set up one of your family, one of your own children, to succeed you and I will establish his kingdom.   [2 Sam. 7:8–12]

This promise of a special relationship between Yahweh and David and his descendants is likened to the relationship of a father to a son. When a son does wrong he is punished.

I will be his father, and he shall be my son. When he does wrong, I will punish him as any father might, and not spare the rod.
[2 Sam. 7:14]

No matter how disobedient David and his descendants may be, God will never cease to love them and work through them.

My love will never be withdrawn from him as I withdrew it from Saul, whom I removed from your path. Your family shall be established and your kingdom shall stand for all time in my sight, and your throne shall be established for ever." '   [2 Sam. 7:15–16]

From this promise Israel later derived consolation in its darkest hours. And from this promise rose the hope and expectation of a Messiah—an "Anointed One" who would rise from the descendants of David to establish God's purpose on earth.

Nathan recounted to David all that had been said to him and all that had been revealed. Then King David went into the presence of the Lord and took his place there and said, 'What am I, Lord God,

and what is my family, that thou hast brought me thus far? And now
what more can I say? for well thou knowest thy servant David, O Lord
God.'   [2 Sam. 7:17–18, 20]

From God nothing can be hidden; the secrets of all hearts are
known to him.

David humbly acknowledges that his triumphs are not his
own, but the result of God's acting *through* him for his people.

Thou hast made good thy word; it was thy purpose to spread thy
servant's fame, and so thou hast raised me to this greatness. Great
indeed art thou, O Lord God; we have never heard of one like thee;
there is no god but thee. And thy people Israel, to whom can they
be compared? Is there any other nation on earth whom thou, O God,
hast set out to redeem from slavery to be thy people? Thou hast established thy people Israel as thy own for ever, and thou, O Lord,
hast become their God. Thou, O Lord God, art God; thou hast made
these noble promises to thy servant, and thy promises come true; be
pleased now to bless thy servant's house that it may continue always
before thee; thou, O Lord God, hast promised, and thy blessing shall
rest upon thy servant's house for evermore.

[2 Sam. 7:21–23a, 24, 28–29]

DAVID AND BATHSHEBA

The superpowers on the Nile and Euphrates lay in a state of
internal turmoil, and David had conquered all the lesser nearby
powers except the Phoenicians, with whom he concluded an
advantageous treaty. With agriculture and trade undisturbed by
war, and enriched by the tribute and booty of those it had conquered, Israel under David entered upon its golden age.

Yet the Israelites were not used to such power and wealth.
David's court soon began to resemble that of an oriental potentate. Men who have great power are subject to especially
great temptations to misuse it for themselves. David was no
exception. He came to regard his kingly office less and less as a
sacred responsibility to Yahweh and his people, and more and
more as an instrument of self-indulgence.

Affected by the restless emptiness that comes with late middle
age, David knows what he wants:

One evening David got up from his couch and, as he walked about
on the roof of the palace, he saw from there a woman bathing, and

she was very beautiful. He sent to inquire who she was, and the answer came, 'It must be Bathsheba daughter of Eliam and wife of Uriah
the Hittite.' So he sent messengers to fetch her, and when she came
to him, he had intercourse with her, though she was still being purified
after her period, and then she went home. She conceived, and sent
word to David that she was pregnant.   [2 Sam. 11:2–5]

In a polygamous society such as Israel, adultery was considered an even greater evil than it is in a society where a man
can have only one wife. David therefore seeks to cover up what
he has done by calling Uriah home from leave. His plan is
simple: Uriah will naturally have intercourse with Bathsheba
and later assume her child by David is his own.

David ordered Joab to send Uriah the Hittite to him. So Joab sent
him to David, and when he arrived, David asked him for news of
Joab and the troops and how the campaign was going; and then
said to him, 'Go down to your house and wash your feet after your
journey.' As he left the palace, a present from the king followed him.
But Uriah did not return to his house; he lay down by the palace gate
with the king's slaves. David heard that Uriah had not gone home,
and said to him, 'You have had a long journey, why did you not go
home?' Uriah answered David, 'Israel and Judah are under canvas,
and so is the Ark, and my lord Joab and your majesty's officers are
camping in the open; how can I go home to eat and drink and to
sleep with my wife? By your life, I cannot do this!'   [2 Sam. 11:6–11]

As a soldier engaged in a holy war, Uriah had sworn the usual
oath to abstain from intercourse. As a man of honor he adheres
to his vow.

Frustrated, David next tries to undermine Uriah's resolve by
getting him drunk.

David then said to Uriah, 'Stay here another day, and tomorrow I
will let you go.' So Uriah stayed in Jerusalem that day. The next day
David invited him to eat and drink with him and made him drunk.
But in the evening Uriah went out to lie down in his blanket among
the king's slaves and did not go home.   [2 Sam. 11:12–13]

Uriah's honesty and noble character bring out all the more
David's deceitfulness and selfishness.

Desperate, David arranges Uriah's death.

The following morning David wrote a letter to Joab and sent Uriah with it. He wrote in the letter, 'Put Uriah opposite the enemy where the fighting is fiercest and then fall back, and leave him to meet his death.' Joab had been watching the city, and he stationed Uriah at a point where he knew they would put up a stout fight. The men of the city sallied out and engaged Joab, and some of David's guards fell; Uriah the Hittite was also killed.

When Uriah's wife heard that her husband was dead, she mourned for him; and when the period of mourning was over, David sent for her and brought her into his house. She became his wife and bore him a son.   [2 Sam. 11:14–17, 26–27a]

Nathan, Israel's religious leader, was close enough to David to realize what David had done. To condone the king's actions by silence would have been a cowardly abdication of responsibility.

The Lord sent Nathan the prophet to David, and when he entered his presence, he said to him, 'There were once two men in the same city, one rich and the other poor. The rich man had large flocks and herds, but the poor man had nothing of his own except one little ewe lamb. He reared it himself, and it grew up in his home with his own sons. It ate from his dish, drank from his cup and nestled in his arms; it was like a daughter to him. One day a traveller came to the rich man's house, and he, too mean to take something from his own flocks and herds to serve to his guest, took the poor man's lamb and served up that.'   [2 Sam. 12:1–4]

The poor man's plight touches David's sensitive and compassionate heart. With righteous indignation, as chief judge of Israel, he pronounces judgment on the wicked man.

David was very angry, and burst out, 'As the Lord lives, the man who did this deserves to die! He shall pay for the lamb four times over, because he has done this and shown no pity.' Then Nathan said to David, 'You are the man. This is the word of the Lord the God of Israel to you: "I anointed you king over Israel, I rescued you from the power of Saul, I gave you your master's daughter and his wives to be your own, I gave you the daughters of Israel and Judah; and, had this not been enough, I would have added other favours as great. Why then have you flouted the word of the Lord by doing what is wrong in my eyes? You have struck down Uriah the Hittite with the sword; the man himself you murdered by the sword of the Ammonites, and you have stolen his wife. Now, therefore, since you have despised me and taken the wife of Uriah the Hittite to be your own wife, your family shall never again have rest from the sword." This is the word of the Lord: "I will bring trouble upon you from within your own family; I will take your wives and give them to another man before your eyes, and he will lie with them in broad daylight. What you did was done in secret; but I will do this in the light of day for all Israel to see." ' David said to Nathan, 'I have sinned against the Lord.'

[2 Sam. 12:5–13a]

Though the story of his selfishness with Bathsheba and his murder of Uriah show David at his worst, David's response to Nathan reveals him at his noblest. A lesser man might have silenced Nathan by putting him to death. But David was aware of the ethical standards God had given Israel. Brought face to face with the evil he has done, David makes no effort to evade responsibility and attempts no self-justification. With abject humility, he makes his starkly simple confession: "I have sinned against the Lord."

David then entered upon a period of fasting and prayer. Parts of Psalm 51 may derive from David's confession:

Be gracious to me, O God, in thy true love;
in the fullness of thy mercy blot out my misdeeds.

Wash away all my guilt
and cleanse me from my sin.
For well I know my misdeeds,
and my sins confront me all the day long.
Against thee, thee only, I have sinned
and done what displeases thee,
so that thou mayest be proved right in thy charge
and just in passing sentence.

In iniquity I was brought to birth
and my mother conceived me in sin;
yet, though thou hast hidden the truth in darkness,
through this mystery thou dost teach me wisdom.
Take hyssop and sprinkle me, that I may be clean;
wash me, that I may become whiter than snow;
let me hear the sounds of joy and gladness,

let the bones dance which thou hast broken.
Turn away thy face from my sins
and blot out all my guilt.

Create a pure heart in me, O God,
and give me a new and steadfast spirit;
do not drive me from thy presence
or take thy holy spirit from me;
revive in me the joy of thy deliverance
and grant me a willing spirit to uphold me.
I will teach transgressors the ways that lead to thee,
and sinners shall return to thee again.
O Lord God, my deliverer, save me from bloodshed,
and I will sing the praises of thy justice.
Open my lips, O Lord,
that my mouth may proclaim thy praise.
Thou hast no delight in sacrifice;
if I brought thee an offering, thou wouldst not accept it.
My sacrifice, O God, is a broken spirit;
a wounded heart, O God, thou wilt not despise.   [Ps. 51:1–17]

When Bathsheba's child was born dead, David regarded this as
divine justice at work.

DAVID AND ABSALOM

Like other eastern potentates, David had a number of wives,
each one of whom bore him children. Inevitably children with
different mothers but the same father were sexually attracted
to one another since they were thrown together in a common
household. A particularly ugly situation arose when Amnon, refused sexual relations by his beautiful half-sister Tamar, raped
her. David adored his children and was an indulgent father
who could rarely bring himself to correct them. Though he was
appalled by Amnon's crime, he could not face up to the situation
and take action, and Amnon was left unpunished. David's attitude outraged Tamar's full brother Absalom who took matters
into his own hands, killed Amnon in retaliation, and fled the
country. After Absalom had been in exile three years David was
persuaded to allow him to return, though at first he was not
allowed to take part in court life.

"No one in all Israel was so greatly admired for his beauty as

Absalom; he was without flaw from the crown of his head to the sole of his feet." (2 Sam. 14:25) The handsome but embittered Absalom, driven by the same force that led him to murder Amnon, now determined to seize power in Israel and began to organize a conspiracy against his father. Below the surface of Israelite society there were, as in every society, streams of discontent. No doubt there were those who chafed under David's centralized and authoritarian administration with its taxes, forced labor, and high-living elitist ruling class. Absalom's intrigue against his father fed on these discontents.

After this, Absalom provided himself with a chariot and horses and an escort of fifty men. He made it a practice to rise early and stand beside the road which runs through the city gate. He would hail every man who had a case to bring before the king for judgement and would ask him what city he came from. When he answered, 'I come, sir, from such and such a tribe of Israel,' Absalom would say to him, 'I can see that you have a very good case, but you will get no hearing from the king.' And he would add, 'If only I were appointed judge in the land, it would be my business to see that everyone who brought a suit or a claim got justice from me.' Whenever a man approached to prostrate himself, Absalom would stretch out his hand, take hold of him and kiss him. By behaving like this to every Israelite who sought the king's justice, Absalom stole the affections of the Israelites.   [2 Sam. 15:1–6]

Having ingratiated himself with many of the people, Absalom was now ready for his coup d'etat. Proceeding to David's old capital at Hebron, Absalom rallied the many in Judah who resented David's decision to move the capital from Hebron to Jerusalem and his abolition of tribal rights. At a signal, Absalom's followers in all the major cities proclaimed him king of Israel.

Absalom's revolt met with great initial success and David was forced to flee Jerusalem. When the priests followed him out of the city with the Ark, David told them to take it back.

'Take the Ark of God back to the city. If I find favour with the Lord, he will bring me back and will let me see the Ark and its dwelling-place again. But if he says he does not want me, then here I am; let him do what he pleases with me.'   [2 Sam. 15:25b–26]

David refused to use the Ark for personal purposes. God would decide who should be Israel's king. That decision would not be affected by the location of the Ark.

David rallied support in the countryside and succeeded in planting one of his own men among Absalom's advisers. In due course, in the forest of Ephron, his army destroyed Absalom's forces. In the rout Absalom, departing through the forest, was lifted off his mule and hung up helplessly as the forked branches of an oak tree caught him by the throat. Though David had instructed his men not to harm Absalom, Joab savagely killed the helpless rebel. He knew that as long as Absalom lived he would be a rallying point for treasonous activities.

David was now an old man. To the heartbreak and sense of shame and failure he felt when his son turned against him, was now added the grief of his son's death. So—after all his trials, all his splendid successes—this is what it had come to.

The king was deeply moved and went up to the roof-chamber over the gate and wept, crying out as he went, 'O, my son! Absalom my son, my son Absalom! If only I had died instead of you! O Absalom, my son, my son.'   [2 Sam. 18:33]

"In every crisis of David's life it was the human being, poet, lover, or father, who predominated over the soldier and the politician. So now his grief outweighed his triumph." [6]

Joab was told that the king was weeping and mourning for Absalom; and that day victory was turned to mourning for the whole army, because they heard how the king grieved for his son; they stole into the city like men ashamed to show their faces after a defeat in battle. The king hid his face and cried aloud, 'My son Absalom; O Absalom, my son, my son.'   [2 Sam. 19:1–4]

Angry at David's total preoccupation with his personal loss, Joab bluntly reproved the king for neglecting the brave and loyal soldiers who had risked their lives to defend him against his rebellious son.

But Joab came into the king's quarters and said to him, 'You have put to shame this day all your servants, who have saved you and your sons and daughters, your wives and your concubines. You love those

that hate you and hate those that love you; you have made us feel,
officers and men alike, that we are nothing to you; for it is plain that
if Absalom were still alive and all of us dead, you would be content.
Now go at once and give your servants some encouragement; if you
refuse, I swear by the Lord that not a man will stay with you tonight,
and that would be a worse disaster than any you have suffered since
your earliest days.' Then the king rose and took his seat in the gate;
and when the army was told that the king was sitting in the gate,
they all appeared before him.   [2 Sam. 19:5–8]

Though he reestablished himself at Jerusalem midst the cheers
of the people, David never recovered from the physical and
mental strain placed on him by Absalom's rebellion, and from
the emotional anguish of Absalom's death. A revolt among the
northern tribes, though quickly put down, was a devastating last
blow. Though still surrounded by the trappings of power and
glory, David was now a pathetic figure.

King David was now a very old man and, though they wrapped
clothes round him, he could not keep warm. So his household said to
him, 'Let us find a young virgin for your majesty, to attend you and
take care of you; and let her lie in your bosom, sir, and make you
warm.' So they searched all over Israel for a beautiful maiden and
found Abishag, a Shunammite, and brought her to the king. She was
a very beautiful girl, and she took care of the king and waited on
him, but he had no intercourse with her.   [1 Kings 1:1–4]

Impotent and alone, his glory mocked by the indignities of old
age, David waited for the inevitable, aware that those who surrounded him were not interested in him as much as they were in
the issue of who would be the next king. In the midst of the
intrigues, David chose Bathsheba's second son Solomon to be
his successor.

Then King David said, 'Call Zadok the priest, Nathan the prophet,
and Benaiah son of Jehoiada.' They came into the king's presence
and he gave them these orders: 'Take the officers of the household
with you; mount my son Solomon on the king's mule and escort him
down to Gihon. There Zadok the priest and Nathan the prophet shall
anoint him king over Israel. Sound the trumpet and shout, "Long live
King Solomon!" Then escort him home again, and he shall come and

sit on my throne and reign in my place; for he is the man that I have appointed prince over Israel and Judah.'

So Zadok the priest, Nathan the prophet, and Benaiah, together with the guards, went down and mounted Solomon on King David's mule and escorted him to Gihon. Zadok the priest took the horn of oil from the Tent of the Lord and anointed Solomon; they sounded the trumpet and all the people shouted, 'Long live King Solomon!' Then all the people escorted him home in procession, with great rejoicing and playing of pipes, so that the very earth split with the noise.

[1 Kings 1:32–35, 38–40, abridged]

David's last words—addressed to Solomon—show the complexity of his character. First, with simple eloquence, he tells him to follow the ways of God.

When the time of David's death drew near, he gave this last charge to his son Solomon: 'I am going the way of all the earth. Be strong and show yourself a man. Fulfil your duty to the Lord your God; conform to his ways, observe his statutes and his commandments, his judgements and his solemn precepts, as they are written in the law of Moses, so that you may prosper in whatever you do and whichever way you turn, and that the Lord may fulfill this promise that he made about me: "If your descendants take care to walk faithfully in my sight with all their heart and with all their soul, you shall never lack a successor on the throne of Israel." [1 Kings 2:1–4]

But his final words are those of a broken, bitter, and vengeful old man.

You know how Joab treated me and what he did to two commanders-in-chief in Israel, Abner and Amasa. Do as your wisdom prompts you, and do not let his grey hairs go down to the grave in peace. Show constant friendship to the family of Barzillai of Gilead; let them have their place at your table; they befriended me when I was a fugitive from your brother Absalom. Do not forget Shimei who cursed me bitterly the day I went to Mahanaim. True, he came down to meet me at the Jordan, and I swore by the Lord that I would not put him to death. But you do not need to let him go unpunished now; you are a wise man and will know how to deal with him; bring down his grey hairs in blood to the grave.' [1 Kings 2:5a, 6–9, abridged]

Fortunately time is forgiving. In later years when Israel looked back on David's reign, it remembered not his mistakes and cruelties, but his masterful leadership, his sensitivity as a musician and poet, his humble acceptance of criticism, and his readiness to love and to forgive.

Chapter 10

SOLOMON

Though his right to succeed David had been contested, once Solomon ascended the throne there was no longer any question about who was king of Israel. To consolidate his position he eliminated all the disappointed contenders and their supporters.

David had grown up, a simple shepherd boy, in Israel's darkest hour; in an heroic struggle the shepherd boy had become a king and had welded a scattered group of bickering tribes into a great nation. Though he achieved power and riches, he remained a man of the common people; the years of insecurity and struggle were never forgotten. Solomon, however, was born to the purple, knew little beyond the sumptuous life of the court, and inherited the throne of a great and prosperous kingdom by the accident of birth.

THE WISDOM OF SOLOMON

Contrary to what we might expect, Solomon, at least at the start of his reign, undertook his obligation as king with humility and dedication.

Now King Solomon went to Gibeon to offer a sacrifice, for that was the chief hill-shrine, and he used to offer a thousand whole-offerings on its altar. There that night the Lord God appeared to him in a dream and said, 'What shall I give you? Tell me.' And Solomon answered, 'Thou didst show great and constant love to thy servant David my father, because he walked before thee in loyalty, righteousness, and integrity of heart; and thou hast maintained this great and constant love towards him and hast now given him a son to succeed him on the throne. Now, O Lord my God, thou hast made thy servant king in place of my father David, though I am a mere child, unskilled in leadership. And I am here in the midst of thy people, the people of thy choice, too many to be numbered or counted. Give thy servant, therefore, a heart with skill to listen, so that he may govern thy people justly and distinguish good from evil. For who is equal to the task of governing this great people of thine?'   [1 Kings 3:4–9]

This picture of Solomon is undoubtedly idealized. History often forgets the imperfections of past heroes. Americans, for example, tend to look back on Washington and Lincoln as nearly perfect. But great men are idealized for a reason: the greatness of some of their deeds tends in retrospect to overshadow and color everything else they did. Solomon probably *was* humble. Those who, like Solomon, have always lived midst the boast of heraldry and the pomp of power often know far better than those who scramble for power and wealth how insignificant human wealth and power are. Even kings undress, eat, and die. And they know better than anyone that "I am but a child."

The Biblical account of God's response to Solomon's prayer is clearly colored by the later historian's knowledge of Solomon's fabulous wealth.

The Lord was well pleased that Solomon had asked for this, and he said to him, 'Because you have asked for this, and not for long life for yourself, or for wealth, or for the lives of your enemies, but have asked for discernment in administering justice, I grant your request; I give you a heart so wise and so understanding that there has been none like you before your time nor will be after you. I give you furthermore those things for which you did not ask, such wealth and honour as no king of your time can match. And if you conform to my ways and observe my ordinances and commandments, as your father David did, I will give you long life.' Then he awoke, and knew it was a dream.

Solomon came to Jerusalem and stood before the Ark of the Covenant of the Lord; there he sacrificed whole-offerings and brought shared-offerings, and gave a feast to all his household.

[1 Kings 3:10–15]

Psalm 72, though edited and revised for the yearly festivals in which kings after Solomon rededicated themselves to God, may originate in part from the prayers of the people for Solomon as he began his reign.

O God, endow the king with thy own justice,
and give thy righteousness to a king's son,

that he may judge thy people rightly
and deal out justice to the poor and suffering.
May hills and mountains afford thy people
peace and prosperity in righteousness.
He shall give judgement for the suffering
and help those of the people that are needy;
he shall crush the oppressor.
He shall live as long as the sun endures,
long as the moon, age after age.
He shall be like rain falling on early crops,
like showers watering the earth.
In his days righteousness shall flourish,
prosperity abound until the moon is no more.
May he hold sway from sea to sea,
from the River to the ends of the earth.
Ethiopians shall crouch low before him;
his enemies shall lick the dust.
The kings of Tarshish and the islands shall bring gifts,
the kings of Sheba and Seba shall present their tribute,
and all kings shall pay him homage,
all nations shall serve him. [Ps. 72:1–11]

Solomon's wisdom was widely celebrated even in his own time. One incident in particular reveals how his discerning mind provided justice for his people.

Then there came into the king's presence two women who were prostitutes and stood before him. The first said, 'My lord, this woman and I share the same house, and I gave birth to a child when she was there with me. On the third day after my baby was born she too gave birth to a child. We were quite alone; no one else was with us in the house; only the two of us were there. During the night this woman's child died because she overlaid it, and she got up in the middle of the night, took my baby from my side while I, your servant, was asleep, and laid it in her bosom, putting her dead child in mine. When I got up in the morning to feed my baby, I found him dead; but when I looked at him closely, I found that it was not the child that I had borne.' The other woman broke in, 'No; the living child is mine; yours is the dead one,' while the first retorted, 'No; the dead child is yours; mine is the living one.' So they went on arguing in the king's presence. The king thought to himself, 'One of them says, "This is my child, the living one; yours is the dead one." The other says, "No; it is your child that is dead and mine that is alive." ' Then he said, 'Fetch me a sword.' They brought in a sword and the king gave the order: 'Cut the living child in two and give half to one and half to the other.' At this the woman who was the mother of the living child, moved with love for her child, said to the king, 'Oh! sir, let her have the baby; whatever you do, do not kill it.' The other said, 'Let neither of us have it; cut it in two.' Thereupon the king gave judgement: 'Give the living baby to the first woman; do not kill it. She is its mother.' When Israel heard the judgement which the king had given, they all stood in awe of him; for they saw that he had the wisdom of God within him to administer justice.

[1 Kings 3:16–28]

Solomon's wisdom extended beyond the realms of morals and justice. None of his achievements is more notable than the wise and skillful way in which he developed and elaborated the rudimentary central administration left him by his father. Solomon was a brilliant organizer. He established a cabinet and gave each of his advisers responsibility for an area of national life. In an effort to break down still further the old tribal organization, he divided the nation into twelve tax districts which did not conform to tribal boundaries. Each district was responsible for the financial maintenance of the government for a month each year.

Looking back on Solomon many years later, when Israel was divided and humiliated by foreign powers, men saw his reign as a golden age of peace and prosperity.

The people of Judah and Israel were countless as the sands of the sea; they ate and they drank, and enjoyed life. Solomon ruled over all the kingdoms from the river Euphrates to Philistia and as far as the frontier of Egypt; they paid tribute and were subject to him all his life.

Solomon's provision for one day was thirty kor of flour and sixty kor of meal, ten fat oxen and twenty oxen from the pastures and a hundred sheep, as well as stags, gazelles, roebucks, and fattened fowl. For he was paramount over all the land west of the Euphrates from Tiphsah to Gaza, ruling all the kings west of the river; and he enjoyed peace on all sides. All through his reign Judah and Israel continued at peace, every man under his own vine and fig-tree, from Dan to Beersheba.

Solomon had forty thousand chariot-horses in his stables and twelve thousand cavalry horses.

The regional governors, each for a month in turn, supplied provisions for King Solomon and for all who came to his table; they never fell short in their deliveries. They provided also barley and straw, each according to his duty, for the horses and chariot-horses where it was required.   [1 Kings 4:20–28]

For years Israel's leaders had been preoccupied with military matters, with protecting the tribes from attack. Solomon basked in the political and military security which his father bequeathed him. He could turn his attention to cultural matters. Under him the intellectual and artistic life of Israel blossomed.

And God gave Solomon depth of wisdom and insight, and understanding as wide as the sand on the sea-shore, so that Solomon's wisdom surpassed that of all the men of the east and of all Egypt. For he was wiser than any man; his fame spread among all the surrounding nations. He uttered three thousand proverbs, and his songs numbered a thousand and five. He discoursed of trees, from the cedar of Lebanon down to the marjoram that grows out of the wall, of beasts and birds, of reptiles and fishes. Men of all races came to listen to the wisdom of Solomon, and from all the kings of the earth who had heard of his wisdom he received gifts.

[1 Kings 4:29–34, abridged]

Ironically, however, the outstanding surviving achievement of the great cultural awakening of Solomon's reign was a literary work quite uncelebrated at the time. Modern scholars call it the "J" or "Yahwist" epic. It is one of the four strands which were combined 400 years later to form the first five books of the Bible. Drawing from vast pools of oral tradition, the author(s) of the J epic attempted to put in writing a comprehensive account of Israel's experience in history, from the earliest times to the Exodus and Sinai. During Solomon's reign, when foreigners were the main cultural influence and Israel's distinctive faith was in danger of being lost, J gathered together the old traditions of the tribal shrines into one dramatically persuasive written document which showed God's distinctive love for Israel and Israel's distinctive call. This document was destined to last longer than all the temples and palaces and literature and art which brought Solomon such fame in his own lifetime.

THE BUILDING OF THE TEMPLE

Solomon's cultural interests found their most striking expression in architecture. David's tastes had been simple; Solomon wished to make Jerusalem a magnificent capital city worthy of a great king. He threw himself with zeal into the complex arrangements for the magnificent buildings he envisioned.

When Hiram King of Tyre heard that Solomon had been anointed king in his father's place, he sent envoys to him, because he had always been a friend of David. Solomon sent this answer to Hiram: 'You know that my father David could not build a house in honour of the name of the Lord his God, because he was surrounded by armed nations until the Lord made them subject to him. But now on every side the Lord my God has given me peace; there is no one to oppose me, I fear no attack. So I propose to build a house in honour of the name of the Lord my God, following the promise given by the Lord to my father David: "Your son whom I shall set on the throne in your place will build the house in honour of my name." If therefore you will now give orders that cedars be felled and brought from Lebanon, my men will work with yours, and I will pay you for your men whatever sum you fix; for, as you know, we have none so skilled at felling timber as your Sidonians.'   [1 Kings 5:1–6]

The Israelites had only recently ceased their semi-nomadic life. Preoccupied with living off the land and defending themselves from enemies, they had, until David's reign, little time for culture. As a result there were no skilled Israelite artists and architects, and Solomon had to turn to the culturally advanced Phoenicians, who had both skilled artisans and the best building materials.

When Hiram received Solomon's message, he was greatly pleased and said, 'Blessed be the Lord today who has given David a wise son to rule over this great people.' And he sent this reply to Solomon: 'I have received your message. In this matter of timber, both cedar and pine, I will do all you wish. My men shall bring down the logs from Lebanon to the sea and I will make them up into rafts to be floated to the place you appoint; I will have them broken up there and you can remove them. You, on your part, will meet my wishes if you provide the food for my household.' So Hiram kept Solomon supplied

with all the cedar and pine that he wanted, and Solomon supplied
Hiram with twenty thousand kor of wheat as food for his household
and twenty kor of oil of pounded olives; Solomon gave this yearly
to Hiram. (The Lord had given Solomon wisdom as he had promised
him; there was peace between Hiram and Solomon and they concluded an alliance.)   [1 Kings 5:7–12]

The price of Hiram's human and material resources—all imported for the building project—was staggering: 220,000 bushels
of wheat and 180,000 gallons of olive oil.

Providing unskilled labor for Solomon's projects were no less
than 180,000 Israelites whom Solomon forced to work one out
of every three months under Hiram's skilled craftsmen.

King Solomon raised a forced levy from the whole of Israel amount-
ing to thirty thousand men. He sent them to Lebanon in monthly relays
of ten thousand, so that the men spent one month in Lebanon and
two at home; Adoniram was superintendent of the whole levy. Solomon
had also seventy thousand hauliers and eighty thousand quarrymen,
apart from the three thousand three hundred foremen in charge of
the work who superintended the labourers. By the king's orders they
quarried huge, massive blocks for laying the foundation of the Lord's
house in hewn stone. Solomon's and Hiram's builders and the Gebalites
shaped the blocks and prepared both timber and stone for the building of the house.   [1 Kings 5:13–18]

Though the Temple was only one of the many buildings in the
vast complex Solomon envisioned, it was the most important one
and gave a pious aura to the whole project. Solomon was human;
his motives were no doubt mixed. On the one hand, he wished
to build a temple and city which would reflect and proclaim his
greatness. On the other hand, he was motivated as well by the
peoples' needs. The Temple was to be a reminder to the people
of God's presence. Though material itself, in the midst of the
material things of the world it would remind them of the God
who had entered into a covenant relationship with them and
who required of them high ethical standards in their daily lives.

Only the most perfect building materials were used in its construction. It was to be a building unexcelled in magnificence,
which would last forever: though men come and go in life, God
is eternally present among his people.

The building was actually quite small (about 30 x 90 x 45 feet); it was the house (or palace) of God, the resting place of the Ark of the Covenant (symbol of God's presence), and not in any sense (like a church) a building for people. Only priests entered the Temple, and only the high priest, once a year, was permitted to enter the "Holy of Holies," the closed-off inner sanctuary in which the Ark rested. Vast areas outside were paved for people to stand in. Naturally the design of the Temple was Phoenician. The First Book of Kings gives an elaborate description of the construction and furnishing. The account, however, is broken in the middle by these sober words:

> Then the word of the Lord came to Solomon, saying, 'As for this house which you are building, if you are obedient to my ordinances and conform to my precepts and loyally observe all my commands, then I will fulfil my promise to you, the promise I gave to your father David, and I will dwell among the Israelites and never forsake my people Israel.'   [1 Kings 6:11–13]

Solomon is reminded that God's presence among his people is not the result of any Temple in their midst. God's presence is conditional: he is present "*if* you are obedient to my ordinances and conform to my precepts and loyally observe all my commands."

Finally after seven years of labor and phenomenal expense, the Temple was completed. The day of dedication was set to coincide with the New Year Feast (celebrated today as Rosh Hashana). One of the psalms still sung at the celebration of this festival is Psalm 132. It may be a revised version of the words spoken and sung as the Ark was brought from the tent in which David had placed it to the new Temple.

The ceremony begins with the king's prayer in the tent before the Ark.

> O Lord, remember David
> in the time of his adversity,
> how he swore to the Lord
> and made a vow to the Mighty One of Jacob:
> 'I will not enter my house
> nor will I mount my bed,
> I will not close my eyes in sleep

or my eyelids in slumber,
until I find a sanctuary for the Lord,
a dwelling for the Mighty One of Jacob.'   [Ps. 132:1–5]

Then the priests lift up the Ark and transport it in a great procession through the crowds to the Temple as the choir sings:

Arise, O Lord, and come to thy resting-place,
thou and the ark of thy power.
Let thy priests be clothed in righteousness
and let thy loyal servants shout for joy.
For thy servant David's sake
reject not thy anointed king.   [Ps. 132:8–10]

Finally God's promise to dwell with David and his descendants (*"if* your sons keep my covenant") is recalled as the Ark is placed in the Holy of Holies:

The Lord swore to David
an oath which he will not break:
'A prince of your own line
will I set upon your throne.
If your sons keep my covenant
and heed the teaching that I give them,
their sons in turn for all time
shall sit upon your throne.'
For the Lord has chosen Zion
and desired it for his home:
'This is my resting-place for ever;
here will I make my home, for such is my desire.' [Ps. 132:11–14]

Solomon's beautiful dedication prayer begins on a note of rapturous praise:

Then Solomon, standing in front of the altar of the Lord in the presence of the whole assembly of Israel, spread out his hands towards heaven and said, 'O Lord God of Israel, there is no god like thee in heaven above or on earth beneath, keeping covenant with thy servants and showing them constant love while they continue faithful to thee in heart and soul. Thou hast kept thy promise to thy servant David my father; by thy deeds this day thou hast fulfilled what thou didst say to him in words. Now therefore, O Lord God of Israel, keep this promise of thine to thy servant David my father: "You shall never

want for a man appointed by me to sit on the throne of Israel, if only
your sons look to their ways and walk before me as you have walked
before me." And now, O God of Israel, let the words which thou
didst speak to thy servant David my father be confirmed.

> O Lord who hast set the sun in heaven,
> but hast chosen to dwell in thick darkness,
> here have I built thee a lofty house,
> a habitation for thee to occupy for ever.'
>
> [1 Kings 8:22–26, 12b–13]

In a dramatic and concrete way the Temple emphasized the
presence of the living God immanent and accessible among his
people. Yet though it contained the Ark, the special symbol and
reminder of God's presence, it was not a "habitation" which
could contain or confine the God who was king of the universe.
God cannot be put in a box. Solomon continues:

> 'But can God indeed dwell on earth? Heaven itself, the highest
> heaven, cannot contain thee; how much less this house that I have
> built! Yet attend to the prayer and the supplication of thy servant,
> O Lord my God, listen to the cry and the prayer which thy servant
> utters this day, that thine eyes may ever be upon this house night
> and day, this place of which thou didst say, "My Name shall be there";
> so mayest thou hear thy servant when he prays towards this place.
> Hear the supplication of thy servant and of thy people Israel when
> they pray towards this place. Hear thou in heaven thy dwelling and,
> when thou hearest, forgive.'   [1 Kings 8:27–30]

Since God's presence was dependent not on buildings made
with hands but on Israel's commitment to follow his ways, Solomon concludes with an exhortation to the people:

> 'Blessed be the Lord who has given his people Israel rest, as he
> promised: not one of the promises he made through his servant Moses
> has failed. The Lord our God be with us as he was with our fore-
> fathers; may he never leave us nor forsake us. May he turn our
> hearts towards him, that we may conform to all his ways, observing
> his commandments, statutes, and judgements, as he commanded our
> forefathers. And may the words of my supplication to the Lord be
> with the Lord our God day and night, that, as the need arises day

by day, he may grant justice to his servant and justice to his people
Israel. So all the peoples of the earth will know that the Lord is
God, he and no other, and you will be perfect in loyalty to the Lord
our God as you are this day, conforming to his statutes and observing
his commandments.'   [1 Kings 8:56–61]

Finally, the people made an immense sacrificial offering of
their possessions:

When the king and all Israel came to offer sacrifices before the
Lord, Solomon offered as shared-offerings to the Lord twenty-two
thousand oxen and a hundred and twenty thousand sheep; thus it
was that the king and the Israelites dedicated the house of the Lord.
                                                [1 Kings 8:62–63]

SOLOMON IN ALL HIS GLORY

Meanwhile work was underway on the vast complex of royal
buildings: Solomon's own palace, the administrative and military
quarters, and a separate palace for his Egyptian wife. Though the
house of God was built in seven years, thirteen were required to
build the house of Solomon, which was considerably larger than
the Temple. Despite high taxes and forced labor, the expense of
the buildings so lavishly exceeded Solomon's income that he was
forced to cede twenty Galilean cities within his boundary to
Hiram, King of Tyre, to pay his debts.

Through most of its history Israel's geographical position—
along the path between the great powers of the Nile and Euphrates—was a terrible disadvantage. Yet in Solomon's time,
with the great powers in internal turmoil, it was advantageous.
Solomon was a shrewd businessman. He built fortified cities to
secure Israel's control of the principal trade routes between the
Nile and Euphrates, and then exacted tolls from all traders.
Excavations of vast stables at Megiddo show also that Solomon
engaged in extensive trade in horses and chariots. He undertook
extensive copper mining and refining in southern Palestine. In
partnership with Hiram, whose people were expert sailors, Solomon built a fleet of ships at the port of Ezion-geber on the Red
Sea, and made a fortune in sea trade with Eastern powers.

This sea trade may have had a devastating effect on the land
caravan trade which had been controlled for years by the people

of Sheba in southern Arabia. Commercial interests may account for the extraordinary visit to Solomon's court of the Queen of Sheba.

The queen of Sheba heard of Solomon's fame and came to test him with hard questions. She arrived in Jerusalem with a very large retinue, camels laden with spices, gold in great quantity, and precious stones. When she came to Solomon, she told him everything she had in her mind, and Solomon answered all her questions; not one of them was too abstruse for the king to answer. When the queen of Sheba saw all the wisdom of Solomon, the house which he had built, the food on his table, the courtiers sitting round him, and his attendants standing behind in their livery, his cupbearers, and the whole-offerings which he used to offer in the house of the Lord, there was no more spirit left in her. Then she said to the king, 'The report which I heard in my own country about you and your wisdom was true, but I did not believe it until I came and saw for myself. Indeed I was not told half of it; your wisdom and your prosperity go far beyond the report which I had of them. Happy are your wives, happy these courtiers of yours who wait on you every day and hear your wisdom! Blessed be the Lord your God who has delighted in you and has set you on the throne of Israel; because he loves Israel for ever, he has made you their king to maintain law and justice.' Then she gave the king a hundred and twenty talents of gold, spices in great abundance, and precious stones. Never again came such a quantity of spices as the queen of Sheba gave to King Solomon.

And King Solomon gave the queen of Sheba all she desired, whatever she asked, in addition to all that he gave her of his royal bounty. So she departed and returned with her retinue to her own land.

[1 Kings 10:1–10, 13]

To the Israelites writing later about Solomon's reign, his wealth seemed to defy belief.

Besides all this, Hiram's fleet of ships, which had brought gold from Ophir, brought in also from Ophir cargoes of almug wood and precious stones. The king used the wood to make stools for the house of the Lord and for the royal palace, as well as harps and lutes for the singers. No such almug wood has ever been imported or even seen since that time.

Now the weight of gold which Solomon received yearly was six hundred and sixty-six talents, in addition to the tolls levied by the customs officers and profits on foreign trade, and the tribute of the kings of Arabia and the regional governors.

King Solomon made two hundred shields of beaten gold, and six hundred shekels of gold went to the making of each one; he also made three hundred bucklers of beaten gold, and three minas of gold went to the making of each buckler. The king put these into the House of the Forest of Lebanon.

The king also made a great throne of ivory and overlaid it with fine gold. Six steps led up to the throne; at the back of the throne there was the head of a calf. There were arms on each side of the seat, with a lion standing beside each of them, and twelve lions stood on the six steps, one at either end of each step. Nothing like it had ever been made for any monarch. All Solomon's drinking vessels were of gold, and all the plate in the House of the Forest of Lebanon was of red gold; no silver was used, for it was reckoned of no value in the days of Solomon. The king had a fleet of merchantmen at sea with Hiram's fleet; once every three years this fleet of merchantmen came home, bringing gold and silver, ivory, apes and monkeys.

Thus King Solomon outdid all the kings of the earth in wealth and wisdom, and all the world courted him, to hear the wisdom which God had put in his heart. Each brought his gift with him, vessels of silver and gold, garments, perfumes and spices, horses and mules, so much year by year.   [1 Kings 10:11-12, 14-25]

Solomon had 700 wives and 300 concubines, many of them foreign. When we have accounted for his sensual needs, and after we realize that the confirming of alliances and treaties sometimes called for marriage to a foreign woman, we are still left with a superabundance of women. Only one thing can account for so vast a number: the need felt by the monarch of a newly established country to make a display of his power and wealth. A man who could support that sort of household was a man indeed, in Solomon's eyes. We might compare Solomon to a nouveau riche American with a fleet of Cadillacs. With the onset of the creeping impotence of age, Solomon apparently felt more need than ever to surround himself with the glitter of wealth and the vulgar display of power. His biographers, seeking to make excuse, put the blame on his women.

He had seven hundred wives, who were princesses, and three
hundred concubines, and they turned his heart from the truth. When
he grew old, his wives turned his heart to follow other gods, and he
did not remain wholly loyal to the Lord his God as his father David
had been. He followed Ashtoreth, goddess of the Sidonians, and
Milcom, the loathsome god of the Ammonites. Thus Solomon did what
was wrong in the eyes of the Lord, and was not loyal to the Lord
like his father David. He built a hill-shrine for Kemosh, the loathsome
god of Moab, on the height to the east of Jerusalem, and for Molech,
the loathsome god of the Ammonites. Thus he did for the gods to
which all his foreign wives burnt offerings and made sacrifices.

[1 Kings 11:3b–8]

Solomon had known in his heart, from boyhood on, that Yahweh was a "jealous" God whose steadfast love was not to be
toyed with. At the great moments in his life he had—at least in
principle, if not purely in practice—committed himself to Yahweh with single-minded devotion. Nevertheless he lost the vision,
and, under the pretense of "tolerance," allowed and even supported the worship of other gods within Yahweh's own city.

His inferiority complex about Israel's still unsophisticated culture—that of a man embarrassed by his family's humble background—led him to grasp at foreign cultures. Even the Temple
was a work of purely Phoenician genius.

In the end, his need for splendor and glitter divided and impoverished his people. Subject peoples such as the Edomites
tired of the heavy tributes he exacted and they revolted. His own
people—especially those in the north—plotted against him, seeking to throw off the heavy taxes and forced labor with which he
oppressed them. The reign which had begun with simple dedication ended in vulgar display and decadent self-indulgence. At
the end, Solomon reigned neither for the glory of God nor the
good of the people, but only for himself.

A thousand years after Solomon's death, Jesus of Nazareth
gave this evaluation of all the great king's accomplishments:
"Consider the lilies of the field, how they grow; they toil not,
neither do they spin; and yet I say unto you that even Solomon
in all his glory was not arrayed like one of these."

Chapter 11

ELIJAH

Immediately after Solomon's death in 922 B.C., his son Rehoboam was proclaimed king of the tribe of Judah at Hebron. Since Israel was a dual monarchy, he had to journey to the old northern shrine at Shechem to receive recognition as king by the northern tribes.

Even in the monarchy's golden age there had always been strong undercurrents of resistance to the single monarchy in the North. Both David and Solomon had to contend with major anti-monarchist revolutions. Fed up with the tyranny they had increasingly experienced under Solomon—high taxes, forced labor, disregard of tribal rights—the northern tribal elders offered their allegiance to Rehoboam only if he promised to abandon Solomon's oppressive measures.

Rejecting the advice of experienced counselors who told him to compromise with the elders, Rehoboam

next consulted those who had grown up with him, the young men in attendance, and asked them, 'What answer do you advise me to give to this people's request that I should lighten the yoke which my father laid on them?' The young men replied, 'Give this answer to the people who say that your father made their yoke heavy and ask you to lighten it; tell them: "My little finger is thicker than my father's loins. My father laid a heavy yoke on you; I will make it heavier. My father used the whip on you; but I will use the lash."' Jeroboam and the people all came back to Rehoboam on the third day, as the king had ordered. And the king gave them a harsh answer. He rejected the advice which the elders had given him and spoke to the people as the young men had advised: 'My father made your yoke heavy; I will make it heavier. My father used the whip on you; but I will use the lash.'   [1 Kings 12:8b–14]

Slapped in the face, the North rejected Rehoboam. The battle song of the revolutionaries over the preceding century now became the North's declaration of independence:

What share have we in David?
We have no lot in the son of Jesse.
Away to your homes, O Israel;
now see to your own house, David.   [1 Kings 12:16b]

In place of Solomon's son, the ten northern tribes elected the prominent revolutionary Jeroboam as their king. Consisting of about two-thirds of the territory of Solomon's Israel, this new northern kingdom called itself Israel. Only the tribe of Benjamin in the south joined with Judah in accepting Rehoboam as king. This small southern kingdom, with its king descended from David and its capital at Jerusalem, became known henceforth as Judah. Fifty years of intrigue and border skirmishes were necessary before the northern and southern kingdoms finally accepted their separateness.

In the north, Jeroboam set out at once to secure Israel's economic well-being by fortifying the shrine cities of Shechem and Penuel, which were located on key trade routes. He next confronted a serious problem in social psychology. Under David and Solomon the old local shrines had been shut down or eclipsed by Jerusalem which, with the Ark, Temple, and priesthood, had become the center of religious life. Since Jeroboam did not want his people to be pilgrims to his rival's capital, he had to reverse the trend. He therefore revived two shrines within the northern kingdom, Bethel in the southern part and Dan in the north. These shrines were far more ancient than Jerusalem, being associated with the patriarchs. Pilgrimages to and worship in them had never completely died out, and the priesthoods established there claimed a direct line of succession from Moses.

Following an old northern tradition which envisioned Yahweh standing invisibly on the back of a young bull, Jeroboam set up golden bulls at both Bethel and Dan, trying to equal the grandeur of Solomon's Temple where two animals stood on either side of the Ark. Unfortunately, however, bulls were a principal symbol of the baals. Since Israel was located on the main trade routes, it had constant encounters and relationships with foreigners, in particular with the Canaanites. The Canaanites' baal fertility religion never ceased to attract the popular imagination. It is not surprising that in the long run many northerners came to Bethel and Dan to worship not the invisible Yahweh enthroned on the bulls, but the bulls themselves as symbols of the baals.

Located on lucrative trade routes, Israel was the more prosperous and powerful of the two kingdoms. However, instability and chaos characterized its political life. In its first forty-six years as a nation, three dynasties rose and fell. Of its 19 kings, no fewer than eight attained the throne as a result of their predecessor's assassination. Kings frequently killed all members of their predecessor's family in order to prevent conspiracy.

After twenty-five years of chaos following Jeroboam's death in 901 B.C., Omri succeeded in capturing the throne and stabilizing the northern kingdom. He gave the north its third and final capital, the new fortress hill city of Samaria. He staved off the threatening Assyrian Empire by promoting an alliance with Judah and, like Solomon, with Phoenicia. His reign ushered in a period of prosperity unknown since Solomon's time.

JEZEBEL

To seal the Phoenician alliance, Omri married his son Ahab to Jezebel, the Phoenician king's daughter. Ahab (who reigned from 869–850 B.C.) tried to make his wife comfortable in her new country. As Solomon had done for his foreign wives, Ahab allowed Jezebel to continue her native baal-worship. He even built a baal temple for her at Samaria. Unlike Solomon's wives, however, Jezebel was not satisfied with these arrangements. She was not content to "do her own thing" and to let Israel do its. She was a zealous and crusading devotee of the Phoenician baal, Melkart, and brought with her 450 baal prophets for whose support she demanded and received funds from Israel's treasury. Though her short-range goal was to have the worship of Baal-Melkart become the official state religion along with Yahweh-worship, her long-range goal was nothing other than the total eradication of Yahweh-worship.

Ahab appears to have been a conventional worshipper of Yahweh. His sons have Yahwistic names, and he seems to have gone through the religious exercises required of the king. Yet he did little to hold his wife in check.

Since Solomon's time, there had been a tolerant attitude toward other religions. Toleration, rightly conceived, is good: I have one opinion, you have another, we agree to listen, argue, and respect one another's viewpoints. But there is a form of mental laziness and lack of moral commitment which disguises itself as "toleration." Since Solomon's time this false type of toleration had more and more characterized the Israelites. The old purity of commitment to Yahweh and his distinctive ethical commandments had been watered down. The attitude that "one god is as good as another" characterized not only the king but most of his subjects. There seemed little that was likely to stand in the way of the strong-minded Jezebel.

Then—as suddenly as a bolt of lightning—there appears on the scene the greatest religious figure to arise in Israel since Moses. Alone and without worldly credentials, Elijah steps forth to challenge the queen. From Tisbeh—from the rough semi-nomadic life on the edge of the desert where the purity of commitment to Yahweh had never faded—Elijah presents himself: unshaven, his hair never having been cut, his tough, lean, strong body scantily clothed in a garment of hair. He had not been sent for; no one sought to consult him. He simply appeared. There he was, suddenly, midst the luxury of the Samarian court with its religious and moral apathy, denouncing the king and his wife.

Perhaps no figure in all Israel's history so gripped the popular imagination as this nobody who dared to challenge the ruler of the land. We are not surprised to discover that accounts of his life acquired all sorts of miraculous and legendary elements as the story of his bravery was told and retold by the people whose imaginations he captured.

The occasion of Elijah's first appearance at the court was one of those periodic droughts which afflict the Middle East. We can only guess at the conversation. Elijah appears to have associated the drought with Ahab's moral and religious laxity and to have warned the king, "I swear by the life of the LORD the God of Israel, whose servant I am, that there shall be neither dew nor rain these coming years unless I give the word." Having so spo-

ken, he left as abruptly as he had arrived. For three years Elijah
wandered from place to place while the drought worsened.

Time went by, and in the third year the word of the Lord came to
Elijah: 'Go and show yourself to Ahab, and I will send rain upon the
land.' So he went to show himself to Ahab. At this time the famine in
Samaria was at its height, and Ahab summoned Obadiah, the comp-
troller of his household, a devout worshipper of the Lord. When
Jezebel massacred the prophets of the Lord, he had taken a hundred
of them and hidden them in caves, fifty by fifty, giving them food
and drink to keep them alive. Ahab said to Obadiah, 'Let us go
through the land, both of us, to every spring and gully; if we can
find enough grass we may keep the horses and mules alive and lose
none of our cattle.' They divided the land between them for their
survey, Ahab going one way by himself and Obadiah another.

As Obadiah was on his way, Elijah met him. Obadiah recognized
him and fell prostrate before him and said, 'Can it be you, my lord
Elijah?' 'Yes,' he said, 'it is I; go and tell your master that Elijah is
here.' 'What wrong have I done?' said Obadiah. 'Why should you
give me into Ahab's hands? He will put me to death. As the Lord your
God lives, there is no nation or kingdom to which my master has not
sent in search of you. If they said, "He is not here", he made that
kingdom or nation swear on oath that they could not find you. Yet
you now say, "Go and tell your master that Elijah is here." What will
happen? As soon as I leave you, the spirit of the Lord will carry you
away, who knows where? I shall go and tell Ahab, and when he
fails to find you, he will kill me. Yet I have been a worshipper of the
lord from boyhood. Have you not been told, my lord, what I did
when Jezebel put the Lord's prophets to death, how I hid a hundred
of them in caves, fifty by fifty, and kept them alive with food and
drink? And now you say, "Go and tell your master that Elijah is
here"! He will kill me.' Elijah answered, 'As the Lord of Hosts lives,
whose servant I am, I swear that I will show myself to him this very
day.' So Obadiah went to find Ahab and gave him the message, and
Ahab went to meet Elijah.

As soon as Ahab saw Elijah, he said to him, 'Is it you, you troubler
of Israel?' 'It is not I who have troubled Israel,' he replied, 'but you
and your father's family, by forsaking the commandments of the
Lord and following Baal. But now, send and summon all Israel to

meet me on Mount Carmel, and the four hundred and fifty prophets
of Baal with them and the four hundred prophets of the goddess
Asherah, who are Jezebel's pensioners.'   [1 Kings 18:1–19]

Who is the figure who dares first to contradict and criticize the
king and then to tell him what to do? The only authority he cites
is the Lord, "whose servant I am." He calls himself a "prophet"
of Yahweh. In the modern world we use the word "prophet" to
describe one who foretells the future. To the Israelites the word
had a much fuller meaning. A prophet is one who *speaks for God*
now, in the present. Any implication a prophet's words may
have for the future is incidental to what he is saying to people of
his own time.

From early times bands of prophets (ecstatically possessed by
God's spirit) roved throughout Israel. Prophets were also associated with the shrines, and kings and others sometimes went to
them for advice. As time went on, individual prophets emerged
out of these bands. They "spoke God's word," alone and often
without being asked, when the Spirit moved them. We have already seen one such figure: Nathan, the prophet who confronted
David with his murder of Bathsheba's husband Uriah. Like Nathan, these individual prophets often said things people didn't
want to hear. Thus Ahab greets Elijah with the words, "Is it
you, you troubler of Israel?"

MT. CARMEL: ELIJAH AND THE PROPHETS OF BAAL

The story of Elijah's confrontation of the prophets of baal on
Mt. Carmel is one of the masterpieces of all literature.

So Ahab sent out to all the Israelites and assembled the prophets
on Mount Carmel. Elijah stepped forward and said to the people,
'How long will you sit on the fence? If the Lord is God, follow him;
but if Baal, then follow him.' Not a word did they answer.
[1 Kings 18:20–21]

Here, with striking simplicity, Elijah reasserts in all its purity
the distinctive faith in Yahweh as experienced and understood by
Israel at the Exodus and Mt. Sinai. Israel may not toy with this
God—the God of the universe. It must either accept him or reject him.

Then, because Yahweh is the only God, Elijah challenges the prophets of baal in order to illustrate vividly that their god is no god at all.

Then Elijah said to the people, 'I am the only prophet of the Lord still left, but there are four hundred and fifty prophets of Baal. Bring two bulls; let them choose one for themselves, cut it up and lay it on the wood without setting fire to it, and I will prepare the other and lay it on the wood without setting fire to it. You shall invoke your god by name and I will invoke the Lord by name; and the god who answers by fire, he is God.' And all the people shouted their approval.

Then Elijah said to the prophets of Baal, 'Choose one of the bulls and offer it first, for there are more of you; invoke your god by name, but do not set fire to the wood.' So they took the bull provided for them and offered it, and they invoked Baal by name from morning until noon, crying, 'Baal, Baal, answer us'; but there was no sound, no answer. They danced wildly beside the altar they had set up. At midday Elijah mocked them: 'Call louder, for he is a god; it may be he is deep in thought, or engaged, or on a journey; or he may have gone to sleep and must be woken up.' They cried still louder and, as was their custom, gashed themselves with swords and spears until the blood ran. All afternoon they raved and ranted till the hour of the regular sacrifice, but still there was no sound, no answer, no sign of attention.

Then Elijah said to all the people, 'Come here to me.' They all came, and he repaired the altar of the Lord which had been torn down. He took twelve stones, one for each tribe of the sons of Jacob, the man named Israel by the word of the Lord. With these stones he built an altar in the name of the Lord; he dug a trench round it big enough to hold two measures of seed; he arranged the wood, cut up the bull and laid it on the wood. Then he said, 'Fill four jars with water and pour it on the whole-offering and on the wood.' They did so, and he said, 'Do it again.' They did it again, and he said, 'Do it a third time.' They did it a third time, and the water ran all round the altar and even filled the trench.   [1 Kings 18:22–35]

He soaks what is to be set afire to emphasize the wonder of what follows. Then he calls on the God who had revealed himself so distinctively to Israel in the past to show that he is the living Lord of the present.

At the hour of the regular sacrifice the prophet Elijah came forward and said, 'Lord God of Abraham, of Isaac, and of Israel, let it be known today that thou art God in Israel and that I am thy servant and have done all these things at thy command. Answer me, O Lord, answer me and let this people know that thou, Lord, art God and that it is thou that hast caused them to be back-sliders.' Then the fire of the Lord fell. It consumed the whole-offering, the wood, the stones, and the earth, and licked up the water in the trench. When all the people saw it, they fell prostrate and cried, 'The Lord is God, the Lord is God.' Then Elijah said to them, 'Seize the prophets of Baal; let not one of them escape.' They seized them, and Elijah took them down to the Kishon and slaughtered them there in the valley.

Elijah said to Ahab, 'Go back now, eat and drink, for I hear the sound of coming rain.' He did so, while Elijah himself climbed to the crest of Carmel. There he crouched on the ground with his face between his knees. He said to his servant, 'Go and look out to the west.' He went and looked; 'There is nothing to see', he said. Seven times Elijah ordered him back, and seven times he went. The seventh time he said, 'I see a cloud no bigger than a man's hand, coming up from the west.' 'Now go', said Elijah, 'and tell Ahab to harness his chariot and be off, or the rain will stop him.' Meanwhile the sky had grown black with clouds, the wind rose, and heavy rain began to fall. Ahab mounted his chariot and set off for Jezreel; but the power of the Lord had come upon Elijah: he tucked up his robe and ran before Ahab all the way to Jezreel.   [1 Kings 18:36–46]

This is a wild, fantastic story, containing primitive folk tale and exaggeration. We need not try to rationalize the fire as a timely bolt of lightning. We need not try to explain away the vengeful slaughter of the prophets of baal or recoil in embarrassment at the sympathetic magic Elijah uses (pouring out water in order to bring rain). These are elements of wonder added by a still primitive people as they told and retold the story of Elijah's amazing courage. While not literally true, the story is true in a deeper non-literal way. A nobody confronted the king alone and, against enormous odds, presented afresh the pure faith of the Exodus and Mt. Sinai, and challenged the spirit of compromise and half-hearted commitment which had infected Israel since Solomon.

IN THE WILDERNESS

Jezebel was a formidable adversary.

Ahab told Jezebel all that Elijah had done and how he had put all the prophets to death with the sword. Jezebel then sent a messenger to Elijah to say, 'The gods do the same to me and more, unless by this time tomorrow I have taken your life as you took theirs.' He was afraid and fled for his life. When he reached Beersheba in Judah, he left his servant there and himself went a day's journey into the wilderness. He came upon a broom-bush, and sat down under it and prayed for death: 'It is enough,' he said; 'now, Lord, take my life, for I am no better than my fathers before me.'　　[1 Kings 19:1–4]

Israel was never ashamed that its heroes were human. Even the most zealously committed man of God—willing to risk his life to serve his God—can experience despair unto death. In his lonely discouragement, Elijah receives practical advice from someone whose presence is like a messenger ("angel") from God: "Don't wallow in your despair. Get up and have something to eat and you'll feel better."

He lay down under the bush and, while he slept, an angel touched him and said, 'Rise and eat.' He looked, and there at his head was a cake baked on hot stones, and a pitcher of water. He ate and drank and lay down again. The angel of the Lord came again and touched him a second time, saying, 'Rise and eat; the journey is too much for you.' He rose and ate and drank and, sustained by this food, he went on for forty days and forty nights to Horeb, the mount of God. He entered a cave and there he spent the night.　　[1 Kings 19:5–9]

In his confusion and despair, Elijah wisely returns to his roots to renew himself. Journeying "forty days and forty nights" (the Hebrews journeyed in the wilderness forty years) he arrives at Mt. Horeb (an alternate name for Mt. Sinai), the holy place where Israel had entered into its covenant with God.

Suddenly the word of the Lord came to him: 'Why are you here, Elijah?' 'Because of my great zeal for the Lord the God of Hosts', he said. 'The people of Israel have forsaken thy covenant, torn down thy altars and put thy prophets to death with the sword. I alone am left, and they seek to take my life.' The answer came: 'Go and stand

on the mount before the Lord.' For the Lord was passing by: a great
and strong wind came rending mountains and shattering rocks before him, but the Lord was not in the wind; and after the wind there
was an earthquake, but the Lord was not in the earthquake; and
after the earthquake fire, but the Lord was not in the fire; and after
the fire a low murmuring sound. When Elijah heard it, he muffled
his face in his cloak and went out and stood at the entrance of the
cave.   [1 Kings 19:9–13a]

Wind, earthquake, and fire are all traditional symbols of God's
presence. Yet God appears at times in quite unexpected ways. To
the despairing Elijah he came "in a low murmuring sound," a
soft whisper, in the silence of reflection at this sacred spot.

Then there came a voice: 'Why are you here, Elijah?' 'Because of
my great zeal for the Lord the God of Hosts', he said. 'The people
of Israel have forsaken thy covenant, torn down thy altars and put
thy prophets to death with the sword. I alone am left, and they seek
to take my life.'
    The Lord said to him, 'Go back by way of the wilderness of Damas-
cus, enter the city and anoint Hazael to be king of Aram; anoint
Jehu to be king of Israel, and Elisha to be prophet in your place.
Anyone who escapes the sword of Hazael Jehu will slay, and anyone
who escapes the sword of Jehu Elisha will slay. But I will leave seven
thousand in Israel, all who have not bent the knee to Baal, all whose
lips have not kissed him.'   [1 Kings 19:13b–18, abridged]

In discouragement things seem worse than they are. God tells
the whining Elijah, "There are 7000 in Israel who have not bowed
the knee to baal. You're not the only one. Go back and continue
where you left off." Among other things he is instructed to fo-
ment revolution against Ahab.

NABOTH'S VINEYARD

We have so far seen Elijah as the champion of a true understanding of God against a false understanding. Upon his return
we see him as the champion of social justice and mercy against
injustice and oppression. To Elijah, of course, these were not different concerns but two aspects of the same concern. Commitment to Yahweh, if it was genuine, automatically entailed a certain quality of life.

Naboth of Jezreel had a vineyard near the palace of Ahab king of Samaria. One day Ahab made a proposal to Naboth: 'Your vineyard is close to my palace; let me have it for a garden; I will give you a better vineyard in exchange for it or, if you prefer, its value in silver.' But Naboth answered, 'The Lord forbid that I should let you have land which has always been in my family.'   [1 Kings 21:1–3]

Naboth's vineyard was a family vineyard. He inherited it from his family and he was honor bound to pass it on to his family. It is interesting to note that even the king was not above the law. All he could do was return home and sulk.

So Ahab went home sullen and angry because Naboth would not let him have his ancestral land. He lay down on his bed, covered his face and refused to eat. His wife Jezebel came in to him and said, 'What makes you so sullen and why do you refuse to eat?' He told her, 'I proposed to Naboth of Jezreel that he should let me have his vineyard at its value or, if he liked, in exchange for another; but he would not let me have the vineyard.' 'Are you or are you not king in Israel?' said Jezebel.   [1 Kings 21:4–7a]

Jezebel's religion was divorced from ethics. She loathed the egalitarianism of her husband's nation, and was determined to have her way in spite of Israel's absurd laws.

'Come, eat and take heart; I will make you a gift of the vineyard of Naboth of Jezreel.' So she wrote a letter in Ahab's name, sealed it with his seal and sent it to the elders and notables of Naboth's city, who sat in council with him. She wrote: 'Proclaim a fast and give Naboth the seat of honour among the people. And see that two scoundrels are seated opposite him to charge him with cursing God and the king, then take him out and stone him to death.' So the elders and notables of Naboth's city, who sat with him in council, carried out the instructions Jezebel had sent them in her letter: they proclaimed a fast and gave Naboth the seat of honour, and these two scoundrels came in, sat opposite him and charged him publicly with cursing God and the king. Then they took him outside the city and stoned him, and sent word to Jezebel that Naboth had been stoned to death.

As soon as Jezebel heard that Naboth had been stoned and was dead, she said to Ahab, 'Get up and take possession of the vineyard which Naboth refused to sell you, for he is no longer alive; Naboth

of Jezreel is dead.' When Ahab heard that Naboth was dead, he got
up and went to the vineyard to take possession. Then the word of
the Lord came to Elijah the Tishbite: 'Go down at once to Ahab king
of Israel, who is in Samaria; you will find him in Naboth's vineyard,
where he has gone to take possession.'   [1 Kings 21:7b–18]

Though Jezebel was responsible for framing Naboth and ar-
ranging his death, Elijah pronounces Yahweh's judgment not
against her, but against her husband. To hold a position of power
and to fail to use it to anticipate and prevent injustice is as evil
as committing an act of injustice. Since David's time, monarchs
had more and more disregarded the rights of the little man.
Elijah's confrontation of the king is a dramatic reassertion of the
ethical demands Yahweh made equally upon all his people—
rich and poor, high and low—at Mt. Sinai.

'Say to him, "This is the word of the Lord: Have you killed your man,
and taken his land as well?" Say to him, "This is the word of the
Lord: Where dogs licked the blood of Naboth, there dogs shall lick
your blood." ' Ahab said to Elijah, 'Have you found me, my enemy?'
'I have found you', he said, 'because you have sold yourself to do
what is wrong in the eyes of the Lord.'   [1 Kings 21:19–20]

Here, in crude terms, Elijah asserts the principle of divine justice:
in the end, somehow under God's providence, good is rewarded
and evil punished.

'I will bring disaster upon you; I will sweep you away and destroy
every mother's son of the house of Ahab in Israel, whether under
protection of the family or not. And I will deal with your house as
I did with the house of Jeroboam because you have provoked my
anger and led Israel into sin.' And the Lord went on to say of Jezebel,
'Jezebel shall be eaten by dogs by the rampart of Jezreel. Of the
house of Ahab, those who die in the city shall be food for the dogs,
and those who die in the country shall be food for the birds.' When
Ahab heard this, he rent his clothes, put on sackcloth and fasted; he
lay down in his sackcloth and went about muttering to himself.
                    [1 Kings 21:21–24, 27, abridged]

Though we hear of no such repentance on Jezebel's part, Ahab
seems truly penitent. His own repentance brings, again in a rather
crudely conceived way, forgiveness.

Then the word of the Lord came to Elijah the Tishbite: 'Have you seen how Ahab has humbled himself before me? Because he has thus humbled himself, I will not bring disaster upon his house in his own lifetime, but in his son's.'   [1 Kings 21:28–29]

TRUE AND FALSE PROPHETS

Two other prophets of Elijah's time merit our attention: Micaiah and Elisha.

With his ally Jehoshaphat, King of Judah, Ahab was engaged in another of a long succession of wars with the Syrians (who were called "Aramaeans"). Jehoshaphat proposes that they consult God about the upcoming battle.

Then Jehoshaphat said to the king of Israel, 'First let us seek counsel from the Lord.' The king of Israel assembled the prophets, some four hundred of them, and asked them, 'Shall I attack Ramoth-gilead or shall I refrain?' 'Attack,' they answered; 'the Lord will deliver it into your hands.'   [1 Kings 22:5–6]

This band of 400 prophets—professionals financially supported by the king—give the king the answer they suppose he wants to hear. Yet Jehoshaphat is suspicious.

Jehoshaphat asked, 'Is there no other prophet of the Lord here through whom we may seek guidance?' 'There is one more,' the king of Israel answered, 'through whom we may seek guidance of the Lord, but I hate the man, because he prophesies no good for me; never anything but evil. His name is Micaiah son of Imlah.' Jehoshaphat exclaimed, 'My lord king, let no such word pass your lips!' So the king of Israel called one of his eunuchs and told him to fetch Micaiah son of Imlah with all speed.

The king of Israel and Jehoshaphat king of Judah were seated on their thrones, in shining armour, at the entrance to the gate of Samaria, and all the prophets were prophesying before them. One of them, Zedekiah son of Kenaanah, made himself horns of iron and said, 'This is the word of the Lord: "With horns like these you shall gore the Aramaeans and make an end of them."' In the same vein all the prophets prophesied, 'Attack Ramoth-gilead and win the day; the Lord will deliver it into your hands.' The messenger sent to fetch Micaiah told him that the prophets had with one voice given the king a favourable answer. 'And mind you agree with them,' he added. 'As the Lord lives,' said Micaiah, 'I will say only what the Lord tells me to say.'

When Micaiah came into the king's presence, the king said to him, 'Micaiah, shall we attack Ramoth-gilead or shall we refrain?' Then Micaiah said, 'I saw all Israel scattered on the mountains, like sheep without a shepherd; and I heard the Lord say, "They have no master, let them go home in peace." ' The king of Israel said to Jehoshaphat, 'Did I not tell you that he never prophesies good for me, nothing but evil?' Then the king of Israel ordered Micaiah to be arrested and committed to the custody of Amon the governor of the city and Joash the king's son.   [1 Kings 22:7–15a, 17–18, 26]

No incident better illustrates the distinction between true and false prophets. Alone against the yes-men, Micaiah told the king not what he wanted to hear but what he ought to hear. The king responded by clapping him into prison. A true prophet is one who, like Elijah and Micaiah, speaks God's word with regard neither for his own safety nor the recipient's comfort and reaction.

Though Ahab was killed in the battle, just as Micaiah had warned, Jezebel's influence remained strong during the reign of her son. It remained for Elisha, Elijah's friend, the worthy successor he commissioned, to bring about her final downfall.

Nothing reflects more credit on Elijah than that he was able to pass on to another the spirit of the work God had given him to do. Those who saw Elisha in action were led to remark, "The spirit of Elijah rests on Elisha." Around Elisha cluster stories as primitive and wonder-filled as those about Elijah. Though his was a personality very different from Elijah's, Elisha continued Elijah's lonely stance against false religion and social injustice. He succeeded in overthrowing Ahab's dynasty and placing the reformer Jehu on the throne. Jehu wasted no time in massacring Jezebel and all her family, and eliminating baal-worship.

Fleming James has written, "If now we turn to the Elijah narratives as a whole and ask what he did for Israel we shall find that his service lay not so much in any definite accomplishment as in the impulse that he gave. He was one of those rare men through whom the elemental power of God bursts afresh into humanity. He was above all things a man of God. That is what we still feel as we read. When he enters, the familiar scenery of

man's world falls away and God appears. Winds begin to blow
from out the deep, breaking in pieces the rocks before Yahweh.
Earthquake and fire follow. Historians may lament that the sheer
miraculous in these narratives thrusts aside the sober reality. But
deeper reflection will perhaps convince us that this atmosphere
of the supernatural *must* surround the figure of Elijah if we are
to see him as Israel felt and knew him—yes, as he really was. The
Spirit of Yahweh that conveyed him hither and yon, the prayer
that called down fire from heaven; the angel that ministered to
the weary sleeper; the theophany with its wind, earthquake, fire
and sound of gentle stillness—these are indeed legend, but they
are something else also. They are the bold primitive outlines and
colours wherewith natural artists portrayed a reality which would
otherwise escape us. For in this man actuality was *not* sober. God
was there! This was what he made men feel. He 'turned their
hearts back again.' That was his greatness." [7]

Chapter 12

AMOS AND HOSEA

Under Jeroboam II (786–746 B.C.) the northern kingdom enjoyed a period of national greatness and prosperity unknown since Solomon's time. This was partly because of Jeroboam's ability as an administrator, military technician, and builder, but mostly because Syria and Assyria, which had continually threatened Israel since Solomon, were temporarily in a state of internal turmoil. Israel was therefore able to increase her territory and, by her unchallenged control of the principal trade routes, to grow wealthy. Below the surface of peace and prosperity, however, were problems not unlike those of twentieth-century America. Not all of Israelite society partook of the prosperity. There was widespread poverty and injustice.

Nowhere were these social inequities more apparent than in Samaria, the northern kingdom's capital, where luxurious palaces stood side by side with ghastly slums. The respectable and satisfied upper classes went through all the outward rituals of Yahweh-worship, but their daily lives were selfish. The lower classes, on the other hand, were infected by the baal-worship of the surrounding countryside.

AMOS: THE RIGHTEOUSNESS OF GOD

Into Samaria, probably to sell wool, came Amos, a shepherd and vine-dresser from Tekoa, the farm country south of Jerusalem on the edge of the desert. Amos could not reconcile what he saw in Samaria with the commandments of Yahweh as he had learned them. Each time he returned home from Samaria to his solitary life in Tekoa he thought about what he had seen. Amos was only a simple layman; he was not a paid professional prophet. But finally in 752 B.C. he felt compelled by God to speak out in Samaria against what he saw.

Perhaps in order to attract a crowd, he began by condemning

the evils of Israel's nearby foreign neighbors, capitalizing on the rampant nationalism which characterized most of the people of Samaria. His indictment of Syria is typical:

These are the words of the Lord:

> For crime after crime of Damascus
> I will grant them no reprieve,
> because they threshed Gilead under threshing-sledges spiked
>   with iron.
> Therefore will I send fire upon the house of Hazael,
> fire that shall eat up Ben-hadad's palaces;
> I will crush the great men of Damascus
> and wipe out those who live in the Vale of Aven
> and the sceptred ruler of Beth-eden;
> the people of Aram shall be exiled to Kir.
> It is the word of the Lord. [Amos 1:3–5]

No doubt his listeners were well satisfied, until, suddenly and unexpectedly, he included Israel itself among the nations deserving condemnation.

These are the words of the Lord:

> For crime after crime of Israel
> I will grant them no reprieve,
> because they sell the innocent for silver
> and the destitute for a pair of shoes.
> They grind the heads of the poor into the earth
> and thrust the humble out of their way,
> Father and son resort to the same girl,
> to the profanation of my holy name.
> Men lie down beside every altar
> on garments seized in pledge,
> and in the house of their God they drink liquor
> got by way of fines. [Amos 2:6–8]

Amos is speaking of his listeners. It is *their* hypocrisy he is attacking. And it is God's judgment on *them* that he announces.

Yahweh was popularly misconceived as a national deity who automatically favored Israel. "God is on our side" was the cry. God was a sort of automatic vending machine who dispensed favor to those who went through the motions of worshiping him.

Amos, however, declared that God was Lord of all the nations and that he would not tolerate men mistreating other men in *any* nation, including Israel. God judges nations not by their political power or by their economic success. He cares about the quality of men's lives, how men treat one another. God chose Israel not to indulge her with unconditional favor. He chose her not to give her privileges but to lay on her a heavy responsibility. God singled out Israel to be an example of right living for other nations.

Listen, Israelites, to these words that the Lord addresses to you, to the whole nation which he brought up from Egypt:

> For you alone have I cared
> among all the nations of the world;
> therefore will I punish you
> for all your iniquities.   [Amos 3:1–2]

The key word is *therefore*. Because he has given the Israelites special opportunities, they have an especially high calling. *Therefore* Israel is not exempt from judgment, she is specially liable to it.

> The lion has roared; who is not terrified?
> The Lord God has spoken; who will not prophesy?

> Stand upon the palaces in Ashdod
> and upon the palaces of Egypt,
> and proclaim aloud:
> 'Assemble on the hills of Samaria,
> look at the tumult seething among her people
> and at the oppression in her midst;
> what do they care for honesty
> who hoard in their palaces the gains of crime and violence?'
> This is the very word of the Lord.

Therefore these are the words of the Lord God:

> An enemy shall surround the land;
> your stronghold shall be thrown down
> and your palaces sacked.   [Amos 3:8–11]

Israel has ignored her calling. She has turned from serving God to indulging herself. Ignoring the poor, the rich live in sumptuous luxury:

> I will break down both winter-house and summer-house;
> houses of ivory shall perish,
> and great houses be demolished.
> This is the very word of the Lord.   [Amos 3:15]

The women are fat, self-indulgent cows.

> Listen to this,
> you cows of Bashan who live on the hill of Samaria,
> you who oppress the poor and crush the destitute,
> who say to your lords, 'Bring us drink':
> the Lord God has sworn by his holiness
> that your time is coming
> when men shall carry you away on their shields
> and your children in fish-baskets.
> You shall each be carried straight out
> through the breaches in the walls
> and pitched on a dunghill.
> This is the very word of the Lord.   [Amos 4:1–3]

Injustice is rampant in the land.

> You that turn justice upside down
> and bring righteousness to the ground,
> you that hate a man who brings the wrongdoer to court
> and loathe him who speaks the whole truth:
> for all this, because you levy taxes on the poor
> und extort a tribute of grain from them,
> though you have built houses of hewn stone,
> you shall not live in them,
> though you have planted pleasant vineyards,
> you shall not drink wine from them.
> For I know how many your crimes are
> and how countless your sins,
> you who persecute the guiltless, hold men to ransom
> and thrust the destitute out of court.   [Amos 5:7, 10–12]

Religion as practiced is an hypocrisy. The people go through
all the cultic motions of religion at the lavishly supported shrines,
but their worship is an abomination because it is divorced from
how they live.

> I hate, I spurn your pilgrim-feasts;
> I will not delight in your sacred ceremonies.

> When you present your sacrifices and offerings
> I will not accept them,
> nor look on the buffaloes of your shared-offerings.
> Spare me the sound of your songs;
> I cannot endure the music of your lutes.   [Amos 5:21–23]

Religion is a little compartment of life. These hypocrites cannot wait till the Sabbath services are over to go back to cheating people and getting rich.

> Listen to this, you who grind the destitute and plunder the humble, you who say, 'When will the new moon be over so that we may sell corn? When will the sabbath be past so that we may open our wheat again, giving short measure in the bushel and taking overweight in the silver, tilting the scales fraudulently, and selling the dust of the wheat; that we may buy the poor for silver and the destitute for a pair of shoes?'

> Let justice roll on like a river
> and righteousness like an ever-flowing stream. [Amos 8:4–6; 5:24]

But justice and righteousness are nowhere to be found. Israel is not a nation characterized by love and justice, but by smug arrogance.

> Shame on you who live at ease in Zion,
> and you, untroubled on the hill of Samaria,
> men of mark in the first of nations,
> you to whom the people of Israel resort!
> Go, look at Calneh,
> travel on to Hamath the great,
> then go down to Gath of the Philistines—
> are you better than these kingdoms?
> Or is your territory greater than theirs?
> You who thrust the evil day aside
> and make haste to establish violence.

> You who loll on beds inlaid with ivory
> and sprawl over your couches,
> feasting on lambs from the flock
> and fatted calves,
> you who pluck the strings of the lute

and invent musical instruments like David,
you who drink wine by the bowlful
and lard yourselves with the richest of oils,
but are not grieved at the ruin of Joseph—
now, therefore,
you shall head the column of exiles;
that will be the end of sprawling and revelry.

The Lord God has sworn by himself:

I loathe the arrogance of Jacob,
I loathe his palaces;
city and all in it I will abandon to their fate.
Can horses gallop over rocks?
Can the sea be ploughed with oxen?
Yet you have turned into venom the process of law
and justice itself into poison,
you who are jubilant over a nothing and boast,
'Have we not won power by our own strength?'
O Israel, I am raising a nation against you,
and they shall harry your land
from Lebo-hamath to the gorge of the Arabah.
This is the very word of the Lord the God of Hosts.

[Amos 6:1–8, 12–14]

Again and again God had brought suffering upon Israel as a
remedial punishment, so that it would turn from its evil ways.
Again and again Israel had persisted in selfishness.

It was I who kept teeth idle
in all your cities,
who brought famine on all your settlements;
yet you did not come back to me.
This is the very word of the Lord.

It was I who withheld the showers from you
while there were still three months to harvest.
I would send rain on one city
and no rain on another;
rain would fall on one field,
and another would be parched for lack of it.

From this city and that, men would stagger to another
for water to drink, but would not find enough;
yet you did not come back to me.
This is the very word of the Lord.
Therefore, Israel, this is what I will do to you;
and, because this is what I will do to you,
Israel, prepare to meet your God.   [Amos 4:6–8, 12]

AMOS: THE JUDGMENT OF GOD

Men want a god who makes no demands on them, who is remote from the way they live, who is not concerned about what
they do in life. But, says Amos, the God of all the nations is,
above all, a God of justice and righteousness. Though God chose
the Israelites to enter into a special relationship with him and
reached out to them with love again and again, they have not
responded. By their lives they have repudiated their relationship
with Yahweh. Judgment is therefore inevitable. A teacher may go
to great lengths—in time, energy, and devotion—to reach out to
and help a student. But if the student persistently ignores the
offered help and refuses to study, the teacher, if he is just, must
ultimately fail the student. Israel has ignored God and persisted
in indulging itself and avoiding responsibility. Judgment is inevitable.

God has tried so often that there is no reason to hope that
another try will do any good. But even now, says Amos, it may
not be too late for Israel to return to the covenant it made with
Yahweh at Mt. Sinai.

Seek good and not evil,
that you may live,
that the Lord the God of Hosts may be firmly on your side,
as you say he is.
Hate evil and love good;
enthrone justice in the courts;
it may be that the Lord the God of Hosts
will be gracious to the survivors of Joseph.   [Amos 5:14–15]

But those who are self-satisfied never listen. Amos, therefore,
concludes on a note of unrelieved gloom. In a vision he sees God
as a builder using a plumb line to test whether a wall is straight
and true.

This was what the Lord showed me: there was a man standing by a wall with a plumb-line in his hand. The Lord said to me, 'What do you see, Amos?' 'A plumb-line', I answered, and the Lord said, 'I am setting a plumb-line to the heart of my people Israel; never again will I pass them by. The hill-shrines of Isaac shall be desolated and the sanctuaries of Israel laid waste; I will rise, sword in hand, against the house of Jeroboam.'   [Amos 7:7–9]

Naturally the people found Amos' message intolerable. Among other things it was unpatriotic.

Amaziah, the priest of Bethel, reported to Jeroboam king of Israel: 'Amos is conspiring against you in Israel; the country cannot tolerate what he is saying. He says, "Jeroboam shall die by the sword, and Israel shall be deported far from their native land." ' To Amos himself Amaziah said, 'Be off, you seer! Off with you to Judah! You can earn your living and do your prophesying there. But never prophesy again at Bethel, for this is the king's sanctuary, a royal palace.'
[Amos 7:10–13]

Amos is the descendant of a great prophetic tradition. Nathan and Elijah never feared to speak against the king if the king had done evil. Amos responds that he is not a prophet, that is, he is not a paid prophet, one of the yes-men whose salary is paid by the king. He is a plain man whose duty to God demands that he speak the truth, whatever the cost.

'I am no prophet,' Amos replied to Amaziah, 'nor am I a prophet's son; I am a herdsman and a dresser of sycomore-figs. But the Lord took me as I followed the flock and said to me, "Go and prophesy to my people Israel." '   [Amos 7:14–15]

Each year at the New Year festival the people celebrated with smug anticipation the coming "day of Yahweh" when God would wipe out all their enemies and make Israel rich and all-powerful. Amos warned them that the day of Yahweh would be very different from what they expected. Doom was certain.

> Fools who long for the day of the Lord,
> what will the day of the Lord mean to you?
> It will be darkness, not light.
> It will be as when a man runs from a lion,
> and a bear meets him,

> or turns into a house and leans his hand on the wall,
> and a snake bites him.
> On that day, says the Lord God,
> I will make the sun go down at noon
> and darken the earth in broad daylight.
> I will turn your pilgrim-feasts into mourning
> and all your songs into lamentation.
> The day of the Lord is indeed darkness, not light,
> a day of gloom with no dawn.   [Amos 5:18–19; 8:9–10a; 5:20]

Historical records tell nothing of the end of Amos' life. He appears to have escaped and become, probably in Judah, the teacher of a small circle of disciples who wrote down what he said.

HOSEA: ISRAEL—THE UNFAITHFUL WIFE

Shortly after Amos was driven out of Israel, Jeroboam II died (746 B.C.). By his brilliant leadership and with excellent luck (the great powers were in a state of temporary weakness) this latter-day Solomon had brought Israel strength and prosperity unequaled in 200 years. When Jeroboam died everything went wrong. Within seven months two successor kings had been murdered along with their followers. Egypt and Assyria both rose from their slumbers to menace Israel. The kings—in Israel's unstable last 25 years there were no less than six—embarked on a desperate policy of appeasing and paying off first one power and then the other. Now the smug confidence of Israel's ruling class in Amos' time was seen to have been unwarranted.

The Book of Hosea gives us a clear picture of these declining days. Hosea spoke out publicly on the events of Israel's national life about 740 B.C. Like Amos, he perceived Israel's hypocrisy and faithlessness, and, like Amos, he believed Israel was doomed.

Israel's political disintegration was accompanied by further moral deterioration. People would do anything to make money.

> False scales are in merchants' hands,
> and they love to cheat;
> so Ephraim says,
> 'Surely I have become a rich man, I have made my fortune';
> but all his gains will not pay
> for the guilt of his sins.   [Hos. 12:7–8]

(Ephraim is an alternate name which Hosea uses for Israel.)

The social structure crumbles to ruin as people pursue their own selfish goals without regard for others.

> There is no good faith or mutual trust,
> no knowledge of God in the land,
> oaths are imposed and broken, they kill and rob;
> there is nothing but adultery and licence,
> one deed of blood after another. [Hos. 4:1b–2]

While exploitation of the poor and social injustice are rampant at home, Israel desperately prostitutes herself to foreign powers to gain protection.

> Ephraim is an oppressor trampling on justice,
> doggedly pursuing what is worthless.
> So when Ephraim found that he was sick,
> Judah that he was covered with sores,
> Ephraim went to Assyria,
> he went in haste to the Great King;
> but he has no power to cure you
> or to heal your sores.
> Ephraim is a silly senseless pigeon,
> now calling upon Egypt, now turning to Assyria for help.
> [Hos. 5:11, 13; 7:11]

Israel cares about power and riches, not about faithfulness to her covenant with Yahweh.

> King after king falls from power,
> but not one of them calls upon me.
> They make kings, but not by my will;
> they set up officers, but without my knowledge;
> they have made themselves idols of their silver and gold.
> [Hos. 7:7b; 8:4]

Religious ceremonies are a blasphemous sham. The shrines of Yahweh are cluttered with Canaanite idols and polluted by the sexual orgies of baal-worship.

> For they have forsaken the Lord
> to give themselves to sacred prostitution.
> New wine and old steal my people's wits:

they ask advice from a block of wood
and take their orders from a fetish;
for a spirit of [harlotry] has led them astray
and in their lusts they are unfaithful to their God.
Your men sacrifice on mountain-tops
and burn offerings on the hills,
under oak and poplar
and the terebinth's pleasant shade.
Therefore your daughters play the [harlot]
and your sons' brides commit adultery.
I will not punish your daughters for playing the wanton
nor your sons' brides for their adultery,
because your men resort to wanton women
and sacrifice with temple-prostitutes.
A people without understanding comes to grief;
they are a mother turned [harlot].
Ephraim, keeping company with idols,
has held a drunken orgy,
they have practised sacred prostitution,
they have preferred dishonour to glory.
  Your calf-gods stink, O Samaria;
my anger flares up against them.
Long will it be before they prove innocent.
For what sort of a god is this bull?
It is no god,
a craftsman made it;
the calf of Samaria will be broken in fragments.
  Their misdeeds have barred their way back to their God;
for a [harlot] spirit is in them.
and they care nothing for the Lord.
Israel's arrogance cries out against him;
Ephraim's guilt is his undoing,
and Judah no less is undone.
They go with sacrifices of sheep and cattle
to seek the Lord, but do not find him.
He has withdrawn himself from them;
for they have been unfaithful to him,
and their sons are bastards.

[Hos. 4:10b–15a, 17–18; 8:5–6; 5:4–7a]

Even the religious leaders are corrupt:

> Like robbers lying in wait for a man,
> priests are banded together
> to do murder on the road to Shechem;
> their deeds are outrageous.
> Priest? By day and by night you blunder on,
> you and the prophet with you.
> My people are ruined for lack of knowledge;
> Your own countrymen are brought to ruin.
> You have rejected knowledge,
> and I will reject you from serving me as priest. [Hos. 6:9; 4:5–6a]

What penitence there is consists of such slight and superficial gestures that it amounts to toying with God who, they imagine, will grant forgiveness the second they snap their fingers:

> Come, let us return to the Lord;
> for he has torn us and will heal us,
> he has struck us and he will bind up our wounds;
> after two days he will revive us,
> on the third day he will restore us,
> that in his presence we may live.   [Hos. 6:1–2]

God has repeatedly offered Israel his love. Again and again she has responded half-heartedly.

> O Ephraim, how shall I deal with you?
> How shall I deal with you, Judah?
> Your loyalty to me is like the morning mist,
> like dew that vanishes early.
> Therefore have I lashed you through the prophets
> and torn you to shreds with my words;
> loyalty is my desire, not sacrifice,
> not whole-offerings but the knowledge of God.   [Hos. 6:4–6]

Israel no longer knows God. She ignores what he has shown himself to be. She ignores the God who chose and loved her at the Exodus and she repudiates the covenant she entered into with him on Mt. Sinai. Since she ignores him she cannot know him deeply from the heart, she cannot respond to him and enter into relationship with him.

Israel ignores Yahweh; for her he is dead. Israel sacrifices to a god, but the god, though called Yahweh, is not really Yahweh but a god of her own creation. Because of her idolatrous infidelity, doom is inevitable. "Israel has sown the wind; she will now reap the whirlwind." (8:7)

Most of us understand the world around us in terms of our own particular experiences. That is true for Hosea in an especially striking way. His whole understanding of God's relationship to Israel is colored by his own experience with his wife Gomer.

Hosea's wife repudiated and betrayed his love. She was unfaithful to him and went off with other men as a harlot. From his own resulting bitterness and despair Hosea came to an awareness of how God must feel about Israel's infidelity, about her running off with and chasing after the fertility baals of Canaan.

Hosea turns to his children to ask them to plead with their mother to return.

> Plead my cause with your mother;
> is she not my wife and I her husband?
> Plead with her to forswear those [harlot] looks,
> to banish the lovers from her bosom.   [Hos. 2:2]

If she does not, he will have to divorce her. An adulterous woman in Israel was disowned by her husband and publicly disgraced by being stripped naked (a symbolic reversal of the promise to clothe that is part of the marriage covenant):

> Or I will strip her and expose her
> naked as the day she was born.   [Hos. 2:3a]

In a like manner God will have to divorce and strip the unfaithful Israel naked as the day she was born (i.e., in slavery in Egypt).

> I will make her bare as the wilderness,
> parched as the desert,
> and leave her to die of thirst.
> I will show no love for her children;
> they are the offspring of [harlotry],
> and their mother is a [harlot].
> She who conceived them is shameless;

she says, 'I will go after my lovers;
they give me my food and drink,
my wool and flax, my oil and my perfumes.'   [Hos. 2:3b–5]

Like Gomer, Israel ignores the one who loves her,

For she does not know that it is I who gave her
corn, new wine, and oil,
I who lavished upon her silver and gold
which they spent on the Baal.   [Hos. 2:8]

There is no recourse but divorce, the ending of the relationship. The ignored love and generosity will be withdrawn.

Therefore I will take back
my corn at the harvest and my new wine at the vintage,
and I will take away the wool and the flax
which I gave her to cover her naked body;
so I will show her up for the lewd thing she is,
and no lover will want to steal her from me.
I will ravage the vines and the fig-trees,
which she says are the fee
with which her lovers have hired her,
and turn them into jungle where wild beasts shall feed.
I will put a stop to her merrymaking,
her pilgrimages and new moons, her sabbaths and festivals.
I will punish her for the holy days
when she burnt sacrifices to the Baalim,
when she decked herself with earrings and necklaces,
ran after her lovers and forgot me.
This is the very word of the Lord.   [Hos. 2:9–13]

HOSEA: GOD'S LOVING ANGER

Yet, unlike Amos, Hosea's last word is not doom. Though hurt and embittered by his wife's infidelity, Hosea had entered into a life-long marriage covenant with her and he realizes that he still loves her and longs to be reconciled with her. He therefore goes out to find her, to receive her back.

The Lord said to me,
Go again and love a woman
loved by another man, an adulteress,

and love her as I, the Lord, love the Israelites
although they resort to other gods
and love the raisin-cakes offered to their idols.
So I got her back for fifteen pieces of silver, a homer of barley
and a measure of wine; and I said to her,
Many a long day you shall live in my house
and not play the [harlot],
and have no intercourse with a man, nor I with you. [Hos. 3:1–3]

Gomer was to be punished; she was to live in solitude without
the outward signs of her husband's love. Israel's unfaithfulness
would also be punished.

For the Israelites shall live many a long day
without king or prince,
without sacrifice or sacred pillar,
without image or household gods;
but after that they will again seek
the Lord their God and David their king,
and turn anxiously to the Lord for his bounty in days to come.

[Hos. 3:4–5]

In suffering, however, Gomer/Israel will turn back to her true
husband. God's "anger," his punishment, is not capricious or
vengeful, but redemptive. It is a holy love which seeks to restore
and heal a broken relationship. After she has been chastened she
will come to her senses and see the love being poured out upon
her, which she has so long ignored.

But now listen,
I will woo her, I will go with her into the wilderness
and comfort her:
there I will restore her vineyards,
turning the Vale of Trouble into the Gate of Hope,
and there she will answer as in her youth,
when she came up out of Egypt.
On that day she shall call me 'My husband'
and shall no more call me 'My Baal';
and I will wipe from her lips the very names of the Baalim;
never again shall their names be heard.
This is the very word of the Lord.   [Hos. 2:14–17]

Then a new and more perfect marriage covenant will be established.

> I will betroth you to myself for ever, betroth you in lawful wedlock with unfailing devotion and love; I will betroth you to myself to have and to hold, and you shall know the Lord. At that time I will give answer, says the Lord, I will answer for the heavens and they will answer for the earth, and the earth will answer for the corn, the new wine, and the oil, and they will answer for Jezreel. Israel shall be my new sowing in the land, and I will show love to Loruhamah and say to Lo-ammi, 'You are my people', and he will say, 'Thou art my God.'   [Hos. 2:19–23]

Amos remained focused on man's evil and the inevitable doom which would result from man's rejection of God. Hosea, too, knew Israel would be punished, but he saw beyond it. The God who loved Israel would use the suffering and disgrace which was coming to bring his people to their senses so that they would return and accept his love. Hosea, then, marveled not so much at man's evil, as at God's love which seeks men out.

In a final analogy, Hosea sets out the whole record of God's relationship with Israel, from the Exodus, to the infidelity in Canaan, to the inevitable sufferings which result from ignoring God, to the new awareness and relationship which will come out of those sufferings.

> When Israel was a boy, I loved him;
> I called my son out of Egypt;
> but the more I called, the further they went from me;
> they must needs sacrifice to the Baalim
> and burn offerings before carved images.
> It was I who taught Ephraim to walk,
> I who had taken them in my arms;
> but they did not know that I harnessed them in leading-strings
> and led them with bonds of love—
> that I had lifted them like a little child to my cheek,
> that I had bent down to feed them.
> Back they shall go to Egypt,
> the Assyrian shall be their king;
> for they have refused to return to me.

The sword shall be swung over their blood-spattered altars
and put an end to their prattling priests
and devour my people in return for all their schemings,
bent on rebellion as they are.
Though they call on their high god,
even then he will not reinstate them.
How can I give you up, Ephraim,
how surrender you, Israel?
My heart is changed within me,
my remorse kindles already.
I will not let loose my fury,
I will not turn round and destroy Ephraim;
for I am God and not a man,
the Holy One in your midst.   [Hos. 11:1–9, abridged]

Though in peace and prosperity Israel had denied God, in suffering and exile she would come again to know him and witness to him.

Inevitably, disaster befell Israel. In 722 B.C. Sargon II of Assyria overran Israel. To insure against rebellion he took with him 27,290 members of the upper classes into captivity. (From these captives, incidentally, arises the legend of the ten lost tribes of Israel.) To destroy Israel's distinctive culture and her will to resist, Sargon sent Assyrians to colonize Israel and marry Israelite women. Many Israelites fled south; others refused intermarriage. Those who did intermarry (and their children) became known as Samaritans and have persisted as a distinctive group in Palestine down to the present.

Chapter 13

ISAIAH

In the last three chapters we have focused on the northern kingdom. To the south was the smaller, more compact kingdom of Judah. With its orderly descent of kings from the dynasty of David and Solomon it experienced little of the North's political instability. Located in the hill country quite far removed from the main trade routes, Judah was neither as prosperous nor as dangerously exposed to invasion as Israel.

GOD'S HOLINESS

With the great powers of the Nile and Euphrates temporarily in internal turmoil, Judah, like Israel, enjoyed a happy period of peace and prosperity in the mid-eighth century B.C. But peace and prosperity were as mixed a blessing for Judah as they had been for Israel. Peace brought a false sense of security and national arrogance, while prosperity led to corruption and injustice. In 742 B.C., as leprosy brought King Uzziah's long and glorious reign to an end, a sophisticated aristocrat of Jerusalem stepped forth to speak out.

Isaiah's "calling"—the experience which compelled him to address the people of his land—came suddenly and unexpectedly while he was worshiping God in the great Jerusalem Temple. Perhaps the occasion was the annual New Year Festival in which the people celebrated Yahweh's enthronement. As the leprous king of Judah (symbolic of his unclean, corrupted people) lay dying, Isaiah had a vision of God as eternal king enthroned in transcendent majesty.

In the year of King Uzziah's death I saw the Lord seated on a throne, high and exalted, and the skirt of his robe filled the temple. About him were attendant seraphim, and each had six wings; one pair covered his face and one pair his feet, and one pair was spread in flight. They were calling ceaselessly to one another,

> Holy, holy, holy is the Lord of Hosts:
> the whole earth is full of his glory.

And, as each one called, the threshold shook to its foundations, while the house was filled with smoke.   [Isa. 6:1–4]

The Hebrews used the word "holy" (*kodesh*), just as we use it, to describe what is morally pure. But the principal meaning of the Hebrew word is "cut off," "separated." Isaiah uses the word to emphasize the fact that God is totally *other* than man, separate, transcendent. Amos had emphasized God's justice, his desire for moral excellence. Hosea stressed God's steadfast love for his people even as he punishes them. The heart of Isaiah's message is God's holiness. His understanding of God is far removed from the primitive anthropomorphism of early Israel. God is not man. God is holy, wholly other. God is present among his people, but is at the same time transcendent, utterly beyond man's control or manipulation. God enters the world he has created, but he is not captive in it.

The experience of God makes Isaiah acutely aware of his own temporariness and moral weakness.

> Then I cried,
> Woe is me! I am lost,
> for I am a man of unclean lips
> and I dwell among a people of unclean lips;
> yet with these eyes I have seen the King, the Lord of Hosts.

Then one of the seraphim flew to me carrying on his hand a glowing coal which he had taken from the altar with a pair of tongs. He touched my mouth with it and said,

> See, this has touched your lips;
> your iniquity is removed,
> and your sin is wiped away.   [Isa. 6:5–7]

The experience of God changes men's lives, sends them off in new directions.

Then I heard the Lord saying, Whom shall I send? Who will go for me? And I answered, Here am I; send me. He said, Go and tell this people:

You may listen and listen, but you will not understand.
You may look and look again, but you will never know.
This people's wits are dulled,
   their ears are deafened and their eyes blinded,
so that they cannot see with their eyes
nor listen with their ears
nor understand with their wits,
so that they may turn and be healed.   [Isa. 6:8–10]

Though Isaiah knows what he must do with his life, what he must say, he also knows that what he does and what he says will have no effect on his people. He has no illusions that his words will change them. So often in life we say, "What good can *I* do? Why should I beat my head against a stone wall?" But in every generation there rise up, like Isaiah, people who do and say what is right, because it is right, without regard for "success" and without being discouraged by the hopelessness of their earthly tasks. And apparently Isaiah's task *is* hopeless:

Then I asked, How long, O Lord? And he answered,

   Until cities fall in ruins and are deserted,
   houses are left without people,
   and the land goes to ruin and lies waste,
   until the Lord has sent all mankind far away,
   and the whole country is one vast desolation.
   Even if a tenth part of its people remain there,
   they too will be exterminated.   [Isa. 6:11–13a]

CONFRONTING THE PEOPLE

First, Isaiah points out that the people live as if God doesn't even exist.

   Hark you heavens, and earth give ear,
   for the Lord has spoken:
   I have sons whom I reared and brought up,
   but they have rebelled against me.
   The ox knows its owner
   and the ass its master's stall;
   but Israel, my own people,
   has no knowledge, no discernment.

> O sinful nation, people loaded with iniquity,
> race of evildoers, wanton destructive children
> who have deserted the Lord,
> spurned the Holy One of Israel
> and turned your backs on him.   [Isa. 1:2–4]

Jerusalem is likened to the evil cities of Sodom and Gomorrah which were destroyed for their wickedness.

> Hear the word of the Lord, you rulers of Sodom;
> attend, you people of Gomorrah, to the instruction of our God.
>   [Isa. 1:10]

In the elaborate religious ceremonies and sacrifices the people worship God with their lips, but not their lives.

> Your countless sacrifices, what are they to me?
> says the Lord.
> I am sated with whole-offerings of rams
> and the fat of buffaloes;
> I have no desire for the blood of bulls,
> of sheep and of he-goats.
> Whenever you come to enter my presence—
> who asked you for this?
> No more shall you trample my courts.
> The offer of your gifts is useless,
> the reek of sacrifice is abhorrent to me.
> New moons and sabbaths and assemblies,
> sacred seasons and ceremonies, I cannot endure.
> I cannot tolerate your new moons and your festivals;
> they have become a burden to me,
> and I can put up with them no longer.
> When you lift your hands outspread in prayer,
> I will hide my eyes from you.
> Though you offer countless prayers,
> I will not listen.
> There is blood on your hands;
> wash yourselves and be clean.
> Put away the evil of your deeds,
> away out of my sight.   [Isa. 1:11–16]

Ceremonial worship which is not connected with the way a person lives and acts in everyday life is blasphemous.

> Cease to do evil and learn to do right,
> pursue justice and champion the oppressed;
> give the orphan his rights, plead the widow's cause.
> How the faithful city has played the whore,
> once the home of justice where righteousness dwelt—
> but now murderers!
> Your very rulers are rebels, confederate with thieves;
> every man of them loves a bribe
> and itches for a gift;
> they do not give the orphan his rights,
> and the widow's cause never comes before them.
> Money-lenders strip my people bare,
> and usurers lord it over them.
> The Lord opens the indictment
> against the elders of his people and their officers:
> You have ravaged the vineyard,
> and the spoils of the poor are in your houses.
> Is it nothing to you that you crush my people
> and grind the faces of the poor?
> This is the very word of the Lord, the Lord of Hosts.
> Shame on you! you who rise early in the morning
> to go in pursuit of liquor
> and draw out the evening inflamed with wine,
> at whose feasts there are harp and lute,
> tabor and pipe and wine,
> who have no eyes for the work of the Lord,
> and never see the things that he has done.
> Shame on you! you mighty topers, valiant mixers of drink,
> who for a bribe acquit the guilty
> and deny justice to those in the right.
> Shame on you! you who call evil good and good evil.
> [Isa. 1:17, 21, 23; 3:12a, 14–15; 5:11–12, 22–23, 20a]

Those who call evil good are those whose ethic is self-serving: whatever is good *for me* (even if it is said to be evil) is good. Such persons ridicule unselfishness in others.

Finally, there are the smug and self-assured who are too sophisticated to believe in God, who think they "have the world by the tail":

> Shame on you! you who are wise in your own eyes
> and prudent in your own esteem.   [Isa. 5:21]

God has reached out again and again to Judah, but Judah has ignored God and rejected his ways. Isaiah likens Judah to a vineyard on which the owner has expended every effort so that it may produce good fruit.

> I will sing for my beloved
> my love-song about his vineyard:
> My beloved had a vineyard
> high up on a fertile hill-side.
> He trenched it and cleared it of stones
> and planted it with red vines;
> he built a watch-tower in the middle
> and then hewed out a winepress in it.
> He looked for it to yield grapes,
> but it yielded wild grapes.
> Now, you who live in Jerusalem,
> and you men of Judah,
> judge between me and my vineyard.
> What more could have been done for my vineyard
> that I did not do in it?
> Why, when I looked for it to yield grapes,
> did it yield wild grapes?
> Now listen while I tell you
> what I will do to my vineyard:
> I will take away its fences and let it be burnt,
> I will break down its walls and let it be trampled underfoot,
> and so I will leave it derelict;
> it shall be neither pruned nor hoed,
> but shall grow thorns and briars.
> Then I will command the clouds
> to send no more rain upon it.
> The vineyard of the Lord of Hosts is Israel,
> and the men of Judah are the plant he cherished.
> He looked for justice and found it denied,
> for righteousness but heard cries of distress.   [Isa. 5:1–7]

These concluding words are filled with poignant disappointment and sadness. God has done all that he can do for Israel. But his love has brought no response. The fruitless vineyard must now be plowed under.

CONFRONTING THE KING

By the time Ahaz succeeded to Judah's throne (735–715 B.C.) the mighty Assyrian Empire had awakened from her slumbers to threaten the whole Fertile Crescent. Syria and Israel formed an alliance against Assyria and tried to persuade Judah to join them. Sensing that Judah was so small that it might be overlooked and spared in the ensuing international conflict, King Ahaz wisely refused alliance with either side. In 733 B.C., therefore, Syria and Israel invaded Judah. The Judeans—king and people—"were shaken like forest trees in the wind." The choice had to be made to accept defeat by the more powerful invaders, or to appeal for help to Assyria and become her vassal.

At this critical juncture, as the king tries to secure the city water supply, Isaiah goes to the king. Urging him not to make an alliance with Assyria, but to remain aloof from all alliances, Isaiah tells him to trust in God alone: "Be on your guard, keep calm; do not be frightened or unmanned by these two smouldering stumps of firewood. . . . Have firm faith, or you will not stand firm." (7:4,9c) Isaiah's point is telling: on one side are two mortal men (the kings of Syria and Assyria) who temporarily rule earthly kingdoms; on the other side is God, whose kingdom is the universe, and whose rule is forever.

We can imagine the king's response. The enemy is at the gates and this well-meaning but meddlesome man of God comes to offer him a lot of pious impractical God-talk. The king "believes" in Yahweh, but when it comes right down to a concrete situation, for him Yahweh really doesn't exist.

Isaiah offers Ahaz a sign. But the king, anxious to avoid having to reject the prophet's advice when backed up by a divine sign, answers him with false piety, "No, I will not put the Lord to the test by asking for a sign."

Provoked now to anger, Isaiah gives him the sign anyway.

Then the answer came: Listen, house of David. Are you not content to wear out men's patience? Must you also wear out the patience of my

God? Therefore the Lord himself shall give you a sign: A young woman
is with child, and she will bear a son, and will call him Immanuel.

[Isa. 7:13–14]

The young woman may be Ahaz's queen. "Immanuel" in Hebrew
means "God with us." These words of expectation are well known
to Christians because they were later applied to the birth of Jesus.
In this context, Isaiah is giving the king a sign or pledge that,
whatever occurs, God will be with Judah.

Ahaz ignored Isaiah's advice and entered into a vassal relationship with Assyria. To Assyria went the treasures of the Jerusalem Temple, and plans were made for erection of an Assyrian
altar in the Temple.

Isaiah's exhortations of the people had fallen on deaf ears. His
advice to the king had been rejected. For the rest of Ahaz's
reign, therefore, Isaiah withdrew from public life into a small
circle of friends.

THE LORD OF HISTORY

In 715 B.C. the wise and forceful Hezekiah succeeded Ahaz as
king. Hezekiah reformed religious practices by suppressing the
local shrines (which were infected by baal-worship) and cen-
tralizing worship at the Temple in Jerusalem, and by removing
the Assyrian altars. He secured Jerusalem's water supply by
building a remarkable tunnel through 1,777 feet of solid rock,
and he standardized weights and measures to prevent the poor
from being cheated.

In 705 B.C., when Sargon of Assyria died, Hezekiah was confronted with the decision of whether or not to join with others in
revolting against Assyria, which appeared to be in a state of
decline.

Isaiah gave Hezekiah the same advice he had earlier given
Ahaz: "do not become part of the conspiracy." Isaiah claimed
no special insights into the particularities of the political situation. His advice was based on his conviction that history is not
governed by chance but by the living God, who is Lord of history.
Safety was to be found not in conspiracies with men, but in trust
in God.

Yahweh alone is God. He is not only the God of Judah; he is
the God of all nations, and he uses all nations to achieve his

purpose. God could even use Assyria, and, ironically, he could use Assyria to chastise his own people.

> The Assyrian! He is the rod that I wield in my anger,
> and the staff of my wrath is in his hand.
> I send him against a godless nation,
> I bid him march against a people who rouse my wrath,
> to spoil and plunder at will
> and trample them down like mud in the streets.   [Isa. 10:5–6]

Isaiah therefore condemned Judah's headlong rush to ally itself with Egypt in revolt against Assyria. Judah must put its trust in God, not men.

> The Egyptians are men, not God,
> their horses are flesh, not spirit;
> and, when the Lord stretches out his hand,
> the helper will stumble and he who is helped will fall,
> and they will all vanish together.
>   Oh, rebel sons! says the Lord,
> you make plans, but not of my devising,
> you weave schemes, but not inspired by me,
> piling sin upon sin;
> you hurry down to Egypt without consulting me,
> to seek protection under Pharaoh's shelter
> and take refuge under Egypt's wing.
> Pharaoh's protection will bring you disappointment
> and refuge under Egypt's wing humiliation;
> for, though his officers are at Zoan
> and his envoys reach as far as Hanes,
> all are left in sorry plight by that unprofitable nation,
> no help they find, no profit, only disappointment and disgrace.
>   For they are a race of rebels, disloyal sons,
> sons who will not listen to the Lord's instruction;
> they say to the seers, 'You shall not see',
> and to the visionaries, 'You shall have no true visions;
> give us smooth words and seductive visions.
> Turn aside, leave the straight path,
> and rid us for ever of the Holy One of Israel.'

These are the words of the Holy One of Israel:

> Because you have rejected this warning
> and trust in devious and dishonest practices,
> resting on them for support,
> therefore you shall find this iniquity will be
> like a crack running down
> a high wall, which bulges
> and suddenly, all in an instant, comes crashing down,
> as an earthen jar is broken with a crash,
> mercilessly shattered,
> so that not a shard is found among the fragments
> to take fire from the glowing embers,
> or to scoop up water from a pool.   [Isa. 31:3; 30:1–5, 9–14]

Security lies not in frantic political maneuvering. It lies in quiet trust in the Lord of the universe, in the goodness of whose purpose we can have absolute confidence:

These are the words of the Lord God the Holy One of Israel:

> Come back, keep peace, and you will be safe;
> in stillness and in staying quiet, there lies your strength.
>
> [Isa. 30:15]

But king and people would not listen. Trusting in political maneuvering, they would bring doom upon themselves. Consumed in the pursuit of wealth they would devour themselves with selfishness.

THE REMNANT

Though doom was inevitable, it was not the last chapter. Like Hosea, Isaiah saw Judah's sufferings as chastening and remedial.

This therefore is the word of the Lord, the Lord of Hosts, the Mighty One of Israel:

> Enough! I will secure a respite from my foes
> and take vengeance on my enemies.
> Once again I will act against you
> to refine away your base metal as with potash
> and purge all your impurities;
> I will again make your judges what once they were
> and your counsellors like those of old.

Then at length you shall be called
the home of righteousness, the faithful city.   [Isa. 1:24–26]

Isaiah named his son Shear-jashub, meaning "A Remnant Shall Return." The name is symbolically both a threat and a promise. Because of her faithlessness, Judah is doomed. Out of the purifying fires of punishment and suffering will emerge *only* a remnant. And yet that remnant is the hope of the future.

A remnant shall turn again, a remnant of Jacob,
to God their champion.
Your people, Israel, may be many as the sands of the sea,
but only a remnant shall turn again,
the instrument of final destruction,
justice in full flood;
for the Lord, the Lord of Hosts, will bring final destruction
upon all the earth.

The survivors left in Judah shall strike fresh root under ground and yield fruit above ground, for a remnant shall come out of Jerusalem and survivors from Mount Zion. The zeal of the Lord of Hosts will perform this.   [Isa. 10:21–23; 37:31–32]

At the heart of that remnant would be a kingly figure from the House of David ("Jesse's stock") through whose leadership a new world order would be established.

Look, the Lord, the Lord of Hosts,
cleaves the trees with a flash of lightning,
the tallest are hewn down, the lofty laid low,
the heart of the forest is felled with the axe,
and Lebanon with its noble trees has fallen.
Then a shoot shall grow from the stock of Jesse,
and a branch shall spring from his roots.
The spirit of the Lord shall rest upon him,
a spirit of wisdom and understanding,
a spirit of counsel and power,
a spirit of knowledge and the fear of the Lord.
    He shall not judge by what he sees
he shall judge the poor with justice
and defend the humble in the land with equity;
his mouth shall be a rod to strike down the ruthless,

and with a word he shall slay the wicked.
Round his waist he shall wear the belt of justice,
and good faith shall be the girdle round his body.
     Then the wolf shall live with the sheep,
and the leopard lie down with the kid;
the calf and the young lion shall grow up together,
and a little child shall lead them;
the cow and the bear shall be friends,
and their young shall lie down together.
The lion shall eat straw like cattle;
the infant shall play over the hole of the cobra,
and the young child dance over the viper's nest.
They shall not hurt or destroy in all my holy mountain;
for as the waters fill the sea,
so shall the land be filled with the knowledge of the Lord.
     The people who walked in darkness
have seen a great light:
light has dawned upon them,
dwellers in a land as dark as death.
Thou hast increased their joy and given them great gladness;
they rejoice in thy presence as men rejoice at harvest,
or as they are glad when they share out the spoil;
for thou hast shattered the yoke that burdened them.
     For a boy has been born for us, a son given to us
to bear the symbol of dominion on his shoulder;
and he shall be called
in purpose wonderful, in battle God-like,
Father for all time, Prince of peace.
Great shall the dominion be,
and boundless the peace
bestowed on David's throne and on his kingdom,
to establish it and sustain it
with justice and righteousness
from now and for evermore.
The zeal of the Lord of Hosts shall do this.

                    [Isa. 10:33–11:9; 9:2–4a, 6–7]

As a magnet, this figure and the remnant he leads will draw together all men and nations at Jerusalem, Zion, City of God, city of peace.

On that day a scion from the root of Jesse
shall be set up as a signal to the peoples;
the nations shall rally to it,
and its resting-place shall be glorious.
    On this mountain the Lord of Hosts will prepare
a banquet of rich fare for all the peoples,
a banquet of wines well matured and richest fare,
well-matured wines strained clear.
On this mountain the Lord will swallow up
that veil that shrouds all the peoples,
the pall thrown over all the nations;
he will swallow up death for ever.
Then the Lord God will wipe away the tears
from every face
and remove the reproach of his people from the whole earth.
The Lord has spoken.
    In days to come
the mountain of the Lord's house
shall be set over all other mountains,
lifted high above the hills.
All the nations shall come streaming to it,
and many peoples shall come and say,
'Come, let us climb up on to the mountain of the Lord,
to the house of the God of Jacob,
that he may teach us his ways
and we may walk in his paths.'
For instruction issues from Zion,
and out of Jerusalem comes the word of the Lord;
he will be judge between nations,
arbiter among many peoples.
They shall beat their swords into mattocks
and their spears into pruning-knives;
nation shall not lift sword against nation
nor ever again be trained for war.   [Isa. 11:10; 25:6–8; 2:2–4]

THE SIEGE OF JERUSALEM

Down the centuries the vision of the peace and serenity which
comes from quiet, confident trust in the Lord of history has in-
spired men. But only rarely have men in the throes of the realities
of political decision-making acted as if these words were true.

"Have firm faith, or you will not stand firm," said Isaiah. But
Hezekiah's faith in God was not firm. He turned to politics for
salvation, and joined the revolt against Assyria. Assyria quickly
recovered its balance and in rapid succession wiped out one after
another of the countries which had revolted against it. By 701
B.C. Assyria was at the gates of Jerusalem and Judah was "shut up
like a bird in a cage."

In this apparently hopeless situation, Isaiah comes forth with
a message of hope: though Judah will be punished, he says, Jerusalem will not fall into Assyria's hands.

Then, as Jerusalem verged on collapse, the Assyrian army suddenly—and inexplicably—withdrew and returned to Nineveh.
We are uncertain what caused this abrupt departure. Perhaps a
contagious disease struck the encamped army. Perhaps reports
of Babylonian aggression forced Sennacherib, the Assyrian king,
to move his army to another trouble spot. Most likely, though, he
had by now gotten all he wanted from Hezekiah—a huge pay-
ment and part of Judah's land. Why should he waste men and
money on a lengthy siege? Isaiah had been right: Judah had
been punished but Jerusalem spared. What had happened
seemed to confirm Isaiah's view of the course of history. Though
chastisement and suffering would fall on Judah, a remnant, here
symbolized by the reduced and impoverished Judah, would be
left to form the nucleus of a new and faithful community.

Unfortunately, most Judeans interpreted Jerusalem's miraculous escape as evidence that God had given the city an unconditional guarantee: it could never fall. Isaiah knew differently.
God's protection of Jerusalem was conditional.

> Come now, let us argue it out,
> says the Lord.
> Though your sins are scarlet,
> they may become white as snow;
> though they are dyed crimson,
> they may yet be like wool.
> Obey with a will,
> and you shall eat the best that earth yields;
> but, if you refuse and rebel,
> locust-beans shall be your only food.
> The Lord himself has spoken.   [Isa. 1:18–20]

Isaiah knew that Jerusalem was eventually doomed. Midst the wild rejoicings he stands, a lonely figure, picturing the inevitable sufferings which his people believe will never come.

> Tell me, what is amiss
> that you have all climbed on to the roofs,
> O city full of tumult, town in ferment
> and filled with uproar,
> whose slain were not slain with the sword
> and did not die in battle?
> On that day the Lord, the Lord of Hosts,
> called for weeping and beating the breast,
> for shaving the head and putting on sackcloth;
> but instead there was joy and merry-making,
> slaughtering of cattle and killing of sheep,
> eating of meat and drinking of wine, as you thought,
> Let us eat and drink; for tomorrow we die.

The Lord of Hosts has revealed himself to me; in my hearing he swore:

> Your wickedness shall never be purged
> until you die.
> This is the word of the Lord, the Lord of Hosts.

[Isa. 22:1–2, 12–14]

Isaiah did not live to see Jerusalem's destruction. Tradition holds that he was put to death in the reign of Hezekiah's successor Manasseh. Manasseh was forced by the political situation to become Assyria's obedient vassal. He reintroduced the Assyrian gods at Jerusalem and restored the old local shrines at which baal-worship flourished. He brought foreign astrologers and magicians to the capital and allowed pagan worship in the Temple. And he revived the cult of the dead and reintroduced the primitive practice of child sacrifice. Those who spoke out against these outrages were, like Isaiah, put to death.

Chapter 14

JEREMIAH

Manasseh's policies were gradually reversed by his grandson Josiah, who became king as a boy and reigned over Judah from 640 to 600 B.C. Though Judah was still a vassal of Assyria and was, as well, threatened from the north by the Scythians, Josiah set about trying to eradicate foreign pagan practices from Judah's worship. With quiet persistence he worked to achieve the dream of a reunited Judah and Israel free of foreign domination.

In 626 B.C., a young man named Jeremiah (perhaps no more than 18 years old) from the village of Anathoth, near Jerusalem, emerged as a public figure in Judah. We have his own revealing description of the experience which compelled him to speak out in public:

The word of the Lord came to me: 'Before I formed you in the womb I knew you for my own; before you were born I consecrated you, I appointed you a prophet to the nations.'   [Jer. 1:4–5]

The God who knows Jeremiah intimately and who has shaped his life from the very beginning is also the God of the nations, the Lord of history. The utterly transcendent God—whose being and ways are beyond man's comprehension—is intimately immanent in the world and in men's individual lives.

'Ah! Lord God,' I answered, 'I do not know how to speak; I am only a child.'   [Jer. 1:6]

Jeremiah's response reveals his inexperience, modesty, and shyness, as well as a natural human tendency to shrink when faced with a heavy responsibility.

Yet if he speaks for God, he will not be speaking his *own* words, but the words which God is compelling him to speak.

But the Lord said, 'Do not call yourself a child; for you shall go to whatever people I send you and say whatever I tell you to say. Fear none of them, for I am with you and will keep you safe.' [Jer. 1:7–8]

Like Isaiah, Jeremiah knew that, if he was doing God's will, God would in the end keep him safe. This trust would be severely tested as Jeremiah endured the hatred and rejection of his compatriots.

This was the very word of the Lord. Then the Lord stretched out his hand and touched my mouth, and said to me, 'I put my words into your mouth. This day I give you authority over nations and over kingdoms, to pull down and to uproot, to destroy and to demolish, to build and to plant.' [Jer. 1:9–10]

Jeremiah—in and of himself—has no authority. God is his authority if he speaks God's words to men. Jeremiah's whole life work is summarized in these words: he is "to pull down and uproot, to destroy and to demolish." He will proclaim destruction and doom to his people. And he is "to build and to plant." The old is torn down in order that what is new and better can take its place.

As Jeremiah contemplates his future, his eyes fall on an almond tree:

The word of the Lord came to me: 'What is it that you see, Jeremiah?' 'An almond in early bloom', I answered. 'You are right', said the Lord to me, 'for I am early on the watch to carry out my purpose.'
[Jer. 1:11–12]

The Hebrew words for almond tree (*shaked*) and for watch (*shoked*) are nearly the same. The tree somehow reminds Jeremiah that God keeps watch and does not slumber. Though the almond tree appears to be dead during the winter, suddenly in the spring it blossoms into life. God is ever awake and at work in his creation, though worldly events sometimes seem to belie his presence.

Jeremiah's eyes then fall on another object. All his surroundings appear to speak to him of his experience:

The word of the Lord came to me a second time: 'What is it that you see?' 'A cauldron', I said, 'on a fire, fanned by the wind; it is tilted away from the north.' The Lord said:

> From the north disaster shall flare up
> against all who live in this land;
> for now I summon all peoples and kingdoms of the north,
> says the Lord.   [Jer. 1:13–15a]

The kettle, with its mouth tilted south, points to destruction coming from the north (at the hands of the Scythians or the Assyrians).

> Their kings shall come and each shall set up his throne
> before the gates of Jerusalem,
> against her walls on every side,
> and against all the cities of Judah.
> I will state my case against my people
> for all the wrong they have done in forsaking me,
> in burning sacrifices to other gods,
> worshipping the work of their own hands.   [Jer. 1:15b–16]

Doom will fall on Judah because she has forsaken God's ways. Jeremiah realizes from the outset how unpopular this message of judgment will be.

> Brace yourself, Jeremiah;
> stand up and speak to them.
> Tell them everything I bid you,
> do not let your spirit break at sight of them,
> or I will break you before their eyes.
> This day I make you a fortified city,
> a pillar of iron, a wall of bronze,
> to stand fast against the whole land,
> against the kings and princes of Judah,
> its priests and its people.
> They will make war on you but shall not overcome you,
> for I am with you and will keep you safe.
> This is the very word of the Lord.   [Jer. 1:17–19]

Jeremiah's message will be primarily a negative one "against" the whole land and he will be rejected and persecuted. Nevertheless, he must not lose heart: "for I am with you and will keep you safe."

Jeremiah's outlook as he begins to speak out publicly is similar to that of Amos and Hosea. Like Hosea he sees Judah rejecting God's loyal, devoted love, repudiating her marriage, and chasing after other gods like a whore.

> But my people have exchanged their Glory
> for a god altogether powerless.
> Stand aghast at this, you heavens,
> tremble in utter despair,
> says the Lord.
> Two sins have my people committed:
> they have forsaken me,
> a spring of living water,
> and they have hewn out for themselves cisterns,
> cracked cisterns that can hold no water. [Jer. 2:11b–13]

Rejecting fresh, flowing waters, the people have chosen instead stale water stored up in cisterns no better than sieves.

Like Amos he proclaims that the people merely go through the outward motions of religion, while their lives are selfish.

> How well you pick your way in search of lovers!
> Why! even the worst of women can learn from you.
> Yes, and there is blood on the corners of your robe—
> the life-blood of the innocent poor.
> You did not get it by housebreaking
> but by your sacrifices under every oak.
> You say, 'I am innocent;
> surely his anger has passed away.'
> But I will challenge your claim
> to have done no sin. [Jer. 2:33–35]

Though he has tried again and again without success, God gives his people still another chance.

> If you will but come back, O Israel,
> if you will but come back to me, says the Lord,
> if you will banish your loathsome idols from my sight,
> and stray no more,
> if you swear by the life of the Lord,
> in truth, in justice and uprightness,
> then shall the nations pray to be blessed like you
> and in you shall they boast. [Jer. 4:1–2]

But Judah will not listen; she brings judgment upon herself.
Jeremiah proclaims the inevitable with hyperbolic eloquence.

These are the words of the Lord to the men of Judah and Jerusalem:
Break up your fallow ground,
do not sow among thorns,
circumcise yourselves to the service of the Lord,
circumcise your hearts,
men of Judah and dwellers in Jerusalem,
lest the fire of my fury blaze up and burn unquenched,
because of your evil doings.
Tell this in Judah,
proclaim it in Jerusalem,
blow the trumpet throughout the land,
sound the muster,
give the command, Stand to!—and let us fall back
on the fortified cities.
Raise the signal—To Zion!
make for safety, lose no time,
for I bring disaster out of the north,
and dire destruction.
A lion has come out from his lair,
the destroyer of nations;
he has struck his tents, he has broken camp,
to harry your land
and lay your cities waste and unpeopled.
    You cast me off, says the Lord,
you turned your backs on me.
So I stretched out my hand and ruined you;
I was weary of relenting.
    Your own ways, your own deeds
have brought all this upon you;
this is your punishment,
and all this comes of your rebellion.   [Jer. 4:3–7; 15:6; 4:18]

JOSIAH'S REFORM

As part of a more and more forthright nationalist policy, Josiah
had decided to remove all traces of Assyrian religion from the
Temple at Jerusalem. In 621 B.C., in the midst of the construction

work, a book was discovered in the Temple which increased Josiah's desire for reform. The Book of the Torah (part of our present Book of Deuteronomy), though cast in the form of a farewell address by Moses, had been written no more than 100 years before Josiah's reign. It is based on early oral traditions and is a restatement of Moses' faith in the light of the insights of the later prophets.

The book's intention was to confront the people afresh with the Covenant. The book emphasizes that the Covenant is not just an ancient pact between God and Israel's ancestors, but that God presents the Covenant to his people in *every* age and, in every age, they must accept or reject it.

Listen, O Israel, to the statutes and the laws which I proclaim in your hearing today. Learn them and be careful to observe them. The Lord our God made a covenant with us at Horeb. It was not with our forefathers that the Lord made this covenant, but with us, all of us who are alive and are here this day.   [Deut. 5:1b–3]

Again the people must hear what Yahweh commands and again they must decide whether to respond. Yahweh has chosen them:

It was not because you were more numerous than any other nation that the Lord cared for you and chose you, for you were the smallest of all nations; it was because the Lord loved you and stood by his oath to your forefathers, that he brought you out with his strong hand and redeemed you from the land of slavery, from the power of Pharaoh king of Egypt.   [Deut. 7:7–8]

They are asked only to respond to his love:

Hear, O Israel, the Lord is our God, one Lord, and you must love the Lord your God with all your heart and soul and strength.
                                                      [Deut. 6:4–5]

To love God means to live by his commandments. Belief in God does not necessarily involve temples and sacrifices; it absolutely requires an ethical life. God has been generous to Israel; Israel is called to imitate that generosity.

What then, O Israel, does the Lord your God ask of you? Only to fear the Lord your God, to conform to all his ways, to love him and to serve him with all your heart and soul. This you will do by keeping the commandments of the Lord and his statutes which I give you this day for your good. To the Lord your God belong heaven itself, the highest heaven, the earth and everything in it; yet the Lord cared for your forefathers in his love for them and chose their descendants after them. Out of all nations you were his chosen people as you are this day. So now you must circumcise the foreskin of your hearts and not be stubborn any more, for the Lord your God is God of gods and Lord of lords, the great, mighty, and terrible God. He is no respecter of persons and is not to be bribed; he secures justice for widows and orphans, and loves the alien who lives among you, giving him food and clothing. You too must love the alien, for you once lived as aliens in Egypt.   [Deut. 10:12–19]

The book concludes with a challenge:

'Today I offer you the choice of life and good, or death and evil. If you obey the commandments of the Lord your God which I give you this day, by loving the Lord your God, by conforming to his ways and by keeping his commandments, statutes, and laws, then you will live and increase, and the Lord your God will bless you in the land which you are entering to occupy. But if your heart turns away and you do not listen and you are led on to bow down to other gods and worship them, I tell you this day that you will perish; you will not live long in the land which you will enter to occupy after crossing the Jordan. I summon heaven and earth to witness against you this day: I offer you the choice of life or death, blessing or curse. Choose life and then you and your descendants will live; love the Lord your God, obey him and hold fast to him: that is life for you and length of days in the land which the Lord swore to give to your forefathers, Abraham, Isaac and Jacob.'   [Deut. 30:15–20]

This new book had a tremendous impact of King Josiah and he summoned all the people to Jerusalem to read it to them. Then with great solemnity the king and his people renewed the Covenant.

The discovery of the book gave fresh impetus to Josiah's reform. Pagan forms of worship were suppressed everywhere. Once again local shrines, infected as they were by baal-worship, were closed, and all worship was concentrated at the Jerusalem Temple. Josiah also reinstituted the celebration of the Passover.

This reform seems to have had great effect at first, and Jeremiah supported it strongly. Disillusion swiftly followed, however, as it became apparent that change was only outward and not inward. As foreign religious practices were abolished they were replaced not by a renewal of commitment to Yahweh, but by a strident nationalism. The centralization of worship at Jerusalem led to the popular belief that Jerusalem was thereby magically protected from defeat. The book itself in places encouraged an "insurance policy" or "success" religion, a conviction that if one obeyed God all would automatically go well in earthly life.

Josiah's reform was brought to a halt by international events. In 612 B.C., the Babylonians, Medes, and Scythians forever destroyed the Assyrian Empire, razing its capital, Nineveh, to dust. At the same time Egypt, under Neccho, began to emerge again as a great power. In 609 B.C. King Josiah, in alliance with Babylonia, went out to meet the advancing Egyptian army at Megiddo. Judah was defeated and the king killed. Then in 605 B.C. Babylonia, under Nebuchadrezzar, defeated Egypt (which lapsed henceforth into military insignificance) at Carchemish.

Josiah was dead, and so were all his hopes for national reunification and reform. Judah had freed itself first of Assyrian, then of Egyptian domination, only to fall under the yoke of Babylonia.

JEREMIAH AGAINST THE NATION

Under King Jehoiakim all pretense of reform was dropped and the nation slid back into paganism. Going to the Temple—the heart of the nation—Jeremiah now bursts forth with a message of condemnation.

> But I am full of the anger of the Lord,
> I cannot hold it in.
> I must pour it out on the children in the street
> and on the young men in their gangs.

These are the words of the Lord of Hosts the God of Israel: Mend your ways and your doings, that I may let you live in this place. You keep saying, 'This place is the temple of the Lord, the temple of the Lord, the temple of the Lord!' This catchword of yours is a lie; put no trust in it.   [Jer. 6:11a; 7:3–4]

Because of Jerusalem's deliverance from invaders in Isaiah's time, and as the result of increasing nationalism and concentration on the Temple in Josiah's time, the idea that the Temple guaranteed Jerusalem against conquest had more and more captured the minds of the people. Jeremiah denounces this idea as magic. Men must put their trust not in the Temple, but in God.

God will be present among his people only if they show—by the quality of their lives—that they deserve his presence.

Mend your ways and your doings, deal fairly with one another, do not oppress the alien, the orphan, and the widow, shed no innocent blood in this place, do not run after other gods to your own ruin. Then will I let you live in this place, in the land which I gave long ago to your forefathers for all time. You gain nothing by putting your trust in this lie.   [Jer. 7:5–8]

Judah's security rests not in the Temple, but in the presence of justice and mercy in the lives of its inhabitants.

But justice and mercy are notably absent.

You steal, you murder, you commit adultery and perjury, you burn sacrifices to Baal, you run after other gods whom you have not known; then you come and stand before me in this house, which bears my name, and say, 'We are safe'; safe, you think, to indulge in all these abominations. Do you think that this house, this house which bears my name, is a robbers' cave? I myself have seen all this, says the Lord. Therefore what I did to Shiloh I will do to this house which bears my name, the house in which you put your trust, the place I gave to you and your forefathers; I will fling you away out of my sight, as I flung away all your kinsfolk, the whole brood of Ephraim.
                    [Jer. 7:9–11, 14–15]

The formalities of temple worship are an abomination since they are not accompanied by commitment to the Covenant in everyday life. The Temple will therefore be razed.

Jeremiah's speech naturally caused uproar and outrage.

The priests, the prophets, and all the people heard Jeremiah say this in the Lord's house and, when he came to the end of what the Lord had commanded him to say to them, priests, prophets, and people seized him and threatened him with death. 'Why', they demanded, 'have you prophesied in the Lord's name that this house shall become like Shiloh and this city waste and uninhabited?' The people all gathered against Jeremiah in the Lord's house. The officers of Judah heard what was happening, and they went up from the royal palace to the Lord's house and took their places there at the entrance of the new gate. Then the priests and the prophets said to the officers and all the people, 'Condemn this fellow to death. He has prophesied against this city: you have heard it with your own ears.' [Jer. 26:7–11]

Jeremiah escapes, however, and continues to speak out. Not only did Judah wallow in religious and moral abominations; nothing revealed the magnitude of her corruption more than her unwillingness even to admit her hypocrisy, not to mention her refusal to change.

> You shall say to them, These are the words of the Lord:
> If men fall, can they not also rise?
> If a man breaks away, can he not return?
> Then why are this people so wayward,
> incurable in their waywardness?
> Why have they clung to their treachery
> and refused to return to their obedience?
> I have listened to them
> and heard not one word of truth,
> not one sinner crying remorsefully,
> 'Oh, what have I done?'
> Are they ashamed when they practise their abominations?
> Ashamed? Not they!
> They can never be put out of countenance.
> Therefore they shall fall with a great crash,
> and be brought to the ground on the day of my reckoning.
> The Lord has said it.
> The enemy come; they devour the land and all its store,
> city and citizens alike.
> Beware, I am sending snakes against you,
> vipers, such as no man can charm,
> and they shall bite you.
> This is the very word of the Lord.   [Jer. 8:4–6a, 12, 16b–17]

These hard words did not come easily to Jeremiah. He loved his people and his city. Many of us have had the terrible experience of trying to point out to someone we love that what he is

doing is wrong and harmful to himself. We can share Jeremiah's
anguish as he watches his people relentlessly steer a course to
their own ruin.

> How can I bear my sorrow?
> I am sick at heart.
> Hark, the cry of my people
> from a distant land:
> 'Is the Lord not in Zion?
> Is her King no longer there?'
> Why do they provoke me with their images
> and foreign gods?
> Harvest is past, summer is over,
> and we are not saved.   [Jer. 8:18–20]

There were two harvests: the grain harvest and then the summer
fruit harvest. If the grain harvest failed, the country could hope
for winter's food from the fruit harvest. If both failed, famine
overshadowed the land. Jeremiah uses this as a parable: Judah's
time is up. Disaster is at hand.

> I am wounded at the sight of my people's wound;
> I go like a mourner, overcome with horror.
> Is there no balm in Gilead,
> no physician there?
> Why has no new skin grown over their wound?
>
> Would that my head were all water,
> my eyes a fountain of tears,
> that I might weep day and night
> for my people's dead!   [Jer. 8:21–9:1]

Jeremiah's vision of Jerusalem's end is eerily modern. One can
imagine a nuclear holocaust reversing the whole process of evo-
lution, reducing the earth to primeval chaos:

> I saw the earth, and it was without form and void;
> the heavens, and their light was gone.
> I saw the mountains, and they reeled;
> all the hills rocked to and fro.
> I saw, and there was no man,
> and the very birds had taken flight.
> I saw, and the farm-land was wilderness,

and the towns all razed to the ground,
before the Lord in his anger.   [Jer. 4:23–26]

Then, in a dramatic public demonstration in the Valley of
Hinnon, where human sacrifice had been reinstituted, Jeremiah
breaks a clay jar. "These are the words of the Lord of Hosts:
Thus will I shatter this people and this city as one shatters an
earthen vessel so that it cannot be mended."

As a result Jeremiah was arrested and beaten. He then appears
to have retired from public life for a time to dictate his spoken
words to his secretary, Baruch. The scroll which Jeremiah dic-
tated concluded with a summary in which he envisioned Nebuchadrezzar, King of Babylon, as God's agent appointed to destroy
Judah:

For twenty-three years, from the thirteenth year of Josiah son of
Amon, king of Judah, to the present day, I have been receiving the
words of the Lord and taking pains to speak to you, but you have
not listened. The Lord has taken pains to send you his servants the
prophets, but you have not listened or shown any inclination to listen.
If each of you will turn from his wicked ways and evil courses, he has
said, then you shall for ever live on the soil which the Lord gave to
you and to your forefathers. You must not follow other gods, serving
and worshipping them, nor must you provoke me to anger with the
idols your hands have made; then I will not do you harm. But you
did not listen to me, says the Lord; you provoked me to anger with
the idols your hands had made and so brought harm upon yourselves.

Therefore these are the words of the Lord of Hosts: Because you
have not listened to my words, I will summon all the tribes of the
north, says the Lord: I will send for my servant Nebuchadrezzar king
of Babylon. I will bring them against this land and all its inhabitants
and all these nations round it; I will exterminate them and make them
a thing of horror and derision, a scandal for ever. I will silence all
sounds of joy and gladness among them, the voices of bridegroom
and bride, and the sound of the handmill; I will quench the light of
every lamp. For seventy years this whole country shall be a scandal
and a horror; these nations shall be in subjection to the king of
Babylon.   [Jer. 25:3–11]

To the people these words—read by Baruch, because Jeremiah
was now barred from the Temple—were simply treason; "God

is on our side and this man tells us that a foreigner is God's servant." King Jehoiakim slashed the scroll to pieces and hurled it
into the fire.

THE DARK NIGHT OF THE SOUL

Hunted as a traitor, Jeremiah remained in seclusion. At this
juncture in his career, Jeremiah periodically descended into the
depths of despair and loneliness. Rejected, ridiculed, and persecuted, Jeremiah was overcome with self-pity, doubt, and, occasionally, even vengefulness.

Perhaps the bitterest experience of all was his rejection by his
family and friends at Anathoth. Associated as they were with the
local shrine at Anathoth, they had probably been angered by his
support of the abolition of local shrines. Or perhaps, having
known him as a child, they felt his speaking out with authority
was inappropriate. At any rate they were outraged by what he
said and plotted to silence him. When the plot came to Jeremiah's
attention he was overcome with desire for revenge.

I had been like a sheep led obedient to the slaughter; I did not know
that they were hatching plots against me and saying, 'Let us cut down
the tree while the sap is in it; let us destroy him out of the living,
so that his very name shall be forgotten.'

> O Lord of Hosts who art a righteous judge,
> testing the heart and mind,
> I have committed my cause to thee;
> let me see thy vengeance upon them.   [Jer. 11:19–20]

Those who seek to accomplish great things have to endure the
most bitter frustrations. Those who commit themselves completely to great causes, and who then experience rejection or persecution, are most prone to resentfulness and vengefulness. Jeremiah at times was overcome with desire to strike out in revenge.
Though almost incredibly courageous, his occasional bitter vengefulness shows that he did not possess the confidence and generosity which come from the certain faith that God is ultimately
faithful to those who do his will.

He poured out his deepest doubts to God. "If God exists, why
is human life so cruelly unfair?"

O Lord, I will dispute with thee, for thou art just;
yes, I will plead my case before thee.
Why do the wicked prosper
and traitors live at ease?
Alas, alas, my mother, that you ever gave me birth!
a man doomed to strife, with the whole world against me.
I have borrowed from no one, I have lent to no one,
Yet all men abuse me.
Lord, thou knowest;
remember me, Lord, and come to visit me,
take vengeance for me on my persecutors.
Be patient with me and take me not away,
see what reproaches I endure for thy sake.
Why then is my pain unending,
my wound desperate and incurable?
Thou art to me like a brook that is not to be trusted,
whose waters fail.   [Jer. 12:1; 15:10, 15, 18]

In his heart he knew that such sentiments were base, and in the
depths of doubt and despair he battled against his baser inclina-
tions. Then in his inner being he was able to hear God rebuke
his doubts.

This was the Lord's answer:
If you will turn back to me, I will take you back
and you shall stand before me.
If you choose noble utterance and reject the base,
you shall be my spokesman.
This people will turn again to you,
but you will not turn to them.
To withstand them I will make you impregnable,
a wall of bronze.
They will attack you but they will not prevail,
for I am with you to deliver you
and save you, says the Lord;
I will deliver you from the wicked,
I will rescue you from the ruthless.   [Jer. 15:19–21]

We see Jeremiah descend into the pit of self-righteous self-
pity, wallowing in the very self-centeredness he condemned in

others. Jeremiah's greatness lies in daring to face the less noble
aspects of his character, in working through his angry vengefulness, and in fighting to regain his perspective. J. S. Bezzant has
written, "Those who try to chart the Christian spiritual life . . .
distinguish in it a period which they call 'the dark night of the
soul' during which all the comforts and certitudes of the truth
seem to be withdrawn. They have persisted and triumphed. This
is the hard way and it is ours in this age. Christians sing in a
saint's day hymn,

> 'They wrestled hard, as we do now,
> With sins, and doubts, and fears.'

This is often precisely what we do *not* do. We wish to make
religion an escape from the conflict, a haven of refuge, . . . for-
getting that it is he who shall endure to the end who shall be
saved." [8]

NATIONAL DISASTER

An intensifying of misguided nationalist sentiment in Judah
led King Jehoiakim in 600 B.C. to dare to withhold tribute from
Babylonia. Though occupied elsewhere at the time, Babylonia
crushed Judah in 597 B.C., emptied the Temple of its treasures,
and took the king and queen and many of the national leaders
into captivity.

Zedekiah, the weak and vacillating youngest son of Josiah, was
placed on the throne. Jeremiah agonized over the demagogues
who now took over leadership roles. Jeremiah denounced their
petty nationalism and their political maneuvering as they plotted
to ally the nation with Egypt and to overthrow Babylonia. He
insisted that the security of Judah and other small nations lay
not in political scheming, jumping from liaison first with one
great power and then another. God was working out his purpose
in history and, for the moment, he chose to give domination to
Nebuchadrezzar, who was therefore his "servant." Jeremiah proclaims this message in a symbolic act:

These are the words of the Lord to me: Take the cords and bars of a
yoke and put them on your neck. Then send to the kings of Edom,
Moab, Ammon, Tyre, and Sidon by the envoys who have come from
them to Zedekiah king of Judah in Jerusalem, and give them the

following message for their masters: These are the words of the Lord of Hosts the God of Israel: Say to your masters: I made the earth with my great strength and with outstretched arm, I made man and beast on the face of the earth, and I give it to whom I see fit. I now give all these lands to my servant Nebuchadrezzar king of Babylon, and I give him also all the beasts of the field to serve him. All nations shall serve him, and his son and his grandson, until the destined hour of his own land comes, and then mighty nations and great kings shall use him as they please.

I have said all this to Zedekiah king of Judah: If you will submit to the yoke of the king of Babylon and serve him and his people, then you shall save your lives. Why should you and your people die by sword, famine, and pestilence, the fate with which the Lord has threatened any nation which does not serve the king of Babylon? Do not listen to the prophets who tell you not to become subject to the king of Babylon; they are prophesying falsely to you. I have not sent them, says the Lord; they are prophesying falsely in my name, and so I shall banish you and you will perish, you and these prophets who prophesy to you.

I said to the priests and all the people, These are the words of the Lord: Do not listen to your prophets who tell you that the vessels of the Lord's house will very soon be brought back from Babylon; they are only prophesying falsely to you. Do not listen to them; serve the king of Babylon, and save your lives. Why should this city become a ruin? If they are prophets, and if they have the word of the Lord, let them intercede with the Lord of Hosts to grant that the vessels still left in the Lord's house, in the royal palace, and in Jerusalem, may not be carried off to Babylon.   [Jer. 27:2-7, 12-18]

Then he denounces the cocky priests and false prophets:

> Do not listen to what the prophets say,
> who buoy you up with false hopes;
> the vision they report springs from their own imagination,
> it is not from the mouth of the Lord.
> They say to those who spurn the word of the Lord,
> 'Prosperity shall be yours';
> and to all who follow the promptings of their own stubborn heart
>   they say,
> 'No disaster shall befall you.'
> But which of them has stood in the council of the Lord,

seen him and heard his word?
Which of them has listened to his word and obeyed?
See what a scorching wind has gone out from the Lord,
a furious whirlwind;
it whirls round the heads of the wicked.
The Lord's anger is not to be turned aside,
until he has accomplished and fulfilled his deep designs.

[Jer. 23:16b–20a]

Outraged, the priest Hananiah breaks the yoke which Jeremiah symbolically wears. Hananiah and other nationalists then put King Zedekiah under pressure until he repeated his predecessor's disastrous mistake and withheld the yearly tribute from Babylonia in 588 B.C. Nebuchadrezzar at once laid siege to Jerusalem. In the ensuing struggle the Judean nationalists demanded that Jeremiah be put to death.

Then the officers said to the king, 'The man must be put to death. By talking in this way he is discouraging the soldiers and the rest of the people left in the city. He is pursuing not the people's welfare but their ruin.' King Zedekiah said, 'He is in your hands; the king is powerless against you.' So they took Jeremiah and threw him into the pit, in the court of the guard-house, letting him down with ropes. There was no water in the pit, only mud, and Jeremiah sank in the mud. Now Ebed-melech the Cushite, a eunuch, who was in the palace, heard that they had thrown Jeremiah into the pit and went to tell the king, who was seated in the Benjamin Gate. 'Your majesty,' he said, 'these men have shown great wickedness in their treatment of the prophet Jeremiah. They have thrown him into the pit, and when there is no more bread in the city he will die of hunger where he lies.' Thereupon the king told Ebed-melech the Cushite to take three men with him and hoist Jeremiah out of the pit before he died. So Ebed-melech went to the palace with the men and took some tattered, cast-off clothes from the wardrobe and let them down with ropes to Jeremiah in the pit. Ebed-melech the Cushite said to Jeremiah, 'Put these old clothes under your armpits to ease the ropes.' Jeremiah did this, and they pulled him up out of the pit with the ropes; and he remained in the court of the guard-house.   [Jer. 38:4–13]

Though he was arrested, beaten, and imprisoned, Jeremiah continued to proclaim that the nation was doomed.

In July 587 B.C. the Babylonian army poured into the city. The king was forced to watch the execution of his children, his eyes were then put out, and he was carried in chains to Babylon. The Temple, palace, and fortifications of Jerusalem were razed. Seven thousand of the leading families were deported, and a governor was appointed over the remaining rabble. Jeremiah was released and, given the option of going to Babylon, chose to stay among his people in the devastated city.

THE NEW COVENANT

A prophet of doom when his fellow countrymen were consumed with unrealistic and arrogant confidence, Jeremiah became, to his humbled and devastated people, a prophet of hope and of promise. Even in Judah's worst hour Jeremiah never lost confidence that God was involved and present in all events of the nation's history. When in the last and worst stages of the siege a cousin offered Jeremiah a piece of property on the outskirts of the city, Jeremiah saw it as an opportunity to demonstrate concretely his confident hope for the future:

I knew that this was the Lord's message; so I bought the field at Anathoth from my cousin Hanamel and weighed out the price, seventeen shekels of silver. In the presence of them all I gave my instructions to Baruch: These are the words of the Lord of Hosts the God of Israel: Take these copies of the deed of purchase, the sealed and the unsealed, and deposit them in an earthenware jar so that they may be preserved for a long time. For these are the words of the Lord of Hosts the God of Israel: The time will come when houses, fields, and vineyards will again be bought and sold in this land.

[Jer. 32:8c–9, 13–15]

To Jeremiah even the ghastly tragedy which had befallen the nation was an opportunity given by God for growth. Judah was an incorrigible child whose parent had reached out to her again and again in love. Now for her own good Judah was being punished. Her chastisement, though it inevitably involved suffering, was ultimately for her own good. Only after her egotistical illusions were shattered could she become what she was intended to be.

> For I am with you and will save you, says the Lord.
> I will make an end of all the nations
> amongst whom I have scattered you,
> but I will not make an end of you;
> though I punish you as you deserve,
> I will not sweep you clean away.
> I will cause the new skin to grow
> and heal your wounds, says the Lord,
> although men call you the Outcast,
> Zion, nobody's friend.
> A people that survived the sword
> found favour in the wilderness;
> Israel journeyed to find rest;
> long ago the Lord appeared to them:
> I have dearly loved you from of old,
> and still I maintain my unfailing care for you.
> I will build you up again, O virgin Israel,
> and you shall be rebuilt.   [Jer. 30:11, 17; 31:2b–4a]

Jeremiah knew that laws do not change men. Josiah's reforms had changed men's outward practices but their hearts remained selfish and they quickly learned how to adapt any outward law or ritual to serve their self-interest.

> The time is coming, says the Lord, when I will make a new covenant with Israel and Judah. It will not be like the covenant I made with their forefathers when I took them by the hand and led them out of Egypt. Although they broke my covenant, I was patient with them, says the Lord.   [Jer. 31:31–32]

Men had abused the Mosaic covenant by turning it into a business deal in which they agreed to do certain outward acts in return for God's favor. Men's lives are changed—made new—when they *know* God, accept his love in their hearts, and respond to that love.

> But this is the covenant which I will make with Israel after those days, says the Lord; I will set my law within them and write it on their hearts; I will become their God and they shall become my people. No longer need they teach one another to know the Lord; all of

them, high and low alike, shall know me, says the Lord, for I will forgive their wrongdoing and remember their sin no more.

[Jer. 31:33–34]

Men are made new, not by new and better laws and rituals, but by *God*. From his own experience Jeremiah knew that when men know God in their hearts, that relationship affects and transforms everything they do. Obedience to God's laws follows naturally and spontaneously.

Jeremiah envisions a world transformed as people come to know and respond to God. Though not until the end of time will all men know God in their hearts, every individual has the opportunity to enter *now*, on his own, into this new covenant. That is the message of hope that Jeremiah offers to all men of all times.

Shortly after the Babylonians set up Gedaliah as Judah's governor, Judean conspirators assassinated him. Fearing reprisal, a large segment of Jerusalem's population fled to Egypt. They forced Jeremiah to go with them and tradition holds that his compatriots murdered him there.

The world did its worst. It humiliated and then silenced the lonely Jeremiah. Today, however, we don't even know the *names* of those "powerful" men who crushed the "weaker" Jeremiah. But Jeremiah's name has remained on the lips of countless millions for 2500 years. That is just one of the ways in which God was faithful to his promise to Jeremiah when he called him as a boy:

They will make war on you but shall not overcome you,
for I am with you and will keep you safe.
This is the very word of the Lord.   [Jer. 1:19]

Chapter 15 ———————————

EZEKIEL

As we have seen, when Babylonia first conquered Judah in 597 B.C. she carted the king and upper classes of Jerusalem into captivity. Among the exiles was Ezekiel, a young man in his twenties, who was a member of a distinguished priestly family. For Ezekiel, as for most of the exiles, life in Babylon was not unpleasant. The Jews (the word comes from "Judeans") in Babylon were quite free to establish businesses and engage in trade. Most of them were prosperous and comfortable in their new surroundings. Ezekiel, for example, seems to have had a private house and complete freedom of speech and religion.

The word "weird" was made for Ezekiel. No other personality in Jewish history holds together such versatile and conflicting elements. Auvray describes Ezekiel thus: "Ecstatic and man of reason, utopian and idealist, a poet with an unrestrained imagination and the most precise of jurists, priest and prophet, a prolix, coarse, and popular writer, yet sometimes also obscure . . . and difficult to grasp." [9]

THE VISION OF YAHWEH

Ezekiel's public life began in 593 B.C., when he was thirty. His ecstatic visionary experience at that time reveals his strange, complex mind and his lurid imagination. What touched off the vision we do not know. Perhaps it was one of the spectacular electrical storms for which the Euphrates River valley is so notorious. His vision weaves elements of Jerusalem priestly practices together with glimpses of the monumental splendor of the city of Babylon.

On the fifth day of the fourth month in the thirtieth year, while I was among the exiles by the river Kebar, the heavens were opened and I saw a vision of God. On the fifth day of the month in the fifth year of the exile of King Jehoiachin, the word of the Lord came to Ezekiel son of Buzi the priest, in Chaldaea, by the river Kebar, and there the hand of the Lord came upon him.

I saw a storm wind coming from the north, a vast cloud with flashes of fire and brilliant light about it; and within was a radiance like brass, glowing in the heart of the flames. In the fire was the semblance of four living creatures in human form. Each had four faces and each four wings; their legs were straight, and their hooves were like the hooves of a calf, glittering like a disc of bronze. Under the wings on each of the four sides were human hands; all four creatures had faces and wings, and their wings touched one another. They did not turn as they moved; each creature went straight forward. Their faces were like this: all four had the face of a man and the face of a lion on the right, on the left the face of an ox and the face of an eagle.   [Ezek. 1:1–10]

"The symbolism of the faces is well explained by the rabbis: 'Man is exalted among creatures; the eagle is exalted among birds; the ox is exalted among domestic animals; the lion is exalted among wild beasts; and all of them have reached dominion and greatness has been given them, yet they are stationed below the chariot of the Holy One.'" [10] Christianity took over these symbols to describe the four evangelists—Matthew, Mark, Luke, and John.

Their wings were spread; each living creature had one pair touching its neighbours', while one pair covered its body. They moved straight forward in whatever direction the spirit would go, they never swerved in their course. The appearance of the creatures was as if fire from burning coals or torches were darting to and fro among them; the fire was radiant, and out of the fire came lightning.

As I looked at the living creatures, I saw wheels on the ground, one beside each of the four. The wheels sparkled like topaz, and they were all alike: in form and working they were like a wheel inside a wheel, and when they moved in any of the four directions they never swerved in their course.   [Ezek. 1:11–17]

These celebrated "wheels in the middle of the wheels" are wheels set at right angles so that the chariot could move in any direction. Eyes from the chariot likewise point in every direction.

All four had hubs and each hub had a projection which had the power of sight, and the rims of the wheels were full of eyes all round. When the living creatures moved, the wheels moved beside them; when the creatures rose from the ground, the wheels rose; they moved in whatever direction the spirit would go; and the wheels rose together with them, for the spirit of the living creatures was in the wheels. When the one moved, the other moved; when the one halted, the other halted; when the creatures rose from the ground, the wheels rose together with them, for the spirit of the creatures was in the wheels.

Above the heads of the living creatures was, as it were, a vault glittering like a sheet of ice, awe-inspiring, stretched over their heads above them. Under the vault their wings were spread straight out, touching one another, while one pair covered the body of each. I heard, too, the noise of their wings; when they moved it was like the noise of a great torrent or of a cloud-burst, like the noise of a crowd or of an armed camp; when they halted their wings dropped. A sound was heard above the vault over their heads, as they halted with drooping wings. Above the vault over their heads there appeared, as it were, a sapphire in the shape of a throne, and high above all, upon the throne, a form in human likeness. I saw what might have been brass glowing like fire in a furnace from the waist upwards; and from the waist downwards I saw what looked like fire with encircling radiance. Like a rainbow in the clouds on a rainy day was the sight of that encircling radiance; it was like the appearance of the glory of the Lord.   [Ezek. 1:18–28a]

The fantastic elements which Ezekiel brings together to convey the majesty and glory of the divine presence both impress and bewilder us. Even more extraordinary is the fact that his vision occurs in Babylon. The God once so firmly associated with the promised land—and specially in the minds of the Judeans with Jerusalem and the Temple—is present in Babylon amongst his exiled people!

When I saw this I threw myself on my face, and heard a voice speaking to me: Man, he said, stand up, and let me talk with you.
                                    [Ezek. 1:28b–2:1]

The experience literally sweeps Ezekiel off his feet. Like a man in the midst of a vast ocean, Ezekiel is overcome by a sense

of his own smallness. He is utterly "man"—a temporary speck
on a temporary speck in the universe. And yet, despite his humanness, he is called to a divine role as a fellow worker with God:
"Stand up and let me talk with you." Then Ezekiel knows what
he must do with his life.

As he spoke, a spirit came into me and stood me on my feet, and I
listened to him speaking. He said to me, Man, I am sending you to
the Israelites, a nation of rebels who have rebelled against me. Past
generations of them have been in revolt against me to this very day,
and this generation to which I am sending you is stubborn and ob-
stinate.   [Ezek. 2:2–4a]

Unlike Hosea and Jeremiah, Ezekiel perceives that Israel has
from her birth rebelled against God. There was no golden age
when the Israelites were faithful. Ezekiel is called to warn his
people of the inevitable consequences of rebellion. He will have
to steel himself; his words will not be popular.

When you say to them, 'These are the words of the Lord God', they
will know that they have a prophet among them, whether they listen
or whether they refuse to listen, because they are rebels. But you,
man, must not be afraid of them or of what they say, though they
are rebels against you and renegades, and you find yourself sitting
on scorpions. There is nothing to fear in what they say, and nothing
in their looks to terrify you, rebels though they are. You must speak
my words to them, whether they listen or whether they refuse to
listen, rebels that they are. But you, man, must listen to what I say
and not be rebellious like them. Open your mouth and eat what I
give you.
    Then I saw a hand stretched out to me, holding a scroll. He un-
rolled it before me, and it was written all over on both sides with
dirges and laments and words of woe. Then he said to me, 'Man,
eat what is in front of you, eat this scroll; then go and speak to the
Israelites.' So I opened my mouth and he gave me the scroll to eat.
Then he said, 'Man, swallow this scroll I give you, and fill yourself
full.' So I ate it, and it tasted as sweet as honey.   [Ezek. 2:4b–3:3]

In a symbolic act—all still in the imagination—Ezekiel accepts
his commission. It is God's word, not his own, which he is
speaking.

Man, he said to me, go and tell the Israelites what I have to say to them. But the Israelites will refuse to listen to you, for they refuse to listen to me, so brazen are they all and stubborn. But I will make you a match for them. I will make you as brazen as they are and as stubborn as they are. I will make your brow like adamant, harder than flint. Never fear them, never be terrified by them, rebels though they are. And he said to me, Listen carefully, man, to all that I have to say to you, and take it to heart. Go to your fellow-countrymen in exile and speak to them. Whether they listen or refuse to listen, say, 'These are the words of the Lord God.' . . . So I came to the exiles at Tel-abib who were settled by the river Kebar. For seven days I stayed with them, dumbfounded.   [Ezek. 3:4, 7–11, 15]

So powerful has been the effect of his vision that Ezekiel enters into a cataleptic stupor or trance. This is but one of several abnormal psychological experiences which Ezekiel undergoes.

CONFRONTING THE EXILES

We have noted the rising tide of nationalism in Jerusalem between 597 B.C. (when Babylonia first overwhelmed the city and took the upper classes to Babylon) and 587 B.C. (when Babylonia destroyed Jerusalem after the king refused to pay the yearly tribute). Nationalistic fervor was strong among the exiles. It led to widespread belief that their release was just around the corner. Ezekiel's principal task was to convince them that this was a false hope. He perceived and proclaimed that Judah would rebel and that Jerusalem would be destroyed.

Every major town had a tower on which was posted a watchman whose duty it was to keep an eye on the surrounding fields and vineyards and to warn the city against any approaching enemy. Ezekiel perceives his role to be that of a watchman:

Man, I have appointed you a watchman for the Israelites. You will take messages from me and carry my warnings to them. It may be that I pronounce sentence of death on a man because he is wicked; if you do not warn him to give up his ways, the guilt is his and because of his wickedness he shall die, but I will hold you answerable for his death. But if you have warned him to give up his ways, and he has not given them up, he will die because of his wickedness, but you will have saved yourself.   [Ezek. 33:7–9]

Ezekiel regards Jerusalem's destruction as the obvious, necessary, and inevitable result of her faithlessness, her idolatry, her rebellion, and her pursuit of self-interest rather than righteousness. God is God; he must be just. Since he is just, ultimately he must punish evil. There is no tenderness in Ezekiel's stern, relentlessly logical message:

> The word of the Lord came to me: Man, the Lord God says this to the land of Israel: An end is coming, the end is coming upon the four corners of the land. The end is now upon you; I will unleash my anger against you; I will call you to account for your doings and bring your abominations upon your own heads. I will neither pity nor spare you: I will make you suffer for your doings and the abominations that continue in your midst. So you shall know that I am the Lord.
>
> [Ezek. 7:1–4]

"So you shall know that I am the Lord," is the formula which Ezekiel uses over and over to reiterate that now the only way the Israelites can again know Yahweh is if he punishes them. Ezekiel conceives of God as a parent who, having tried every other way, finally has only one way to show his child his deep love: by punishing him.

The exiles' bland optimism, however, made them impervious to Ezekiel's message. Ezekiel no longer tries to persuade them. The situation calls for harshness. Ezekiel is like an enraged mother shrilly threatening her child: "You're going to get it when your father gets home! You just wait!"

> These were the words of the Lord to me: Man, will you judge her, will you judge the murderous city and bring home to her all her abominable deeds? Say to her, These are the words of the Lord God: Alas for the city that sheds blood within her walls and brings her fate upon herself, the city that makes herself idols and is defiled thereby! The guilt is yours for the blood you have shed, the pollution is on you for the idols you have made. You have shortened your days by this and brought the end of your years nearer. This is why I exposed you to the contempt of the nations and the mockery of every country. Lands far and near will taunt you with your infamy and gross disorder. In you the princes of Israel, one and all, have used their power to shed blood; men have treated their fathers and

mothers with contempt, they have oppressed the alien and ill-treated the orphan and the widow. You have disdained what is sacred to me and desecrated my sabbaths. In you, Jerusalem, informers have worked to procure bloodshed; in you are men who have feasted at mountain-shrines and have committed lewdness. In you men have exposed their fathers' nakedness; they have violated women during their periods; they have committed an outrage with their neighbours' wives and have lewdly defiled their daughters-in-law; they have ravished their sisters, their own fathers' daughters. In you men have accepted bribes to shed blood, and they have exacted discount and interest on their loans. You have oppressed your fellows for gain, and you have forgotten me. This is the very word of the Lord God.

See, I strike with my clenched fist in anger at your ill-gotten gains and at the bloodshed within your walls. Will your strength or courage stand when I deal with you? I, the Lord, have spoken and I will act. I will disperse you among the nations and scatter you abroad; thus will I rid you altogether of your defilement. I will sift you in the sight of the nations, and you will know that I am the Lord.   [Ezek. 22:1–16]

Only by being punished will men come again to know God's presence in their lives.

Ezekiel then proceeds to act out Jerusalem's coming punishment. In silence this strange man lies on his left side for 150 days (representing Israel's years of exile) and on his right side 40 days (representing Judah's years of exile). During this time he eats only tiny morsels of food to demonstrate the deprivations the people will endure in exile.

DIVINE JUSTICE AND THE INDIVIDUAL

When the exiles were feeling sorry for themselves they complained to one another that they were being punished for the foolishness and evil of others: "Our fathers sinned and now have died; *we* have to pay for the consequences of *their* iniquities." Inadvertently, Ezekiel's own emphasis on Israel's age-old disobedience played into the hands of those who wished to blame their forefathers for all that was wrong.

The people's complaint was really against God: if God is just, why do children pay for their fathers' crimes? Why must a good individual in the community suffer the consequences of the wrongs of others, and why do those who are evil prosper?

Ezekiel does not provide an adequate answer to these questions; only Second Isaiah, Job, and Daniel deal with these issues in depth. But Ezekiel does set us on the road to the beginnings of an answer. First, he asserts that God is just to both societies and individuals. Of that he is certain, even if he cannot explain it. And secondly, he asserts the concept of individual responsibility, each person's responsibility for his own life:

These were the words of the Lord to me: What do you all mean by repeating this proverb in the land of Israel:

'The fathers have eaten sour grapes,
and the children's teeth are set on edge'?   [Ezek. 18:1–2]

"When the prophets threatened that the spiritual faults and moral vices of the people would bring destruction on the nation, the people answered them with [this] proverb, . . . either to exonerate themselves from blame for the impending calamity or to plead impotence to avert it, since according to the proverb its causes lay in the unalterable past. The proverb gave them both an alibi and an excuse for moral inertia." [11]

As I live, says the Lord God, this proverb shall never again be used in Israel. Every living soul belongs to me; father and son alike are mine. The soul that sins shall die.   [Ezek. 18:3–4]

This is one of the great assertions of the Old Testament: God cares about every individual. Each individual is his. Father and son are treated as individuals; neither is punished for the other's sin. But the man who chooses evil will be punished, since God is just.

Consider the man who is righteous and does what is just and right. He never feasts at mountain-shrines, never lifts his eyes to the idols of Israel, never dishonours another man's wife, never approaches a woman during her periods. He oppresses no man, he returns the debtor's pledge, he never robs. He gives bread to the hungry and clothes to those who have none. He never lends either at discount or at interest. He shuns injustice and deals fairly between man and man. He conforms to my statutes and loyally observes my laws. Such a man is righteous: he shall live, says the Lord God.
He may have a son who is a man of violence and a cut-throat who turns his back on these rules. He obeys none of them, he feasts at

mountain-shrines, he dishonours another man's wife, he oppresses the unfortunate and the poor, he is a robber, he does not return the debtor's pledge, he lifts his eyes to idols and joins in abominable rites; he lends both at discount and at interest. Such a man shall not live. Because he has committed all these abominations he shall die, and his blood will be on his own head.   [Ezek. 18:5–13]

Ezekiel oversimplifies. Good men do not always live and prosper and get rewards; bad men do not always die or receive punishment. And yet Ezekiel was not deterred—even in the face of apparently contradictory evidence—from proclaiming the mystery that good lives and evil dies.

It is sometimes said that Ezekiel ignores the fact that heredity and environment *do* affect the way men live and act. Perhaps he does. But perhaps we, like the exiles, are inclined to ignore the fact that men also have tremendous opportunity and freedom to overcome their backgrounds.

This man in turn may have a son who sees all his father's sins; he sees, but he commits none of them. He never feasts at mountain-shrines, never lifts his eyes to the idols of Israel, never dishonours another man's wife. He oppresses no man, takes no pledge, does not rob. He gives bread to the hungry and clothes to those who have none. He shuns injustice, he never lends either at discount or at interest. He keeps my laws and conforms to my statutes. Such a man shall not die for his father's wrongdoing; he shall live.

His father may have been guilty of oppression and robbery and may have lived an evil life among his kinsfolk, and so has died because of his iniquity. You may ask, 'Why is the son not punished for his father's iniquity?' Because he has always done what is just and right and has been careful to obey all my laws, therefore he shall live. It is the soul that sins, and no other, that shall die; a son shall not share a father's guilt, nor a father his son's. The righteous man shall reap the fruit of his own righteousness, and the wicked man the fruit of his own wickedness.   [Ezek. 18:14–20]

Men are not completely prisoners of the past. Even if the situation in which we live is a consequence of others' evils, we are still free within that situation to determine our own response to it.

Ezekiel is trying to emphasize that men, right now, have the freedom to change their lives. They are not helpless victims of the past, impotent to choose what course their lives will take. They are responsible for their own lives.

It may be that a wicked man gives up his sinful ways and keeps all my laws, doing what is just and right. That man shall live; he shall not die. None of the offences he has committed shall be remembered against him; he shall live because of his righteous deeds. Have I any desire, says the Lord God, for the death of a wicked man? Would I not rather that he should mend his ways and live?

It may be that a righteous man turns back from his righteous ways and commits every kind of abomination that the wicked practice; shall he do this and live? No, none of his former righteousness will be remembered in his favour; he has broken his faith, he has sinned, and he shall die. You say that the Lord acts without principle? Listen, you Israelites, it is you who act without principle, not I. If a righteous man turns from his righteousness, takes to evil ways and dies, it is because of these evil ways that he dies. Again, if a wicked man turns from his wicked ways and does what is just and right, he will save his life. If he sees his offences as they are and turns his back on them all, then he shall live; he shall not die.   [Ezek. 18:21–28]

Ezekiel knows that the exiles are not as innocent as they pretend.

'The Lord acts without principle', say the Israelites. No, Israelites, it is you who act without principle, not I. Therefore, Israelites, says the Lord God, I will judge every man of you on his deeds. Turn, turn from your offences, or your iniquity will be your downfall. Throw off the load of your past misdeeds; get yourselves a new heart and a new spirit. Why should you die, you men of Israel? I have no desire for any man's death. This is the very word of the Lord God.   [Ezek. 18:29–32]

THESE BONES SHALL LIVE

In 587 B.C. that which Ezekiel had anticipated took place. Nebuchadrezzar crushed the foolish and arrogant Judean revolt and destroyed Jerusalem. All the false hopes of the Judean nationalists and of the Jews in Babylon were shattered.

For years Ezekiel had warned that since God is just, punishment was inevitable. When it occurred, he believed, the people would turn back to God because of their suffering. No longer does Ezekiel have to be the harsh watchman sounding the alarm. The devastated people no longer need warning but hope, and Ezekiel's message, though still bluntly stern, begins to acquire overtones of tenderness and consolation.

Characteristically, however, Ezekiel's first reaction to the fall of the city is to strike out with bitterness and anger and to fix blame. One of the reasons for the nation's destruction was its corrupt leadership.

These were the words of the Lord to me: Prophesy, man, against the shepherds of Israel; prophesy and say to them, You shepherds, these are the words of the Lord God: How I hate the shepherds of Israel who care only for themselves! Should not the shepherd care for the sheep? You consume the milk, wear the wool, and slaughter the fat beasts, but you do not feed the sheep. You have not encouraged the weary, tended the sick, bandaged the hurt, recovered the straggler, or searched for the lost; and even the strong you have driven with ruthless severity. They are scattered, they have no shepherd, they have become the prey of wild beasts. My sheep go straying over the mountains and on every high hill, my flock is dispersed over the whole country, with no one to ask after them or search for them.

Therefore, you shepherds, hear the words of the Lord. As surely as I live, says the Lord God, because my sheep are ravaged by wild beasts and have become their prey for lack of a shepherd, because my shepherds have not asked after the sheep but have cared only for themselves and not for the sheep—therefore, you shepherds, hear the words of the Lord. These are the words of the Lord God: I am against the shepherds and will demand my sheep from them. I will dismiss those shepherds: they shall care only for themselves no longer; I will rescue my sheep from their jaws, and they shall feed on them no more.

[Ezek. 34:1–10]

Israel's leaders have been consumed in their own selfishness; Ezekiel envisions the people turning now to God as their ruler. And God himself would be their shepherd.

For these are the words of the Lord God: Now I myself will ask after my sheep and go in search of them. As a shepherd goes in search of his sheep when his flock is dispersed all around him, so I will go in search of my sheep and rescue them, no matter where they were scattered in dark and cloudy days. I will bring them out from every nation, gather them in from other lands, and lead them home to their own soil. I will graze them on the mountains of Israel, by her streams and in all her green fields. I will feed them on good grazing-ground, and their pasture shall be the high mountains of Israel. There they will rest, there in good pasture, and find rich grazing on the mountains of Israel. I myself will tend my flock, I myself pen them in their fold, says the Lord God. I will search for the lost, recover the straggler, bandage the hurt, strengthen the sick, leave the healthy and strong to play, and give them their proper food. [Ezek. 34:11–16]

The shepherd cares about each individual sheep. The weak will be protected from the strong.

As for you, my flock, these are the words of the Lord God: I will judge between one sheep and another. [Ezek. 34:17]

Under Yahweh will be an earthly shepherd, a descendant of David who will not set himself up as a mighty king but who will be Yahweh's servant prince, God's faithful earthly viceroy.

Then I will set over them one shepherd to take care of them, my servant David; he shall care for them and become their shepherd. I, the Lord, will become their God, and my servant David shall be a prince among them. I, the Lord, have spoken. I will make a covenant with them to ensure prosperity; I will rid the land of wild beasts, and men shall live in peace of mind on the open pastures and sleep in the woods. I will settle them in the neighbourhood of my hill and send them rain in due season, blessed rain. Trees in the country-side shall bear their fruit, the land shall yield its produce, and men shall live in peace of mind on their own soil. They shall know that I am the Lord when I break the bars of their yokes and rescue them from those who have enslaved them. You are my flock, my people, the flock I feed, and I am your God. This is the very word of the Lord God. [Ezek. 34:23–27, 31]

One senses that the dour Ezekiel is afraid to be too tender. He fears, perhaps, that God's shepherding concern and protection will be mistaken by the people for soft indulgence. Therefore Ezekiel asserts that God will save Israel not out of tender love, but only to preserve his own reputation:

Man, when the Israelites lived on their own soil they defiled it with their ways and deeds; their ways were foul and disgusting in my sight. I poured out my fury upon them because of the blood they had poured out upon the land, and the idols with which they had defiled it. I scattered them among the nations, and they were dispersed among different countries; I passed on them the sentence which their ways and deeds deserved. When they came among those nations, they caused my holy name to be profaned wherever they came: men said of them, 'These are the people of the Lord, and it is from his land that they have come.' And I spared them for the sake of my holy name which the Israelites had profaned among the nations to whom they had gone.

Therefore tell the Israelites that these are the words of the Lord God: It is not for your sake, you Israelites, that I am acting, but for the sake of my holy name, which you have profaned among the peoples where you have gone. I will hallow my great name, which has been profaned among those nations.   [Ezek. 36:17–23a]

A parent who has been deeply wounded by his child can perhaps understand what Ezekiel is trying to say here. Though deeply hurt, a parent still reaches out again in love to his child. Not willing to risk having his love rejected again, however, the parent *does* what is loving, but he *says*, "I don't want you to think I'm doing this because I love you." He is trying not only to protect himself but to convey a message to the child: "You don't deserve the loving things I am doing for you." We may reject the analogy (God is not an insecure, hurt parent), but it does dramatically make an important point: God's concern for Israel is not merited or earned. It is God's free gift.

As a parent's love can sometimes transform a child, or elicit a loving response, so, Ezekiel imagines, God's free gift of love will touch Israel and make her look on her former way of life with loathing.

When they see that I reveal my holiness through you, the nations will know that I am the Lord, says the Lord God. I will take you out of the nations and gather you from every land and bring you to your own soil. I will sprinkle clean water over you, and you shall be cleansed from all that defiles you; I will cleanse you from the taint of all your idols. I will give you a new heart and put a new spirit within you; I will take the heart of stone from your body and give you a heart of flesh. I will put my spirit into you and make you conform to my statutes, keep my laws and live by them. You shall live in the land which I gave to your ancestors; you shall become my people, and I will become your God. I will save you from all that defiles you; I will call to the corn and make it plentiful; I will bring no more famine upon you. I will make the trees bear abundant fruit and the ground yield heavy crops, so that you will never again have to bear the reproach of famine among the nations. You will recall your wicked ways and evil deeds, and you will loathe yourselves because of your wickedness and your abominations. It is not for your sake that I am acting; be sure of that, says the Lord God. Feel, then, the shame and disgrace of your ways, men of Israel. [Ezek. 36:23b–32]

When men know God and accept his love, then a new way of life follows.

In a vision Ezekiel pictures this new life. His vision was no doubt suggested by hearing the Hebrew phrase "our bones are dried up." "Bone" in Hebrew means "my force," "the strength of my being." The phrase expressed the enfeeblement and despair the exiles felt.

The hand of the Lord came upon me, and he carried me out by his spirit and put me down in a plain full of bones. He made me go to and fro across them until I had been round them all; they covered the plain, countless numbers of them, and they were very dry. He said to me, 'Man, can these bones live again?' I answered, 'Only thou knowest that, Lord God.' He said to me, 'Prophesy over these bones and say to them, O dry bones, hear the word of the Lord. This is the word of the Lord God to these bones: I will put breath into you, and you shall live. I will fasten sinews on you, bring flesh upon you, overlay you with skin, and put breath in you, and you shall live; and you shall know that I am the Lord.' I began to prophesy as he had bidden me, and as I prophesied there was a rustling sound and the bones fitted themselves together. As I looked, sinews appeared upon them, flesh covered them, and they were overlaid with skin, but there was no breath in them. Then he said to me, 'Prophesy to the wind, prophesy, man, and say to it, These are the words of the Lord God: Come, O wind, come from every quarter and breathe into these slain, that they may come to life.' I began to prophesy as he had bidden me: breath came into them; they came to life and rose to their feet, a mighty host. He said to me, 'Man, these bones are the whole people of Israel. They say, "Our bones are dry, our thread of life is snapped, our web is severed from the loom." Prophesy, therefore, and say to them, These are the words of the Lord God: O my people, I will open your graves and bring you up from them, and restore you to the land of Israel. You shall know that I am the Lord when I open your graves and bring you up from them, O my people. Then I will put my spirit into you and you shall live, and I will settle you on your own soil, and you shall know that I the Lord have spoken and will act. This is the very word of the Lord.' [Ezek. 37:1–14]

BY THE WATERS OF BABYLON

Bereft of hope, separated from their homes and the center of their religious life, dazzled by the magnificence and glamour of their Babylonian surroundings, one might have expected the Jews in exile to lose their religious and political identity. Strangely, quite the opposite occurred. Though some fell away, many Jews were intensely determined to maintain their distinctive identity.

> By the rivers of Babylon we sat down and wept
> when we remembered Zion.
> There on the willow-trees
> we hung up our harps,
> for there those who carried us off
> demanded music and singing,
> and our captors called on us to be merry:
> 'Sing us one of the songs of Zion.'
> How could we sing the Lord's song
> in a foreign land?
>
> If I forget you, O Jerusalem,
> let my right hand wither away;
> let my tongue cling to the roof of my mouth
> if I do not remember you,
> if I do not set Jerusalem
> above my highest joy.   [Ps. 137:1–6]

Though this preservation of distinctive identity was commendable, it also unfortunately had its ugly side: a cruelly vindictive, narrow nationalism:

> Remember, O Lord, against the people of Edom
> the day of Jerusalem's fall,
> when they said, 'Down with it, down with it,

down to its very foundations!'
O Babylon, Babylon the destroyer,
happy the man who repays you
for all that you did to us!
Happy is he who shall seize your children
and dash them against the rock.   [Ps. 137:7–9]

Even though there was no Temple, the exiles knew that God could be worshiped anywhere, and they gathered in small groups (synagogues) for instruction and worship. Intensive effort was made during this period to collect, study, and record in writing the ancient traditions of the nation. From this period, most notably, comes the P document, a collection of ancient traditions made by the priests, which was later combined with the J, E, and D collections to form the first five books of our present Bible. Once Israel ceased to be a nation politically, it seemed to discover itself more deeply as a spiritual community. The distinctive initiation rite of circumcision was faithfully practiced, the ancient traditions were carefully read, and the Sabbath and the ancient festivals meticulously celebrated.

Ezekiel's own final vision—though typically exaggerated—reflects this intense preoccupation with Israel's particular identity. His vision is of a new Jerusalem and a new Temple. It is a picture of Israel restored. No thought is given to the rest of mankind. Little attention is paid to the ethical behavior of the people. We have, rather, an elaborately worked out description of the new Temple, new cult, and new government of a stridently Jewish people.

We need not condemn this vision, narrow as it is. We can rather marvel at the phenomenal vitality of Israel's distinctive faith in the worst of circumstances. And yet we can also rejoice in the wider vision of Second Isaiah, in a time, slightly later, when loss of identity was not so distinct a possibility.

Chapter 16

SECOND ISAIAH

Paradoxically Israel's greatest prophet came from the small community of faithful Jews in Babylon in the later years of exile. Even more paradoxically, we know nothing whatsoever about this prophet as a person, not even his name. He was probably attached to a small group or "school" which kept alive the teachings of Isaiah the prophet. His thought was obviously influenced by Isaiah's (even though Isaiah lived two hundred years earlier), and his writings were eventually appended to Isaiah's. For this reason he is known as "Second Isaiah." His writings are found in chapters 40–55 of the Book of Isaiah.

Babylonia was a fast-fading star. Less than fifty years after it attained world dominance (605 B.C.), Cyrus of Persia rose to challenge its supremacy. Second Isaiah's early thought focused on the anticipation that Cyrus would destroy Babylonia and return the Jews to their former homeland. He saw Cyrus as God's anointed instrument to restore Israel. These hopes were realized in 539 B.C. when Cyrus defeated Babylonia and captured the capital city of Babylon.

Though Second Isaiah had expected Cyrus to punish and destroy Babylon, his hopes (if such they were) were disappointed. Cyrus was a benevolent conqueror with extraordinary insight into human nature. He destroyed nothing, protected art treasures, left religious worship unhampered, killed no enemies.

Second Isaiah's public activity appears to have taken place over a two-year period (540–538 B.C.) just before and after Cyrus' conquest. Cyrus' moderate attitude toward Babylonia seems to have influenced Second Isaiah's understanding of God's purpose in history. Second Isaiah's early thought focused entirely on the hopes of the exiled Jewish community. After Cyrus' conquest, however, Second Isaiah came to see that Israel's restoration was only a part of God's overall plan for mankind.

THE GOOD NEWS

To his people disheartened by their long exile, to his people subjected to the constant fear and anxiety of being at the mercy of others, to his people whose God seemed powerless to rescue them from the clutches of the world's great powers, Second Isaiah sounds the trumpet to herald the dawn of a new age. Standing, in imagination, in Yahweh's heavenly council, the prophet is told to proclaim the good news to Jerusalem (to Jews everywhere) that God is acting decisively in the events of history:

> Comfort, comfort my people;
> —it is the voice of your God;
> speak tenderly to Jerusalem
> and tell her this,
> that she has fulfilled her term of bondage,
> that her penalty is paid;
> she has received at the Lord's hand
> double measure for all her sins.   [Isa. 40:1–2]

Israel's suffering is creative. God counts it as in some sense "making up" for the past. God therefore will deliver his people from their second bondage in Babylon (as he did from their first bondage in Egypt) in a second and more marvelous Exodus.

> There is a voice that cries:
> Prepare a road for the Lord through the wilderness,
> clear a highway across the desert for our God.
> Every valley shall be lifted up,
> every mountain and hill brought down;
> rugged places shall be made smooth
> and mountain-ranges become a plain.
> Thus shall the glory of the Lord be revealed,
> and all mankind together shall see it;
> for the Lord himself has spoken.   [Isa. 40:3–5]

God himself will lead his people back to Jerusalem; then *everyone* will know that he is not the seemingly weak or absent god of a handful of exiles, but the mighty Lord of the universe.

Compared to this God, nothing human or worldly has any permanence. Men come and go. God is forever.

> A voice says, 'Cry,'
> and another asks, 'What shall I cry?'
> 'That all mankind is grass,
> they last no longer than a flower of the field.
> The grass withers, the flower fades,
> when the breath of the Lord blows upon them;
> the grass withers, the flowers fade,
> but the word of our God endures for evermore.'   [Isa. 40:6–8]

Though God (by his "breath" or "spirit") affects men and therefore history, he himself remains unchanged above the whole changing process.

Though utterly transcendent, God cares about and involves himself in the lives of men in the world. Second Isaiah pictures God as a shepherd (that is, a strong leader and gentle protector):

> You who bring Zion good news, up with you to the mountain-top;
> lift up your voice and shout,
> you who bring good news to Jerusalem,
> lift it up fearlessly;
> cry to the cities of Judah, 'Your God is here.'
> Here is the Lord God coming in might,
> coming to rule with his right arm.
> His recompense comes with him,
> he carries his reward before him.
> He will tend his flock like a shepherd
> and gather them together with his arm;
> he will carry the lambs in his bosom
> and lead the ewes to water.   [Isa. 40:9–11]

This God who cares about them, who is using their lives for his purpose, is none other than the God who brought everything into being, who is the source of all life. What earthly figure can compare to God?

> Who has gauged the waters in the palm of his hand,
> or with its span set limits to the heavens?
> Who has held all the soil of earth in a bushel,
> or weighed the mountains on a balance
> and the hills on a pair of scales?

> Who has set limits to the spirit of the Lord?
> What counsellor stood at his side to instruct him?
> With whom did he confer to gain discernment?
> Who taught him how to do justice
> or gave him lessons in wisdom?   [Isa. 40:12–14]

The nations of the earth, which exercise their power with such pomp and self-importance, are not really in control of things. Compared to the Lord of the universe they are nothing.

> Why, to him nations are but drops from a bucket,
> no more than moisture on the scales;
> coasts and islands weigh as light as specks of dust.
> All Lebanon does not yield wood enough for fuel
> or beasts enough for a sacrifice.
> All nations dwindle to nothing before him,
> he reckons them mere nothings, less than nought.   [Isa. 40:15–17]

The idea of making an earthly object to represent God is ludicrous.

> What likeness will you find for God
> or what form to resemble his?
> Is it an image which a craftsman sets up,
> and a goldsmith covers with plate
> and fits with studs of silver as a costly gift?
> Or Is It mulberry-wood that will not rot which a man chooses,
> seeking out a skilful craftsman for it,
> to mount an image that will not fall?   [Isa. 40:18–20]

The God who creates the whole process of the universe is also the Lord of history. Creation merely sets the stage upon which God acts to carry out his plan.

> Do you not know, have you not heard,
> were you not told long ago,
> have you not perceived ever since the world began,
> that God sits throned on the vaulted roof of earth,
> whose inhabitants are like grasshoppers?
> He stretches out the skies like a curtain,
> he spreads them out like a tent to live in;

he reduces the great to nothing
and makes all earth's princes less than nothing.   [Isa. 40:21–23]

The Hebrew prophets lived in an era, like most others, in which kings and rulers rose, "full of themselves," for a split second, then fell and were forgotten. Men act so important:

Scarcely are they planted, scarcely sown,
scarcely have they taken root in the earth,
before he blows upon them and they wither away,
and a whirlwind carries them off like chaff.
To whom then will you liken me,
whom set up as my equal?
asks the Holy One.
Lift up your eyes to the heavens;
consider who created it all,
led out their host one by one
and called them all by their names;
through his great might, his might and power,
not one is missing.   [Isa. 40:24–26]

If God is in control of the world, says the prophet, then Israel can take heart. God will strengthen and sustain all who "look to him" as they bear the burdens of daily life.

Why do you complain, O Jacob,
and you, Israel, why do you say,
'My plight is hidden from the Lord
and my cause has passed out of God's notice'?
Do you not know, have you not heard?
The Lord, the everlasting God, creator of the wide world,
grows neither weary nor faint;
no man can fathom his understanding.
He gives vigour to the weary,
new strength to the exhausted.
Young men may grow weary and faint,
even in their prime they may stumble and fall;
but those who look to the Lord will win new strength,
they will grow wings like eagles;
they will run and not be weary,
they will march on and never grow faint.   [Isa. 40:27–31]

ISRAEL: A LIGHT TO THE NATIONS

God chooses Israel not to indulge her with privileges, but to lay upon her special responsibility. Israel is not an end in itself. God is not calling her to national greatness. Israel is called to be the beacon light which guides and attracts *all* men to God.

> Thus speaks the Lord who is God,
> he who created the skies and stretched them out,
> who fashioned the earth and all that grows in it,
> who gave breath to its people,
> the breath of life to all who walk upon it:
> I, the Lord, have called you with righteous purpose
> and taken you by the hand;
> I have formed you, and appointed you
> to be a light to all peoples,
> a beacon for the nations,
> to open eyes that are blind,
> to bring captives out of prison,
> out of the dungeons where they lie in darkness.   [Isa. 42:5–7]

The despairing Jewish exiles are summoned to a great cause: to witness to God, to teach all men about him, to summon all men to him. Israel is called to advertise Yahweh, in the way a merchant calls out in the open market to advertise his wares.

> Come, all who are thirsty, come, fetch water;
> come, you who have no food, buy corn and eat;
> come and buy, not for money, not for a price.
> Why spend money and get what is not bread,
> why give the price of your labour and go unsatisfied?
> Only listen to me and you will have good food to eat,
> and you will enjoy the fat of the land.
> come to me and listen to my words,
> hear me, and you shall have life:
> I will make a covenant with you, this time for ever,
> to love you faithfully as I loved David.
> I made him a witness to all races,
> a prince and instructor of peoples;
> and you in turn shall summon nations you do not know,

and nations that do not know you shall come running to you,
because the Lord your God,
the Holy One of Israel, has glorified you.   [Isa. 55:1–5]

Israel then is chosen for responsibility. Salvation is through
her (she is the means God uses to declare his purpose), but
salvation is for the world, not for Israel alone. Israel is called
to be the nucleus now of what will be God's covenant with all
men. The God who created and who controls all that is—the
only God—calls all men to himself.

Thus says the Lord, the creator of the heavens,
he who is God,
who made the earth and fashioned it
and himself fixed it fast,
who created it no empty void,
but made it for a place to dwell in:
I am the Lord, there is no other.
I do not speak in secret, in realms of darkness,
I do not say to the sons of Jacob,
'Look for me in the empty void.'
I the Lord speak what is right, declare what is just.
                                                    [Isa. 45:18–19]

"Yahweh does not make himself deliberately obscure, so that
men are driven to 'seek' him by superstitious, or occult, or
orgiastic means. He speaks righteousness and declares what is
right. He is not, like the gods of the heathen, accessible only to
those who know the techniques of divination or are expert in the
elaborations of ritual. . . . Old Testament religion is at once
grand and simple; it is the religion of the layman." [12] God openly
discloses what he is like. We are called to gather and respond.

Gather together, come, draw near,
all you survivors of the nations,
you fools, who carry your wooden idols in procession
and pray to a god that cannot save you.
Come forward and urge your case, consult together:
who foretold this in days of old,
who stated it long ago?
Was it not I the Lord?

> There is no god but me;
> there is no god other than I, victorious and able to save.
> Look to me and be saved,
> you peoples from all corners of the earth;
> for I am God, there is no other.   [Isa. 45:20–22]

THE SERVANT OF THE LORD

Israel's history after Mount Sinai was punctuated with attempts to achieve national, military, or financial power and greatness. The genius of Second Isaiah is that he perceived that Israel's true calling was to be a servant. He saw that its true greatness lay in humble service.

Israel's calling is most beautifully expressed by Second Isaiah in four "Servant Songs," which appear to be reflections on or of an anonymous individual. This individual already *is* in the present what all of Israel is called to *become*. His life now reveals what Israel is called to be. Since his life shows what Israel is called to become, the Servant *is* Israel. He is Israel as it begins to become its true self. It is not surprising, then, that Second Isaiah sometimes sees the Servant as an individual (who is to inspire and guide Israel as a whole) and other times sees the Servant as Israel (in that he shows what Israel truly is). Likewise, the Servant is sometimes seen as active now in the present, and yet, since all Israel has not yet realized its calling, the Servant's work is also future.

Second Isaiah sees the life of this individual—this Servant— as a model which God presents to all Israel to show Israel its true calling.

> Here is my servant, whom I uphold,
> my chosen one in whom I delight,
> I have bestowed my spirit upon him,
> and he will make justice shine on the nations.   [Isa. 42:1]

The first song describes how the Servant carries out his work not with armies or with loud denunciations, but by quiet acts of service.

> He will not call out or lift his voice high,
> or make himself heard in the open street.
> He will not break a bruised reed,

or snuff out a smouldering wick;
he will make justice shine on every race,
never faltering, never breaking down,
he will plant justice on earth,
while coasts and islands wait for his teaching.   [Isa. 42:2–4]

In the second song, the Servant himself speaks.

Listen to me, you coasts and islands,
pay heed, you peoples far away:
from birth the Lord called me,
he named me from my mother's womb.
He made my tongue his sharp sword
and concealed me under cover of his hand;
he made me a polished arrow
and hid me out of sight in his quiver.
He said to me, 'You are my servant,
Israel through whom I shall win glory';
so I rose to honour in the Lord's sight
and my God became my strength.   [Isa. 49:1–3]

Israel is called to win honor not through military power or
national greatness, but through service. This service will not be
easy, but demanding and often apparently fruitless:

Once I said, 'I have laboured in vain;
I have spent my strength for nothing, to no purpose';
yet in truth my cause is with the Lord
and my reward is in God's hands.   [Isa. 49:4]

Yet if it is service for the Lord, it is not ever wasted, even
though it seems unfruitful in earthly terms.

And now the Lord who formed me in the womb to be his servant,
to bring Jacob back to him
that Israel should be gathered to him,
now the Lord calls me again:
it is too slight a task for you, as my servant,
to restore the tribes of Jacob,
to bring back the descendants of Israel:
I will make you a light to the nations,
to be my salvation to earth's farthest bounds.   [Isa. 49:5–6]

The third song emphasizes that, though the Servant's role is that of a teacher, unlike many learned men, he has the humility to listen.

> The Lord God has given me
> the tongue of a teacher
> and skill to console the weary
> with a word in the morning;
> he sharpened my hearing
> that I might listen like one who is taught.
> The Lord God opened my ears
> and I did not disobey or turn back in defiance.   [Isa. 50:4–5]

Now, however, he begins to see the costliness of being a servant: the degradation and humiliation which the Lord has called him to endure as part of his service.

> I offered my back to the lash,
> and let my beard be plucked from my chin,
> I did not hide my face from spitting and insult;
> but the Lord God stands by to help me;
> therefore no insult can wound me.
> I have set my face like flint,
> for I know that I shall not be put to shame,
> because one who will clear my name is at my side.
> Who dare argue against me? Let us confront one another.
> Who will dispute my cause? Let him come forward.
> The Lord God will help me;
> who then can prove me guilty?
> They will all wear out like a garment,
> the moths will eat them up.   [Isa. 50:6–9]

THE SUFFERING SERVANT

Only gradually, perhaps from personal experience, did Second Isaiah come to perceive that Israel's calling to be a servant was, in essence, a calling to suffer. God had chosen Israel for suffering. It was in and through her suffering that Israel would be a light to the nations.

In the final song, the Servant has suffered so hideously that men avert their eyes from him. How surprised men are when they discover that it is this humiliated one whom God will exalt.

> Behold, my servant shall prosper,
> he shall be lifted up, exalted to the heights.
> Time was when many were aghast at you, my people;
> so now many nations recoil at sight of him,
> and kings curl their lips in disgust.
> For they see what they had never been told
> and things unheard before fill their thoughts.
> Who could have believed what we have heard,
> and to whom has the power of the Lord been revealed?
> [Isa. 52:13–53:1]

There was nothing about him that would have led anyone to think that this was God's own servant. He has been God's servant incognito.

> He grew up before the Lord like a young plant
> whose roots are in parched ground;
> he had no beauty, no majesty to draw our eyes,
> no grace to make us delight in him;
> his form, disfigured, lost all the likeness of a man,
> his beauty changed beyond human semblance.
> He was despised, he shrank from the sight of men,
> tormented and humbled by suffering;
> we despised him, we held him of no account,
> a thing from which men turn away their eyes.   [Isa. 53:2–3]

For a while men saw in his sufferings nothing but degradation. Then they perceived that he was suffering *on their behalf*.

> Yet on himself he bore our sufferings,
> our torments he endured,
> while we counted him smitten by God,
> struck down by disease and misery;
> but he was pierced for our transgressions,
> tortured for our iniquities;
> the chastisement he bore is health for us
> and by his scourging we are healed.
> We had all strayed like sheep,
> each of us had gone his own way;
> but the Lord laid upon him
> the guilt of us all.   [Isa. 53:4–6]

He who was bruised, degraded, and destroyed, was mysteriously the means by which others were healed and forgiven.

And yet before men realized who he was, he had gone—alone, with quiet resignation, unrecognized, deprived of justice—to an ignominious death.

> He was afflicted, he submitted to be struck down
> and did not open his mouth;
> he was led like a sheep to the slaughter,
> like a ewe that is dumb before the shearers.
> Without protection, without justice, he was taken away;
> and who gave a thought to his fate,
> how he was cut off from the world of living men,
> stricken to the death for my people's transgression?
> He was assigned a grave with the wicked,
> a burial-place among the refuse of mankind,
> though he had done no violence
> and spoken no word of treachery.   [Isa. 53:7–9]

But he who freely offered his life will be vindicated by God.

> Yet the Lord took thought for his tortured servant
> and healed him who had made himself a sacrifice for sin;
> so shall he enjoy long life and see his children's children,
> and in his hand the Lord's cause shall prosper.   [Isa. 53:10]

God will use his faithful servant's freely offered life—his suffering and his death—to make up for the evil which others have done. The servant's suffering and the sacrifice of his life, when understood, will move men to loathe their own self-centeredness.

> After all his pains he shall be bathed in light,
> after his disgrace he shall be fully vindicated;
> so shall he, my servant, vindicate many,
> himself bearing the penalty of their guilt.   [Isa. 53:11]

Though there is no articulate theory of resurrection here, the Servant is clearly vindicated: death is *not* the final chapter of his story. The humiliated victim is the exalted victor. The Servant—whom all Israel is called to be—turns out to have the greatest calling of all: through the Servant's sufferings God reconciles the whole world to his purpose.

> Therefore I will allot him a portion with the great,
> and he shall share the spoil with the mighty,
> because he exposed himself to face death
> and was reckoned among transgressors,
> because he bore the sin of many
> and interceded for their transgressions.   [Isa. 53:12]

Israel's true calling, then, is to serve. It is a calling that requires no special intellectual or physical gifts. It is a calling to which even the humblest can aspire. "Whenever the humble worshipper lives in such close fellowship with God that his suffering is borne willingly, thereby becoming God's power for restoring and renewing mankind, then Israel is fulfilling her task." [13]

Christians, of course, regard Jesus Christ as the historical fulfillment of the Servant whom Second Isaiah envisioned.

Chapter 17

THE MYTHS OF GENESIS

We have discussed how stories about Israel's early years passed by word of mouth and were eventually written down by four different groups between 950 and 550 B.C. (See Introduction and Chapters 10, 14, and 15.)

Two of these groups tried to relate Israel's history to their understanding of God's cosmic activity. J (about 950 B.C.) and P (about 550 B.C.) tried to show how Israel's history was part of a process which God began at the creation of the world.

Obviously neither J nor P had any knowledge about what really happened on earth much before 2000 B.C. Their own experience of God, however, led them to certain conclusions about the overall meaning of the process and about human nature. The first eleven chapters of Genesis contain their conclusions (finally interwoven in writing about 425 B.C.).

J and P use myths to express their insights. "Myth" in popular usage describes an untrue story. Scholars use "myth" in a technical sense, however, to describe a story (usually involving a superhuman figure), which may or may not be based on an historical event, whose main purpose is to express a great truth or insight into reality.

The Genesis myths are not intended to be taken literally. They are "historical" only in that they say something about the meaning of history. In one sense they are like Aesop's fables. No one believes that a real tortoise and hare had a race. While literally untrue, however, Aesop's fable does express a great truth of human (historical) experience: "Slow and steady wins the race." Andrew Greeley writes, "Myth is truth told not abstractly, but

concretely. The mythmaker may be a poet but he is not a superstitious fool; he has chosen to grapple with reality with a story
rather than with a schematic proposition." [14]

The Hebrews focused largely on the concrete events of their
own history. They were neither abstract nor imaginative think-
ers. One scholar speaks of their "prosaic cast of mind." We are
not surprised to find that they borrowed stories from other Near
Eastern people and then reworked them for their own purposes.
Often a story's original purpose is entirely lost as J and P twist
it to suit their own needs. The result is that each story takes
on a strikingly new meaning, in every case more morally and
theologically mature than the original.

When the J and P documents were finally combined in writing,
they were put at the opening of the Bible because the final
editors wished Israel's history to be seen in the context of God's
overall purpose for the world from beginning to end. Their location is especially appropriate since these myths address the basic
questions of human existence: what is the significance of the
universe and who is man?

THE CREATION

The Bible opens with a sublime proclamation: God, the self-
existent Being who existed before the material universe and is
distinct from it, is the cause of everything that is. From his own
created materials he decides to form an orderly universe, one
which is purposeful and regular and one which can respond
to his creative love.

**In the beginning of creation, when God made heaven and earth, the
earth was without form and void, with darkness over the face of the
abyss, and a mighty wind that swept over the surface of the waters.**
[Gen. 1:1–2]

Then he expresses himself; his act of creation begins.

**God said, 'Let there be light,' and there was light; and God saw that
the light was good, and he separated light from darkness. He called
the light day, and the darkness night. So evening came, and morning
came, the first day.** **[Gen. 1:3–5]**

A succession of creative acts follows in which God says "Let there be a firmament, dry land and vegetation, celestial bodies, birds and fish." Until finally

God said, 'Let the earth bring forth living creatures, according to their kind: cattle, reptiles, and wild animals, all according to their kind.' So it was; God made wild animals, cattle, and all reptiles, each according to its kind; and he saw that it was good. Then God said, 'Let us make man in our image and likeness to rule the fish in the sea, the birds of heaven, the cattle, all wild animals on earth, and all reptiles that crawl upon the earth.' So God created man in his own image; in the image of God he created him; male and female he created them.   [Gen. 1:24–27]

"Image" means "likeness." Man is enough like God that he (man) can know God and enter into a conscious relationship with him.

The God of the universe gives to his human companions a "little" universe to preside over:

God blessed them and said to them, 'Be fruitful and increase, fill the earth and subdue it, rule over the fish in the sea, the birds of heaven, and every living thing that moves upon the earth.' God also said, 'I give you all plants that bear seed everywhere on earth, and every tree bearing fruit which yields seed: they shall be yours for food. All green plants I give for food to the wild animals, to all the birds of heaven, and to all reptiles on earth, every living creature.' So it was; and God saw all that he had made, and it was very good.
[Gen. 1:28–30]

"It was very good" because God created it. There is in Hebrew thought no downgrading of the material or physical which one finds in later Greek thought. Though creation is not itself God (who as Creator remains above it), God's creation reflects him in the same way any created object reveals its creator.

Other ancient peoples (like many modern philosophers) viewed the material universe as self-existent, operating by chance, beyond the control of any unifying force. The Hebrews originated the concept of a "universe," of one great system, created by a Being who gives it coherence, purpose, and meaning. Man, in Hebrew thought, is not the helpless victim of the process, but is called into companionship with its Creator and given the opportunity to share in his creative act.

THE FALL

J offers us a much more earthy view of God's creation of the world and man than P's more cosmic account (which we have just read):

When the Lord God made earth and heaven, there was neither shrub nor plant growing wild upon the earth, because the Lord God had sent no rain on the earth; nor was there any man to till the ground. A flood used to rise out of the earth and water all the surface of the ground. Then the Lord God formed a man from the dust of the ground and breathed into his nostrils the breath of life. Thus the man became a living creature.   [Gen. 2:5–7]

J emphasizes that man ("Adam" in Hebrew) is "of the dust"— he is earth-bound, earthy—and not the equal of God.

Then the Lord God planted a garden in Eden away to the east, and there he put the man whom he had formed. The Lord God made trees spring from the ground, all trees pleasant to look at and good for food; and in the middle of the garden he set the tree of life and the tree of the knowledge of good and evil. The Lord God took the man and put him in the garden of Eden to till it and care for it.
                                       [Gen. 2:8–9, 15]

Out of love, God gives man a garden of Eden (which means "delight") to live in and use for his happiness.

Only one thing is forbidden:

He told the man, 'You may eat from every tree in the garden, but not from the tree of the knowledge of good and evil; for on the day that you eat from it, you will certainly die.'   [Gen. 2:16–17]

God warns Adam that there is one way in which he can misuse the delight he has been given. He must not eat the fruit of the "tree of the knowledge of good and evil." The Hebrew words really mean the "tree of all knowledge and experience" (i.e., the knowledge of all things, good and bad). God's one warning to man, then, is that man should not try to play God. Man may eat of the fruit of the tree of life, but not of the tree of all knowledge and experience. Man is not God; the only way man can spoil his happiness is to act as if he were God (who alone possesses all knowledge).

For Adam God then provides a woman ("Eve" in Hebrew) as a companion. J tells us that God formed her from Adam's rib, which is probably an effort on J's part to explain sexual attraction. (Since they were originally one, they seek to become one again.) J also tells us that "they were both naked but they had no feeling of shame toward one another." There is nothing wrong with sexual attraction.

God did not create men and women to be automatons. Human beings are the only creatures to whom God gave free will, the opportunity to follow his way or to reject it. One need not be a very subtle observer of human nature to perceive that, though we *know* what is right, we are frequently inclined to choose instead to *do* what is wrong. We call this inclination "temptation." In the myth which follows, J represents temptation by a serpent because, like a serpent, it is fascinating, stealthy, insinuating, and artful:

The serpent was more crafty than any wild creature that the Lord God had made. He said to the woman, 'Is it true that God has forbidden you to eat from any tree in the garden?' The woman answered the serpent, 'We may eat the fruit of any tree in the garden, except for the tree in the middle of the garden; God has forbidden us either to eat or to touch the fruit of that; if we do, we shall die.' [Gen. 3:1–3]

Eve's growing resentment is evident in her exaggeration: God has not said she may not "touch" the fruit.

The serpent said, 'Of course you will not die. God knows that as soon as you eat it, your eyes will be opened and you will be like gods knowing both good and evil.'   [Gen. 3:4–5]

Her resentment grows. In her imagination she now looks upon God's prohibition (made for her welfare) as selfish. She resents any restriction and reaches out to grasp what she thinks will make her equal to God.

When the woman saw that the fruit of the tree was good to eat, and that it was pleasing to the eye and tempting to contemplate, she took some and ate it. She also gave her husband some and he ate it. Then the eyes of both of them were opened and they discovered that they were naked; so they stitched fig-leaves together and made themselves loincloths.   [Gen. 3:6–7]

After eating the forbidden fruit (which legend, but not the Bible, identifies as an apple), "their eyes were opened," but not in the way they had anticipated. Far from possessing all knowledge, their loss of innocence makes them feel guilty and ashamed.

We should perhaps pause at this point to remind ourselves that this story is a myth. It does not attempt to describe the historical origin of evil in the world. It dramatizes, rather, that even though God created man and the universe, nevertheless evil is very real and very powerful in the universe and in man. The myth accounts for this seeming contradiction by asserting that evil is the result of man's desire to act as if he were God, to rebel at being merely a man. Evil then is the result of man's freely-made decision to misuse what God has given him.

Even after Adam and Eve's disobedience, God in his loving mercy seeks them out, to give them the opportunity to acknowledge their disobedience.

The man and his wife heard the sound of the Lord God walking in the garden at the time of the evening breeze and hid from the Lord God among the trees of the garden. But the Lord God called to the man and said to him, 'Where are you?' He replied, 'I heard the sound as you were walking in the garden, and I was afraid because I was naked, and I hid myself.' God answered, 'Who told you that you were naked? Have you eaten from the tree which I forbade you?' The man said, 'The woman you gave me for a companion, she gave me fruit from the tree and I ate it.' Then the Lord God said to the woman, 'What is this that you have done?' The woman said, 'The serpent tricked me, and I ate.'   [Gen. 3:8–13]

The game of passing the buck is as old as man. As the old joke goes, "Adam blamed Eve, Eve blamed the serpent, and the serpent didn't have a leg to stand on." But man cannot, of course, blame temptation for the evil he commits. Ultimately the responsibility rests upon himself, as do the consequences of an evil act.

Then the Lord God said to the serpent:

'Because you have done this you are accursed
more than all cattle and all wild creatures.

On your belly you shall crawl, and dust you shall eat
all the days of your life.
I will put enmity between you and the woman,
between your brood and hers.
They shall strike at your head,
and you shall strike at their heel.'

To the woman he said:

'I will increase your labour and your groaning,
and in labour you shall bear children.
You shall be eager for your husband,
and he shall be your master.'

And to the man he said:

'Because you have listened to your wife
and have eaten from the tree which I forbade you,
accursed shall be the ground on your account.
With labour you shall win your food from it
all the days of your life.
It will grow thorns and thistles for you,
none but wild plants for you to eat.
You shall gain your bread by the sweat of your brow
until you return to the ground;
for from it you were taken.
Dust you are, to dust you shall return.'

The man called his wife Eve because she was the mother of all who live. The Lord God made tunics of skins for Adam and his wife and clothed them. He said, 'The man has become like one of us, knowing good and evil; what if he now reaches out his hand and takes fruit from the tree of life also, eats it and lives for ever?' So the Lord God drove him out of the garden of Eden to till the ground from which he had been taken. He cast him out, and to the east of the garden of Eden he stationed the cherubim and a sword whirling and flashing to guard the way to the tree of life.   [Gen. 3:14–24]

Though the story is told in language even a child can understand, it is anything but childish. Its authors were profoundly aware of the hardness and sorrow of human existence: the broken relationships ("enmity between you"), the pain and suffering ("in labour you shall bear children"), the endless toil for sur-

vival ("you shall gain your bread by the sweat of your brow"),
and the ultimate reality of death ("dust you are, to dust you
shall return"). But most of all, the story is realistic about man's
tendency to evil: to grab for himself power that belongs to God,
to act as if he were equal to God, to misuse what God has given
him. The Hebrews more clearly than any other ancient people
saw man's immense capacity for good: the Psalmist writes,
"Thou [God] has made man little lower than the angels." And
yet of all ancient people the Hebrews had the greatest insight
into man's innate arrogance and potential for evil.

CAIN AND ABEL

Three Genesis myths deal with the implications of man's arrogance.

In the first, Eve gives birth to two sons, Cain and Abel. In
the background of the story we can sense the Israelites' experiences settling in Canaan in the time of Joshua.

> The man lay with his wife Eve, and she conceived and gave birth
> to Cain. She said, 'With the help of the Lord I have brought a man
> into being.' Afterwards she had another child, his brother Abel. Abel
> was a shepherd and Cain a tiller of the soil.   [Gen. 4:1–2]

Cain (whose name is related to "Canaan") is a settled farmer,
like the Canaanites. Abel is a cattleman, like the nomadic Hebrews when they settled in Canaan. The myth reflects the historical antipathy of Hebrew for Canaanite and also the age-old
conflict of cattleman and farmer over land.

> The day came when Cain brought some of the produce of the
> soil as a gift to the Lord; and Abel brought some of the first-born
> of his flock, the fat portions of them. The Lord received Abel and his
> gift with favour; but Cain and his gift he did not receive. [Gen. 4:3–4]

Abel recognized that he was only the steward of God's land and
offered God his best possessions: "the first-born of his flock, the
fat portions." For some reason, apparently because it was not
offered in the right spirit, God refused Cain's offering.

> Cain was very angry and his face fell. Then the Lord said to Cain,
> 'Why are you so angry and cast down?

If you do well, you are accepted;
if not, sin is a demon crouching at the door.
It shall be eager for you, and you will be mastered by it.'

Cain said to his brother Abel, 'Let us go into the open country.' While they were there, Cain attacked his brother Abel and murdered him. Then the Lord said to Cain, 'Where is your brother Abel?' Cain answered, 'I do not know. Am I my brother's keeper?'   [Gen. 4:5–9]

The Hebrews were not naive about the power of evil. Cain is "mastered" by it, as he was warned. Not only does he murder his brother but he lies to God and then insolently denies any responsibility for his brother.

His relationship with God and man destroyed, Cain is symbolically alienated even from the earth:

The Lord said, 'What have you done? Hark! your brother's blood that has been shed is crying out to me from the ground. Now you are accursed, and banished from the ground which has opened its mouth wide to receive your brother's blood, which you have shed. When you till the ground, it will no longer yield you its wealth. You shall be a vagrant and a wanderer on earth.' Then Cain went out from the Lord's presence and settled in the land of Nod to the east of Eden.   [Gen. 4:10–12, 16]

NOAH AND THE ARK

The story of Noah and the Ark was borrowed from the Babylonian Gilgamesh Epic, a flood story which was widely circulated by 3000 B.C. It is undoubtedly based on one of the many floods which from time to time devastated the Tigris and Euphrates River valleys. As usual, however, the Hebrew mind has transformed the Babylonian story. What was originally a tale about "the unmotivated peevishness of the Babylonian gods has become a parable of the sinfulness of man and the judgment of a righteous God." [15]

This is the story of Noah. Noah was a righteous man, the one blameless man of his time; he walked with God. He had three sons, Shem, Ham and Japheth. Now God saw that the whole world was corrupt and full of violence. In his sight the world had become corrupted, for all men had lived corrupt lives on earth. God said to

Noah, 'The loathsomeness of all mankind has become plain to me, for through them the earth is full of violence. I intend to destroy them, and the earth with them. Make yourself an ark with ribs of cypress; cover it with reeds and coat it inside and out with pitch. This is to be its plan: the length of the ark shall be three hundred cubits, its breadth fifty cubits, and its height thirty cubits. You shall make a roof for the ark, giving it a fall of one cubit when complete; and put a door in the side of the ark, and build three decks, upper, middle, and lower. I intend to bring the waters of the flood over the earth to destroy every human being under heaven that has the spirit of life; everything on earth shall perish. But with you I will make a covenant, and you shall go into the ark, you and your sons, your wife and your sons' wives with you. And you shall bring living creatures of every kind into the ark to keep them alive with you, two of each kind, a male and a female; two of every kind of bird, beast, and reptile, shall come to you to be kept alive. See that you take and store every kind of food that can be eaten; this shall be food for you and for them.' Exactly as God had commanded him, so Noah did.

The Lord said to Noah, 'Go into the ark, you and all your household; for I have seen that you alone are righteous before me in this generation. Take with you seven pairs, male and female, of all beasts that are ritually clean, and one pair, male and female, of all beasts that are not clean; also seven pairs, male and female, of every bird —to ensure that life continues on earth. In seven days' time I will send rain over the earth for forty days and forty nights, and I will wipe off the face of the earth every living thing that I have made.' Noah did all that the Lord had commanded him.

In the year when Noah was six hundred years old, on the seventeenth day of the second month, on that very day, all the springs of the great abyss broke through, the windows of the sky were opened, and rain fell on the earth for forty days and forty nights. On that very day Noah entered the ark with his sons, Shem, Ham and Japheth, his own wife, and his three sons' wives. Wild animals of every kind, cattle of every kind, reptiles of every kind that move upon the ground, and birds of every kind—all came to Noah in the ark, two by two of all creatures that had life in them. Those which came were one male and one female of all living things; they came in as God had commanded Noah, and the Lord closed the door on him. The flood continued upon the earth for forty days, and the waters swelled and lifted up the ark so that it rose high above the ground. They swelled and increased over the earth, and the ark floated on the surface of the waters. More and more the waters increased over the earth until they covered all the high mountains everywhere under heaven. The waters increased and the mountains were covered to a depth of fifteen cubits. Every living creature that moves on earth perished, birds, cattle, wild animals, all reptiles, and all mankind. Everything died that had breath of life in its nostrils, everything on dry land. God wiped out every living thing that existed on earth, man and beast, reptile and bird; they were all wiped out over the whole earth, and only Noah and his company in the ark survived.

When the waters had increased over the earth for a hundred and fifty days, God thought of Noah and all the wild animals and the cattle with him in the ark, and he made a wind pass over the earth, and the waters began to subside. The springs of the abyss were stopped up, and so were the windows of the sky; the downpour from the skies was checked. The water gradually receded from the earth, and by the end of a hundred and fifty days it had disappeared. On the seventeenth day of the seventh month the ark grounded on a mountain in Ararat. The water continued to recede until the tenth month, and on the first day of the tenth month the tops of the mountains could be seen.

After forty days Noah opened the trap-door that he had made in the ark, and released a raven to see whether the water had subsided, but the bird continued flying to and fro until the water on the earth had dried up. Noah waited for seven days, and then he released a dove from the ark to see whether the water on the earth had subsided further. But the dove found no place where she could settle, and so she came back to him in the ark, because there was water over the whole surface of the earth. Noah stretched out his hand, caught her and took her into the ark. He waited another seven days and again released the dove from the ark. She came back to him towards evening with a newly plucked olive leaf in her beak. Then Noah knew for certain that the water on the earth had subsided still further. He waited yet another seven days and released the dove, but she never came back.

By the twenty-seventh day of the second month the whole earth was dry. And God said to Noah, 'Come out of the ark, you and your wife, your sons and their wives. Bring out every living creature that is with you, live things of every kind, bird and beast and every reptile that moves on the ground, and let them swarm over the earth and be fruitful and increase there.' So Noah came out with his sons, his wife, and his sons' wives.

God spoke to Noah and to his sons with him: 'I now make my covenant with you and with your descendants after you, and with every living creature that is with you, all birds and cattle, all the wild animals with you on earth, all that have come out of the ark. I will make my covenant with you: never again shall all living creatures be destroyed by the waters of the flood, never again shall there be a flood to lay waste the earth.'

God said, 'This is the sign of the covenant which I establish between myself and you and every living creature with you, to endless generations:

> My bow I set in the cloud,
> sign of the covenant
> between myself and earth.
> When I cloud the sky over the earth,
> the bow shall be seen in the cloud.

Then will I remember the covenant which I have made between myself and you and living things of every kind. Never again shall the waters become a flood to destroy all living creatures.'

[Gen. 6:9–7:5; 7:11–8:12; 8:14–18; 9:8–15]

The point of this vivid story is that there is an ultimate justice in the universe and that it *is* worthwhile to be morally upright. God gives man freedom. If man abuses that freedom and chooses to do evil, he ultimately brings ruin upon himself; he drowns in his own evil. Modern man not only tends to be naive about human nature, but is inclined as well to sentimentalize God's love. Not only is this myth realistic about man's potential for evil; it is realistic about the consequences of evil for those who commit it.

The flood—as every natural disaster—is a telling reminder to the perceptive man that he does not control the universe. It reminds him that he does not possess all knowledge and power, but that these are God's alone.

The story ends, however, with God's pledge of love for man, of which the rainbow (like a handshake expressing friendship) is the outward and visible sign. The Hebrews concluded that God's mercy can overrule even the demands of absolute justice.

The rainbow is a sign that though men may again and again choose evil and bring destruction on themselves, God's love is always offered, always seeks men's response.

THE TOWER OF BABEL

The myth of the Tower of Babel is based on a story whose original purpose was to explain why men spoke different languages. Its setting is one of the advanced and affluent city-states in the Tigris-Euphrates area well before 2000 B.C. Inhabitants of these cities built towers (called *ziggurats*). Originally these towers served a noble (if naive) purpose: they were an effort to raise men up to God and to provide a place for God to speak to men. Later, however, their original purpose was lost and they became symbols of civic pride, and towns competed with one another for the highest tower. To the lower classes they became symbols of oppression because of the forced labor required to erect them.

The Hebrews used the story to express the human condition: men do not live as brothers, sons of a common father, but mankind is divided racially, linguistically, nationally. Members of the same human family cannot communicate with one another.

Once upon a time all the world spoke a single language and used the same words. As men journeyed in the east, they came upon a plain in the land of Shinar and settled there. They said to one another, 'Come, let us make bricks and bake them hard'; they used bricks for stone and bitumen for mortar. 'Come,' they said, 'let us build ourselves a city and a tower with its top in the heavens, and make a name for ourselves; or we shall be dispersed all over the earth.'

[Gen. 11:1–4]

Note the tower's purpose: "to make a name for ourselves." Ironically, despite the high tower, God must still "come down" to earth-bound man.

Then the Lord came down to see the city and tower which mortal men had built, and he said, 'Here they are, one people with a single language, and now they have started to do this; henceforward nothing they have a mind to do will be beyond their reach. Come, let us go down there and confuse their speech, so that they will not understand what they say to one another.' So the Lord dispersed them from there all over the earth, and they left off building the city. That is why it is called Babel, because the Lord there made a babble of the language of all the world; from that place the Lord scattered men all over the face of the earth.   [Gen. 11:5–9]

Men can become so immersed in building great cities, and in pursuing material possessions with regard for nothing but their own self-interest, that they value things more than people.

But "cultural advance" and material greatness fail to achieve their promise of bringing men full, rich lives. In a world governed by divine justice, man's arrogance and selfishness brings inevitable self-destruction. Each man acts as if he were the center of the universe, as if he were God. Communication breaks down because men no longer recognize or honor their common brotherhood.

Chapter 18

RUTH AND JONAH

Cyrus, the Persian king, was a wise and generous imperial administrator. His policy was to give subject peoples almost complete freedom as long as they paid him the required tribute and showed no signs of revolt. Therefore, shortly after he conquered Babylon, Cyrus freed the Jewish exiles and gave them permission to return to Judah (536 B.C.).

Most Jews had established themselves in reasonable comfort in Babylon and did not avail themselves of the opportunity to go back. Those faithful Jews who did return traded the comparative comfort of Babylonia for the bleak poverty of a ruined land in which they had to start a new life from scratch. The return was not nearly as glorious as Second Isaiah had envisioned. The Jews ("people of the land") who had not been exiled and who remained in Judah took a dim view of the returning exiles, as did the Samarians of the north. At the same time, the returning exiles, descendants of the upper classes, were contemptuous of those who had remained in Judah. Squabbles between the various factions and a series of bad harvests soon resulted in despair and apathy.

In 520 B.C. two prophets, Haggai and Zechariah, finally rallied the returned exiles to rebuild the Temple at Jerusalem. By 515 B.C. the new Temple was dedicated. Though it did not equal Solomon's (destroyed) Temple in splendor, it nevertheless captured the affections of the people and endured as the community center of Jewish heritage and worship until the Romans destroyed it in 70 A.D. Most of the biblical psalms were composed for worship in this Temple and all faithful Jews who could afford to do so made an annual pilgrimage to it. Throughout the countryside local synagogues (congregations) grew up, in which, for convenience, weekly worship, instruction, discussion of community problems, and administration of justice took place.

After Haggai and Zechariah died, apathy again set in. Temple worship degenerated and the Jewish community began to lose its identity as its members married outside the faith.

Then in 445 B.C. Nehemiah, a Jewish cupbearer to the Persian king, heard about conditions in Jerusalem and requested the king to grant him a leave of absence to go there. The king forthwith appointed him governor of Judah.

Nehemiah was a practical man of faith. Stirring the people into action he accomplished the rebuilding of Jerusalem's wall defenses in fifty-two days. The wall, in fact, symbolizes the whole thrust of his policy. Emphasizing the distinctiveness of Judaism, Nehemiah prohibited intermarriage and allowed only people of Jewish paternal descent to be community members.

His work was followed up about 397 B.C. by a remarkable Jewish priest, Ezra. Ezra arrived from Babylon with the "Law," the first five books of our present Bible. Between 450 and 425 B.C. the four strands of ancient traditions (J, E, D, and P) had finally been combined into a single written document. Ezra brought this document to Jerusalem, read it aloud to the people, and secured its acceptance as the definitive official record of the great events of Israel's past.

Israel no longer could hope for political greatness. It had no king, no army, no role in international events. Under Nehemiah and Ezra Israel became more and more a religious community whose life was centered on the carrying out of the Law's ethical and ritual implications. Every effort was made to preserve the distinctive identity of this special community. Ezra carried Nehemiah's exclusivist policies even farther. He viewed Israel's problems as originating with Solomon's foreign wives and the weakening of Israel's distinctive faith which occurred when Solomon allowed worship of foreign gods at Jerusalem. Therefore, Ezra decreed that Jewish men must divorce their foreign wives and disown their children by them. Excommunication and confiscation of property were the penalties of disobedience. Every effort was made to emphasize the separateness and distinctiveness of Judaism and to call attention to the difference between Jews and non-Jews.

While emphasis on the separateness of Jews was important in order to preserve the particular identity and calling of Israel, such emphasis inevitably had bad results as well as good. Extreme concern with the fine points of the Law often led to extravagant attention to legalistic trivialities. Emphasis on the distinctiveness of Jews often led to an attitude of religious superiority and exclusiveness. Gone was Second Isaiah's emphasis on Israel's mission to be a "light to the nations"; Judaism turned its sights inward. Israel's calling was only to be itself—a separate community.

This narrow attitude, however, did not go unchallenged.

RUTH

One of the purposes of the Book of Ruth is to protest the narrow exclusivism of the age of Ezra. Written by a master storyteller, this short story is based on an historic personage, Ruth of Moab (a foreign nation on the other side of the Dead Sea), the great-grandmother of King David. Little is known about the historical Ruth's life; the Book of Ruth is fictional, taking only its subject and setting from history.

Long ago, in the time of the judges, there was a famine in the land, and a man from Bethlehem in Judah went to live in the Moabite country with his wife and his two sons. The man's name was Elimelech, his wife's name was Naomi, and the names of his two sons Mahlon and Chilion. They were Ephrathites from Bethlehem in Judah. They arrived in the Moabite country and there they stayed. Elimelech Naomi's husband died, so that she was left with her two sons. These sons married Moabite women, one of whom was called Orpah and the other Ruth. They had lived there about ten years, when both Mahlon and Chilion died, so that the woman was bereaved of her two sons as well as of her husband. Thereupon she set out with her two daughters-in-law to return home, because she had heard while still in the Moabite country that the Lord had cared for his people and given them food. So with her two daughters-in-law she left the place where she had been living, and took the road home to Judah. Then Naomi said to her two daughters-in-law, 'Go back, both of you, to your mothers' homes. May the Lord keep faith with you, as you have kept faith with the dead and with me; and may he grant each of you security in the home of a new husband.' She kissed them and they wept aloud. [Ruth 1:1–9]

A widow was left without money or protection. Naomi decided to return to her own home and family in Israel where she might hope to find some way to subsist. Knowing that Ruth and Orpah were from Moab, however, she urged them to stay among their own people where they were known and where their prospects were better.

> Then they said to her, 'We will return with you to your own people.' But Naomi said, 'Go back, my daughters. Why should you go with me? Am I likely to bear any more sons to be husbands for you? Go back, my daughters, go. I am too old to marry again. But even if I could say that I had hope of a child, if I were to marry this night and if I were to bear sons, would you then wait until they grew up? Would you then refrain from marrying?' At this they wept again. Then Orpah kissed her mother-in-law and returned to her people, but Ruth clung to her.
>
> 'You see,' said Naomi, 'your sister-in-law has gone back to her people and her gods; go back with her.' 'Do not urge me to go back and desert you,' Ruth answered. 'Where you go, I will go, and where you stay, I will stay. Your people shall be my people, and your God my God. Where you die, I will die, and there I will be buried. I swear a solemn oath before the Lord your God: nothing but death shall divide us.'   [Ruth 1:10–13a, 14–17]

Ruth knew Naomi was old and unable to support herself. Out of their common grief, and because Naomi needs her, Ruth deliberately chooses the bleak prospect of widowhood among a people whose ways are unfamiliar. No reader could miss the point: this foreign woman is faithful to her husband's family far above and beyond what the Law of Israel prescribes. No Jew could have acted more generously.

> When Naomi saw that Ruth was determined to go with her, she said no more, and the two of them went on until they came to Bethlehem. The barley harvest was beginning when they arrived in Bethlehem.
>
> Now Naomi had a kinsman on her husband's side, a well-to-do man of the family of Elimelech; his name was Boaz. Ruth the Moabitess said to Naomi, 'May I go out to the cornfields and glean behind anyone who will grant me that favour?' 'Yes, go, my daughter,' she replied. So Ruth went gleaning in the fields behind the reapers.
>   [Ruth 1:18–19a; 1:22b–2:2]

Gleaning, i.e., following the harvesters and picking up anything left by them, was a privilege given to the poor. The young and able-bodied Ruth now goes out to glean food for Naomi and herself.

As it happened, she was in that strip of the fields which belonged to Boaz of Elimelech's family, and there was Boaz coming out from Bethlehem. He greeted the reapers, saying, 'The Lord be with you'; and they replied, 'The Lord bless you.' Then he asked his servant in charge of the reapers, 'Whose girl is this?' 'She is a Moabite girl,' the servant answered, 'who has just come back with Naomi from the Moabite country. She asked if she might glean and gather among the swathes behind the reapers. She came and has been on her feet with hardly a moment's rest from daybreak till now.' Then Boaz said to Ruth, 'Listen to me, my daughter: do not go and glean in any other field, and do not look any further, but keep close to my girls. Watch where the men reap, and follow the gleaners; I have given them orders not to molest you. If you are thirsty, go and drink from the jars the men have filled.' She fell prostrate before him and said, 'Why are you so kind as to take notice of me when I am only a foreigner?' Boaz answered, 'They have told me all that you have done for your mother-in-law since your husband's death, how you left your father and mother and the land of your birth, and came to a people you did not know before. The Lord reward your deed; may the Lord the God of Israel, under whose wings you have come to take refuge, give you all that you deserve.' When meal-time came round, Boaz said to her, 'Come here and have something to eat, and dip your bread into the sour wine.' So she sat beside the reapers, and he passed her some roasted grain. She ate all she wanted and still had some left over. When she got up to glean, Boaz gave the men orders. 'She,' he said, 'may glean even among the sheaves; do not scold her. Or you may even pull out some corn from the bundles and leave it for her to glean, without reproving her.'

One day Ruth's mother-in-law Naomi said to her, 'My daughter, I want to see you happily settled. Now there is our kinsman Boaz; you were with his girls. Tonight he is winnowing barley at his threshing-floor. Wash and anoint yourself, put on your cloak and go down to the threshing-floor, but do not make yourself known to the man until he has finished eating and drinking. But when he lies down, take note of the place where he lies. Then go in, turn back the covering at his feet and lie down. He will tell you what to do.'

[Ruth 2:3–12, 14–16; 3:1–4]

When a husband died childless, Jewish custom decreed that the husband's next-of-kin should father a child for the deceased man. Naomi therefore directs Ruth to fulfill this Jewish custom. Ruth complies, offering her body to the elderly Boaz in order to do what is fitting, according to Jewish custom, to honor her husband and his family.

'I will do whatever you tell me,' Ruth answered. So she went down to the threshing-floor and did exactly as her mother-in-law had told her. When Boaz had eaten and drunk, he felt at peace with the world and went to lie down at the far end of the heap of grain. She came in quietly, turned back the covering at his feet and lay down. About midnight something disturbed the man as he slept; he turned over and, lo and behold, there was a woman lying at his feet. 'Who are you?' he asked. 'I am your servant, Ruth,' she replied. 'Now spread your skirt over your servant, because you are my next-of-kin.' He said, 'The Lord has blessed you, my daughter. This last proof of your loyalty is greater than the first; you have not sought after any young man, rich or poor. Set your mind at rest, my daughter. I will do whatever you ask; for, as the whole neighbourhood knows, you are a capable woman. Are you sure that I am the next-of-kin? There is a kinsman even closer than I. Spend the night here and then in the morning, if he is willing to act as your next-of-kin, well and good; but if he is not willing, I will do so; I swear it by the Lord. Now lie down till morning.' So she lay at his feet till morning, but rose before one man could recognize another; and he said, 'It must not be known that a woman has been to the threshing-floor.' Then he said, 'Bring me the cloak you have on, and hold it out.' So she held it out, and he put in six measures of barley and lifted it on her back, and she went to the town. When she came to her mother-in-law, Naomi asked, 'How did things go with you, my daughter?' Ruth told her all that the man had done for her. 'He gave me these six measures of barley,' she said; 'he would not let me come home to my mother-in-law empty-handed.' Naomi answered, 'Wait, my daughter, until you see what will come of it. He will not rest until he has settled the matter today.'

Now Boaz had gone up to the city gate, and was sitting there; and, after a time, the next-of-kin of whom he had spoken passed by. 'Here,' he cried, calling him by name, 'come and sit down.' He came and sat down. Then Boaz stopped ten elders of the town, and asked them to sit there, and they did so. Then he said to the next-of-kin, 'You will remember the strip of field that belonged to our brother Elimelech. Naomi has returned from the Moabite country and is selling it. I promised to open the matter with you, to ask you to acquire it in the presence of those who sit here, in the presence of the elders of my people. If you are going to do your duty as next-of-kin, then do so, but if not, someone must do it. So tell me, and then I shall know; for I come after you as next-of-kin.' He answered, 'I will act as next-of-kin.' Then Boaz said, 'On the day when you acquire the field from Naomi, you also acquire Ruth the Moabitess, the dead man's wife, so as to perpetuate the name of the dead man with his patrimony.' Thereupon the next-of-kin said, 'I cannot act myself, for I should risk losing my own patrimony. You must therefore do my duty as next-of-kin. I cannot act.'

Now in those old days, when property was redeemed or exchanged, it was the custom for a man to pull off his sandal and give it to the other party. This was the form of attestation in Israel. So the next-of-kin said to Boaz, 'Acquire it for yourself,' and pulled off his sandal. Then Boaz declared to the elders and all the people, 'You are witnesses today that I have acquired from Naomi all that belonged to Elimelech and all that belonged to Mahlon and Chilion; and, further, that I have myself acquired Ruth the Moabitess, wife of Mahlon, to be my wife, to perpetuate the name of the deceased with his patrimony, so that his name may not be missing among his kindred and at the gate of his native place. You are witnesses this day.' Then the elders and all who were at the gate said, 'We are witnesses. May the Lord make this woman, who has come to your home, like Rachel and Leah, the two who built up the house of Israel.'

So Boaz took Ruth and made her his wife. When they came together, the Lord caused her to conceive and she bore Boaz a son. Then the women said to Naomi, 'Blessed be the Lord today, for he has not left you without a next-of-kin. May the dead man's name be kept alive in Israel. The child will give you new life and cherish you in your old age; for your daughter-in-law who loves you, who has proved better to you than seven sons, has borne him.' Naomi took the child and laid him in her lap and became his nurse. Her neighbours gave him a name: 'Naomi has a son,' they said; 'we will call him Obed.' He was the father of Jesse, the father of David.   [Ruth 3:5–4:11a; 4:13–17]

Boaz represents Israel acknowledging its call to be a light to the nations, an inclusive community. Though Ruth is both a foreigner and a woman, Boaz treats her with respect and provides for her protection in the fields (ironically against the *men* of *Israel*). Finally, without further regard for personal desires, he does his duty and fathers a child by her. Ruth herself shows devotion both to Israel's God and to her husband's family far in excess of what the Law required. The writer is subtly contrasting the foreigner's whole-hearted faith with the hair-splitting legalism of many of his fellow Jews whose preoccupation was discovering how to reduce the demands of the Law to a minimum. And finally, of course, we learn that this foreign woman is no less than the great-grandmother of David, Israel's greatest king. Thus —without polemic—does the author of this tale protest the exclusivist spirit of Judaism and set forth his people's true calling.

JONAH

Not long after Ruth was written, another book appeared with much the same message: Jonah. Though the book's hero was a real person (Jonah) who lived in a real historical setting (eighth-century B.C. Israel), the story is purest fiction, containing deliberate exaggeration and wild fantasy. The author makes Jonah typify the narrow nationalist exclusivism of Ezra and Nehemiah in the fifth century B.C., and then proceeds to lampoon him with humor and affectionate ridicule.

The word of the Lord came to Jonah son of Amittai: 'Go to the great city of Nineveh, go now and denounce it, for its wickedness stares me in the face.'   [Jon. 1:1–2]

Yahweh is Lord of *all* creation, of *all* nations. Jonah is summoned to go to the capital of Assyria to give the people opportunity to turn from their evil ways.

Jonah, disgusted at God's concern for these non-Jews and fearful lest they repent and be spared God's punishment, quickly takes a ship to the farthest possible point in the *opposite* direction. His narrow concept of God as exclusively Israel's God no doubt led him to think he could escape God's command if he left Israel.

But Jonah set out for Tarshish to escape from the Lord. He went down to Joppa, where he found a ship bound for Tarshish. He paid his fare and went on board, meaning to travel by it to Tarshish out of reach of the Lord. But the Lord let loose a hurricane, and the sea ran so high in the storm that the ship threatened to break up. The sailors were afraid, and each cried out to his god for help. Then they threw things overboard to lighten the ship. Jonah had gone down into a corner of the ship and was lying sound asleep when the captain came upon him. 'What, sound asleep?' he said. 'Get up, and call on your god; perhaps he will spare us a thought and we shall not perish.'

[Jon. 1:3–6]

"Jonah remained unworried, for he 'had gone down into the inner part of the ship,' where he lay down and fell asleep. He was apparently a happy man, comforted by the thought that he had outsmarted the Eternal; he was rapidly moving out of God's reach." [16]

At last the sailors said to each other, 'Come and let us cast lots to find out who is to blame for this bad luck.' So they cast lots, and the lot fell on Jonah. 'Now then,' they said to him, 'what is your business? Where do you come from? What is your country? Of what nation are you?' 'I am a Hebrew,' he answered, 'and I worship the Lord the God of heaven, who made both sea and land.' At this the sailors were even more afraid. 'What can you have done wrong?' they asked. They already knew that he was trying to escape from the Lord, for he had told them so. 'What shall we do with you,' they asked, 'to make the sea go down?' For the storm grew worse and worse. 'Take me and throw me overboard,' he said, 'and the sea will go down. I know it is my fault that this great storm has struck you.' The crew rowed hard to put back to land but in vain, for the sea ran higher and higher. At last they called on the Lord and said, 'O Lord, do not let us perish at the price of this man's life; do not charge us with the death of an innocent man. All this, O Lord, is thy set purpose.' Then they took Jonah and threw him overboard, and the sea stopped raging. So the crew were filled with the fear of the Lord and offered sacrifice and made vows to him.   [Jon. 1:7–16]

With great subtlety the author impresses us first with the kindness of these foreign sailors to one who is a foreigner to them, and then with their striking piety toward Israel's God.

But the Lord ordained that a great fish should swallow Jonah, and for three days and three nights he remained in its belly. Jonah prayed to the Lord his God from the belly of the fish. Then the Lord spoke to the fish and it spewed Jonah out on to the dry land.

[Jon. 1:17–2:1; 2:10]

After Israel had been swallowed up by Babylon during the exile, her prophets (especially Jeremiah and Second Isaiah) called her once again to be a light to the nations. Jonah is summoned a second time to go to Nineveh. The size of the city is wildly exaggerated to show the magnitude of Jonah's task.

The word of the Lord came to Jonah a second time: 'Go to the great city of Nineveh, go now and denounce it in the words I give you.' Jonah obeyed at once and went to Nineveh. He began by going a day's journey into the city, a vast city, three days' journey across, and then proclaimed: 'In forty days Nineveh shall be overthrown!' The people of Nineveh believed God's word. They ordered a public fast and put on sackcloth, high and low alike. When the news reached the king of Nineveh he rose from his throne, stripped off his robes of state, put on sackcloth and sat in ashes. Then he had a proclamation made in Nineveh: 'This is a decree of the king and his nobles. No man or beast, herd or flock, is to taste food, to graze or to drink water. They are to clothe themselves in sackcloth and call on God with all their might. Let every man abandon his wicked ways and his habitual violence. It may be that God will repent and turn away from his anger: and so we shall not perish.' God saw what they did, and how they abandoned their wicked ways, and he repented and did not bring upon them the disaster he had threatened.   [Jon. 3:1–10]

Only one man has to proclaim God's word and the vast city with one accord turns wholeheartedly to God. What a contrast to Israel's stubborn rebelliousness and lack of response to God, so well illustrated by Jonah's initial refusal to go to Nineveh.

Jonah responded angrily to God's forgiveness. He didn't want the Ninevites to be spared; he had hoped they wouldn't listen to his warning and that God would destroy them. He perfectly represents those respectable religious people who smugly enjoy watching others get caught in evil-doing. God's forgiveness of Nineveh is also personally galling to Jonah since Jonah had announced that Nineveh would be destroyed.

Jonah was greatly displeased and angry, and he prayed to the Lord: 'This, O Lord, is what I feared when I was in my own country, and to forestall it I tried to escape to Tarshish; I knew that thou art "a god gracious and compassionate, long-suffering and ever constant, and always willing to repent of the disaster". And now, Lord, take my life: I should be better dead than alive.' 'Are you so angry?' said the Lord. Jonah went out and sat down on the east of the city. There he made himself a shelter and sat in its shade, waiting to see what would happen in the city. Then the Lord God ordained that a climbing gourd should grow up over his head to throw its shade over him and relieve his distress, and Jonah was grateful for the gourd. But at dawn the next day God ordained that a worm should attack the gourd, and it withered; and at sunrise God ordained that a scorching wind should blow up from the east. The sun beat down on Jonah's head till he grew faint. Then he prayed for death and said, 'I should be better dead than alive.'   [Jon. 4:1–8]

Destruction of the gourd caused Jonah intense suffering. Not enough, however, to make him rejoice that Nineveh had not had to suffer destruction.

At this God said to Jonah, 'Are you so angry over the gourd?' 'Yes,' he answered, 'mortally angry.' The Lord said, 'You are sorry for the gourd, though you did not have the trouble of growing it, a plant which came up in a night and withered in a night. And should not I be sorry for the great city of Nineveh, with its hundred and twenty thousand who cannot tell their right hand from their left, and cattle without number?'   [Jon. 4:9–11]

Jonah's sympathy for himself and the gourd was not matched by sympathy for the people of a city who had not yet heard God's word and therefore did not know right from wrong.

God is the God of all the universe, of all people and all nations. Even Israel's most hated enemies are his children. And Israel's mission is to witness to God's presence on earth everywhere in every life. Israel's refusal of responsibility, its unwillingness to witness as a light to the nations, is rebuked in the story of Jonah. God's people are not called to be a smug exclusivist sect, but to be missionaries proclaiming to the ends of the earth the good news of Yahweh who is "gracious and compassionate, long-suffering and ever constant, and always willing to repent of the disaster."

Chapter 19

JOB

We have so far neglected the role of the "wise men" in Israelite society. By Jeremiah's time the "wise men" were recognized—along with priests and prophets—as one of the three leadership classes in the Jewish nation. In the reigns of David and Solomon, when a bureaucracy became necessary, a body of educated, cosmopolitan scribes and counselors grew up. These suave and worldly men had much in common with the "wise men" who controlled the bureaucracies of other nations, and their outlook was distinctively international.

After the monarchy ended the wise men were no longer concentrated at court but were dispersed throughout the country. Some sat at the gates of towns publicly and privately making pronouncements and giving counsel. By Ezra's time there were "wisdom schools" where groups of wise men gathered to instruct students in large numbers. The widespread availability of formal educational instruction was one of the great achievements of post-exilic Judaism.

The wise men showed little interest in the distinctive Jewish experience of God. They made no reference to Yahweh's special choice of Israel or to any of the great events (such as the Exodus) in which God revealed himself to his people in their history. They also had no interest in Jewish worship and cult. They found God, rather, in the natural order of things. They felt that men of any race or nation might understand the meaning of the universe by study.

The wise men were interested principally in man. Their goal was human happiness and they sought to offer practical, common-sense guidelines by which men could be happy. Since God was in charge of the universe, the beginning of wisdom was an awareness of the order and meaning which God gave to things. Focusing as they did on the universal study of nature, man, and God, and disinterested as they were in the particular history and worship of Israel, the wise men were an antidote to the exclusivism and legalism of Ezra and his followers.

It was, in fact, in the post-exilic period that the *literature* of the wise men emerged and flourished. Our Bible contains three products of the wisdom movement: Proverbs, Job, and Ecclesiastes.

THE DOCTRINE OF REWARD AND PUNISHMENT

In common with most of the prophets (especially Ezekiel) and with the collectors of the D and P traditions, Israel's wise men held that God governed the world by an easily understood principle: he rewarded goodness and punished evil.

The Book of Proverbs assumes that men can understand the meaning of life and discover the moral and natural principles by which God governs the universe. From such understanding and discovery happiness and prosperity result:

My son, do not forget my teaching,
but guard my commands in your heart;
for long life and years in plenty
will they bring you, and prosperity as well.
Let your good faith and loyalty never fail,
but bind them about your neck.
Thus will you win favour and success
in the sight of God and man.

Honour the Lord with your wealth
as the first charge on all your earnings;
then your granaries will be filled with corn
and your vats bursting with new wine.

Happy he who has found wisdom,
and the man who has acquired understanding;
for wisdom is more profitable than silver,
and the gain she brings is better than gold.
She is more precious than red coral,
and all your jewels are no match for her.
Long life is in her right hand,
in her left hand are riches and honour.
Her ways are pleasant ways
and all her paths lead to prosperity.

> She is a staff of life to all who grasp her,
> and those who hold her fast are safe.
>   Do not emulate a lawless man,
> do not choose to follow his footsteps;
> for one who is not straight is detestable to the Lord,
> but upright men are in God's confidence.
> The Lord's curse rests on the house of the evildoer,
> while he blesses the home of the righteous.
> Though God himself meets the arrogant with arrogance,
> yet he bestows his favour on the meek.
> Wise men are adorned with honour,
> but the coat on a fool's back is contempt.
>
> [Prov. 3:1–4, 9–10, 13–18, 31–35]

Underlying these statements is the conviction that happiness and prosperity come from goodness, while unhappiness and poverty come from evil-doing. It is therefore in man's self-interest to be good.

The books of Ecclesiastes and Job, however, take issue with the premise that good is rewarded and evil punished. The authors of these books reflect on their own bitter experience that life simply is not just: the good are not necessarily happy and successful, nor are the evil unhappy and unsuccessful. Both authors deny that God's ways are simple and understandable; both deny that there are principles which men can discover which will automatically make them happy.

Ecclesiastes says bluntly that God governs the universe in a way which men cannot comprehend:

I applied my mind to acquire wisdom and to observe the business which goes on upon earth, when man never closes an eye in sleep day or night; and always I perceived that God has so ordered it that man should not be able to discover what is happening here under the sun. However hard a man may try, he will not find out; the wise man may think that he knows, but he will be unable to find the truth of it. [Ec. 8:16–17]

Since God's ways are inscrutable, all man's efforts to understand the meaning of life are in vain.

Emptiness, emptiness, says the Speaker, emptiness, all is empty. What does man gain from all his labour and his toil here under the sun?

I set myself to look at wisdom and at madness and folly. Then I perceived that wisdom is more profitable than folly, as light is more profitable than darkness: the wise man has eyes in his head, but the fool walks in the dark. Yet I saw also that one and the same fate overtakes them both. So I said to myself, 'I too shall suffer the fate of the fool. To what purpose have I been wise? What is the profit of it? Even this', I said to myself, 'is emptiness. The wise man is remembered no longer than the fool, for, as the passing days multiply, all will be forgotten. Alas, wise man and fool die the same death!' So I came to hate life, since everything that was done here under the sun was a trouble to me; for all is emptiness and chasing the wind.
[Ec. 1:2–3; 2:12–17]

The author of Job begins with the same assumption as Ecclesiastes: God does not govern the universe by an easily understandable principle of reward of good and punishment of evil. In trying to work out whether human life can have meaning, however, the author of Job reaches a conclusion somewhat different from Ecclesiastes.

The author of Job takes the well-known folk story of Job and uses it as the framework within which to set forth his own philosophy. The author recounts this folk tale in the Prologue and Epilogue of his book: Job is a man of righteousness whose faith is tested by God and whose faithfulness in the test is rewarded by God. The author's real message is contained in his own lengthy poem which he places between the Prologue and Epilogue. Here the author deals with the questions of whether or not God is just and whether or not life has meaning.

JOB'S SUFFERING

Job is introduced as the perfect model of a wise man: good and therefore happy and prosperous.

There lived in the land of Uz a man of blameless and upright life named Job, who feared God and set his face against wrongdoing. He had seven sons and three daughters; and he owned seven thousand sheep and three thousand camels, five hundred yoke of oxen and five hundred asses, with a large number of slaves. Thus Job was the greatest man in all the East.

The day came when the members of the court of heaven took their places in the presence of the Lord, and Satan was there among them. The Lord asked him where he had been. 'Ranging over the earth', he said, 'from end to end.' Then the Lord asked Satan, 'Have you considered my servant Job? You will find no one like him on earth, a man of blameless and upright life, who fears God and sets his face against wrongdoing.' Satan answered the Lord, 'Has not Job good reason to be God-fearing? Have you not hedged him round on every side with your protection, him and his family and all his possessions? Whatever he does you have blessed, and his herds have increased beyond measure. But stretch out your hand and touch all that he has, and then he will curse you to your face.'   [Job 1:1–3, 6–11]

With utmost subtlety, the author (through Satan) mocks the neat orthodox doctrine of rewards and punishments, in which righteousness is motivated by self-interest.

Then the Lord said to Satan, 'So be it. All that he has is in your hands; only Job himself you must not touch.' And Satan left the Lord's presence.   [Job 1:12]

"The patience of Job" is still a widely used phrase. Oddly "patience" is the last word one could use to describe the Biblical Job. His happiness and prosperity removed for no apparent reason, Job suffers with considerable impatience the anxiety which results from the realization that life is unjust and therefore meaningless.

After this Job broke silence and cursed the day of his birth:

Perish the day when I was born
and the night which said, 'A man is conceived'!
May that day turn to darkness; may God above not look for it,
nor light of dawn shine on it.
Why was I not still-born,
why did I not die when I came out of the womb?
Why was I ever laid on my mother's knees
or put to suck at her breasts?
Why was I not hidden like an untimely birth,

like an infant that has not lived to see the light?
For then I should be lying in the quiet grave,
asleep in death, at rest.
   Why should the sufferer be born to see the light?
Why is life given to men who find it so bitter?
They wait for death but it does not come,
they seek it more eagerly than hidden treasure.
They are glad when they reach the tomb,
and when they come to the grave they exult.
Why should a man be born to wander blindly,
hedged in by God on every side?
My sighing is all my food,
and groans pour from me in a torrent.
Every terror that haunted me has caught up with me,
and all that I feared has come upon me.
There is no peace of mind nor quiet for me;
I chafe in torment and have no rest.   [Job 3:1–4, 11–13, 20–26]

Job never doubts that God is in control of the universe. But God's purpose is so hidden that life is deprived of meaning. God afflicts Job with sufferings which far outweigh any evil he has done:

Then Job answered:

O that the grounds for my resentment might be weighed,
and my misfortunes set with them on the scales!
For they would outweigh the sands of the sea:
what wonder if my words are wild?
The arrows of the Almighty find their mark in me,
and their poison soaks into my spirit;
God's onslaughts wear me away.   [Job 6:1–4]

JOB'S FRIENDS "COMFORT" HIM

Job's friends enter the picture to comfort him. Ironically they increase his misery. They perfectly represent the orthodox doctrine of reward and punishment.

With utmost courtesy, his friend Eliphaz insinuates that Job's suffering must be the result of some evil he has committed.

If one ventures to speak with you, will you lose patience?
For who could hold his tongue any longer?

Think how once you encouraged those who faltered,
how you braced feeble arms,
how a word from you upheld the stumblers
and put strength into weak knees.
But now that adversity comes upon you, you lose patience;
it touches you, and you are unmanned.
Is your religion no comfort to you?
Does your blameless life give you no hope?
For consider, what innocent man has ever perished?
Where have you seen the upright destroyed?
This I know, that those who plough mischief and sow trouble
reap as they have sown;
they perish at the blast of God
and are shrivelled by the breath of his nostrils.

    For my part, I would make my petition to God
and lay my cause before him,
who does great and unsearchable things,
marvels without number.
He gives rain to the earth
and sends water on the fields;
he raises the lowly to the heights,
the mourners are uplifted by victory;
he frustrates the plots of the crafty,
and they win no success,
he traps the cunning in their craftiness,
and the schemers' plans are thrown into confusion.
In the daylight they run into darkness,
and grope at midday as though it were night.
He saves the destitute from their greed,
and the needy from the grip of the strong;
so the poor hope again,
and the unjust are sickened.
    Happy the man whom God rebukes!
therefore do not reject the discipline of the Almighty.
We have inquired into all this, and so it is;
this we have heard, and you may know it for the truth.

[Job 4:2–9; 5:8–17, 27]

Bildad is more direct in confronting Job. He appeals to human
experience as proof that the universe is justly governed by a God

who rewards good and punishes evil, and he urges Job to confess the evil which is causing his sufferings.

> How long will you say such things,
> the long-winded ramblings of an old man?
> Does God pervert judgement?
> Does the Almighty pervert justice?
> Your sons sinned against him,
> so he left them to be victims of their own iniquity.
> If only you will seek God betimes
> and plead for the favour of the Almighty,
> if you are innocent and upright,
> then indeed will he watch over you
> and see your just intent fulfilled.
> Then, though your beginnings were humble,
> your end will be great.
> Inquire now of older generations
> and consider the experience of their fathers;
> for we ourselves are of yesterday and are transient;
> our days on earth are a shadow.
> Will not they speak to you and teach you
> and pour out the wisdom of their hearts?
> Be sure, God will not spurn the blameless man,
> nor will he grasp the hand of the wrongdoer.   [Job 8:1b–10, 20]

Zophar also tries to make Job's sufferings fit within the orthodox explanation of suffering. Having identified the cause of Job's problem, he offers him a veritable banquet of moral platitudes.

> Should this spate of words not be answered?
> Must a man of ready tongue be always right?
> Is your endless talk to reduce men to silence?
> Are you to talk nonsense and no one rebuke you?
> You claim that your opinions are sound;
> you say to God, 'I am spotless in thy sight.'
> But if only he would speak
> and open his lips to talk with you,
> and expound to you the secrets of wisdom,
> for wonderful are its effects!
> Know then that God exacts from you less than your sin deserves.
> He surely knows which men are false,
> and when he sees iniquity, does he not take note of it?

> If only you had directed your heart rightly
> and spread out your hands to pray to him!
> If you have wrongdoing in hand, thrust it away;
> let no iniquity make its home with you.
> Then you could hold up your head without fault,
> a man of iron, knowing no fear.
> Then you will forget your trouble;
> you will remember it only as flood-waters that have passed.
>   [Job 11:2–6, 11, 13–16]

There is a tendency, among those who glibly offer interpretations of suffering, to minimize the cost of human suffering. The superficial Zophar remarks that once Job confesses his evil, then "you will forget your trouble." As if Job could forget the death of all his children!

Throughout, however, Job insists that he has done no evil which merits such suffering. The more firmly he insists on his innocence, the more adamant and angry his friends become. Job's stand threatens them. Smugly confident that they understand exactly how God runs the universe, they lash out at Job when he rejects their analyses of what is wrong.

Then Eliphaz the Temanite answered:

> Can man be any benefit to God?
> Can even a wise man benefit him?
> Is it an asset to the Almighty if you are righteous?
> Does he gain if your conduct is perfect?
> Do not think that he reproves you because you are pious,
> that on this count he brings you to trial.
> No: it is because you are a very wicked man,
> and your depravity passes all bounds.   [Job 22:1–5]

JOB'S DEFIANCE

Accused of evil by his friends, afflicted with suffering by God, Job stands alone to proclaim his innocence.

He complains that there is no justice. God is so powerful and so aloof that he (Job) cannot get a fair hearing.

Then Job answered:

> Indeed this I know for the truth,
> that no man can win his case against God.

If a man chooses to argue with him,
God will not answer one question in a thousand.
He is wise, he is powerful;
what man has stubbornly resisted him and survived?
It is God who moves mountains, giving them no rest,
turning them over in his wrath;
who makes the earth start from its place
so that its pillars are convulsed;
who commands the sun's orb not to rise
and shuts up the stars under his seal;
who by himself spread out the heavens
and trod on the sea-monster's back;
who made Aldebaran and Orion,
the Pleiades and the circle of the southern stars;
who does great and unsearchable things,
marvels without number.
   He passes by me, and I do not see him;
he moves on his way undiscerned by me;
if he hurries on, who can bring him back?
Who will ask him what he does?
How much less can I answer him
or find words to dispute with him?
Though I am right, I get no answer,
though I plead with my accuser for mercy.
If I summoned him to court and he responded,
I do not believe that he would listen to my plea—
for he bears hard upon me for a trifle
and rains blows on me without cause;
he leaves me no respite to recover my breath
but fills me with bitter thoughts.
If the appeal is to force, see how strong he is;
if to justice, who can compel him to give me a hearing?
Though I am right, he condemns me out of my own mouth;
though I am blameless, he twists my words.
   'He destroys blameless and wicked alike.'
When a sudden flood brings death,
he mocks the plight of the innocent.
The land is given over to the power of the wicked,
and the eyes of its judges are blindfold.

                     [Job 9:1–12, 14–20, 22b–24]

Job pictures God as an unprincipled tyrant whose actions are unjust, mocking, and cruel.

> If I am to be accounted guilty,
> Why do I labour in vain?
> Though I wash myself with soap
> or cleanse my hands with lye,
> thou wilt thrust me into the mud
> and my clothes will make me loathsome.
> He is not a man as I am, that I can answer him
> or that we can confront one another in court.
> If only there were one to arbitrate between us
> and impose his authority on us both,
> so that God might take his rod from my back,
> and terror of him might not come on me suddenly.
> I would then speak without fear of him;
> for I know I am not what I am thought to be.   [Job 9:29–35]

Passionately Job makes his own defense, scandalizing his friends by his heretical statements about God's injustice, by his daring to argue with and accuse God.

> All this I have seen with my own eyes,
> with my own ears I have heard it, and understood it.
> What you know, I also know;
> in nothing do I fall short of you.
> But for my part I would speak with the Almighty
> and am ready to argue with God,
> while you like fools are smearing truth with your falsehoods,
> stitching a patchwork of lies, one and all.
> Ah, if you would only be silent
> and let silence be your wisdom!
> Now listen to my arguments
> and attend while I put my case.
> Be silent, leave me to speak my mind,
> and let what may come upon me!
> I will put my neck in the noose
> and take my life in my hands.
> If he would slay me, I should not hesitate;
> I should still argue my cause to his face.   [Job 13:1–6, 13–15]

Job realizes the weakness of his position. God is eternal and immortal, all-powerful. Job, like other men, is impermanent, utterly the victim of the circumstances in which God places him.

Man born of woman is short-lived and full of disquiet.
He blossoms like a flower and then he withers;
he slips away like a shadow and does not stay;
he is like a wine-skin that perishes
or a garment that moths have eaten.
Dost thou fix thine eyes on such a creature,
and wilt thou bring him into court to confront thee?
The days of his life are determined,
and the number of his months is known to thee;
thou hast laid down a limit, which he cannot pass.
Look away from him therefore and leave him alone
counting the hours day by day like a hired labourer.

[Job 14:1–3, 5–6]

Man's very impermanence makes life meaningless. In itself it is an injustice. God is perceived as cruelly playing with man.

Job likens God to a savage hunter:

I was at ease, but he set upon me and mauled me,
seized me by the neck and worried me.
He set me up as his target;
his arrows rained upon me from every side;
pitiless, he cut deep into my vitals,
he spilt my gall on the ground.   [Job 16:12–13]

God is morally indifferent. He cares nothing for good men, and the wicked prosper.

Why do the wicked enjoy long life,
hale in old age, and great and powerful?
They live to see their children settled,
their kinsfolk and descendants flourishing;
their families are secure and safe;
the rod of God's justice does not reach them.
Their bull mounts and fails not of its purpose;
their cow calves and does not miscarry.
Their children like lambs run out to play,
and their little ones skip and dance;

> they rejoice with tambourine and harp
> and make merry to the sound of the flute.
> Their lives close in prosperity,
> and they go down to Sheol in peace.
> To God they say, 'Leave us alone;
> we do not want to know your ways.
> What is the Almighty that we should worship him,
> or what should we gain by seeking his favour?'   [Job 21:7–15]

At times Job sees God not as unjust but simply as absent. If only God were accessible then there would be justice.

> My thoughts today are resentful,
> for God's hand is heavy on me in my trouble.
> If only I knew how to find him,
> how to enter his court,
> I would state my case before him
> and set out my arguments in full;
> then I should learn what answer he would give
> and find out what he had to say.
> Would he exert his great power to browbeat me?
> No; God himself would never bring a charge against me.
> There the upright are vindicated before him,
> and I shall win from my judge an absolute discharge.
>
> [Job 23:2–7]

But God is *not* available to man, not present in life.

> If I go forward, he is not there;
> if backward, I cannot find him;
> when I turn left, I do not descry him;
> I face right, but I see him not.   [Job 23:8–9]

Yet he dares hope that even though he cannot find God, nevertheless God will somehow vindicate him if he continues to live righteously.

> But he knows me in action or at rest;
> When he tests me, I prove to be gold.
> My feet have kept to the path he has set me,
> I have followed his way and not turned from it.
> I do not ignore the commands that come from his lips,
> I have stored in my heart what he says.

> But in my heart I know that my vindicator lives
> and that he will rise last to speak in court;
> and I shall discern my witness standing at my side
> and see my defending counsel, even God himself,
> whom I shall see with my own eyes,
> I myself and no other.   [Job 23:10–12; 19:25–27]

But Job's defiance does not long retain this softened and hopeful tone. He ends by demanding acquittal. His life—his model citizenship—is offered as evidence.

> Whoever heard of me spoke in my favour,
> and those who saw me bore witness to my merit,
> how I saved the poor man when he called for help
> and the orphan who had no protector.
> The man threatened with ruin blessed me,
> and I made the widow's heart sing for joy.
> I put on righteousness as a garment and it clothed me;
> justice, like a cloak or a turban, wrapped me round.
> I was eyes to the blind
> and feet to the lame;
> I was a father to the needy,
> and I took up the stranger's cause.
> I broke the fangs of the miscreant
> and rescued the prey from his teeth.
>   I swear by God, who has denied me justice,
> and by the Almighty, who has filled me with bitterness:
> so long as there is any life left in me
> and God's breath is in my nostrils,
> no untrue word shall pass my lips
> and my tongue shall utter no falsehood.
> God forbid that I should allow you to be right;
> till death, I will not abandon my claim to innocence.
> I will maintain the rightness of my cause, I will never give up;
> so long as I live, I will not change.   [Job 29:11–17; 27:2–6]

Finally he sums up his case in a defiant challenge to God:

> Let me but call a witness in my defence!
> Let the Almighty state his case against me!
> If my accuser had written out his indictment,
> I would not keep silence and remain indoors.

No! I would flaunt it on my shoulder
and wear it like a crown on my head;
I would plead the whole record of my life
and present that in court as my defence.   [Job 31:35–37]

GOD'S RESPONSE

God's response is not an "answer." He doesn't explain Job's sufferings and he doesn't give the vindication Job requests.

God simply asserts who he is, and by a series of questions forces Job to consider his own utter humanness:

Who is this whose ignorant words
cloud my design in darkness?
Brace yourself and stand up like a man;
I will ask questions, and you shall answer.
Where were you when I laid the earth's foundations?
Tell me, if you know and understand.
Who settled its dimensions? Surely you should know.
Who stretched his measuring-line over it?
On what do its supporting pillars rest?
Who set its corner-stone in place,
when the morning stars sang together
and all the sons of God shouted aloud?
Who watched over the birth of the sea,
when it burst in flood from the womb?—
when I wrapped it in a blanket of cloud
and cradled it in fog,
when I established its bounds,
fixing its doors and bars in place,
and said, 'Thus far shall you come and no farther,
and here your surging waves shall halt.'
In all your life have you ever called up the dawn
or shown the morning its place?
Have the gates of death been revealed to you?
Have you ever seen the door-keepers of the place of darkness?
Have you comprehended the vast expanse of the world?
Come, tell me all this, if you know.
Which is the way to the home of light
and where does darkness dwell?
And can you then take each to its appointed bound

and escort it on its homeward path?
Doubtless you know all this; for you were born already,
so long is the span of your life!
Have you visited the storehouse of the snow
or seen the arsenal where hail is stored,
which I have kept ready for the day of calamity,
for war and for the hour of battle?
By what paths is the heat spread abroad
or the east wind carried far and wide over the earth?
Has the rain a father?
Who sired the drops of dew?
Whose womb gave birth to the ice,
and who was the mother of the frost from heaven,
which lays a stony cover over the waters
and freezes the expanse of ocean?
Can you bind the cluster of the Pleiades
or loose Orion's belt?
Can you bring out the signs of the zodiac in their season
or guide Aldebaran and its train?
Did you proclaim the rules that govern the heavens,
or determine the laws of nature on earth?
Can you command the dense clouds
to cover you with their weight of waters?
If you bid lightning speed on its way,
will it say to you, 'I am ready'?   [Job 38:2 12, 17–24, 20–35]

Who is Job, then, or any man, to judge how God governs the universe? God reminds Job of the vastness of his creation, of which man is a tiny part.

Do you know when the mountain-goats are born
or attend the wild doe when she is in labour?
Do you count the months that they carry their young
or know the time of their delivery,
when they crouch down to open their wombs
and bring their offspring to the birth,
when the fawns grow and thrive in the open forest,
and go forth and do not return?
Does your skill teach the hawk to use its pinions
and spread its wings towards the south?
Do you instruct the vulture to fly high

> and build its nest aloft?
> It dwells among the rocks and there it lodges;
> its station is a crevice in the rock;
> from there it searches for food,
> keenly scanning the distance.   [Job 39:1–4, 26–29a]

Most of God's creatures are utterly different from man. How then can the Creator's activities be judged (as Job judges) merely in terms of *man's* needs?

How can puny, finite man dare to assess and measure the ways of the God of the universe? But that is exactly what Job has done. He has talked as if he knew how God should run the world. God concludes with his own challenge: let Job be God.

> Have you an arm like God's arm,
> can you thunder with a voice like his?
> Deck yourself out, if you can, in pride and dignity,
> array yourself in pomp and splendour;
> unleash the fury of your wrath,
> look upon the proud man and humble him;
> look upon every proud man and bring him low,
> throw down the wicked where they stand;
> hide them in the dust together,
> and shroud them in an unknown grave.
> Then I in my turn will acknowledge
> that your own right hand can save you.   [Job 40:9–14]

God says nothing about the "evil" of which Job's friends accuse him. God points out not Job's sin but Job's finite, creaturely ignorance. Man is not God.

JOB'S REPENTANCE

How often Job had complained that he should be allowed to defend himself before God. But in the presence of the Lord of the universe of what use are man's twitterings?

And Job answered the Lord:

> What reply can I give thee, I who carry no weight?
> I put my finger to my lips.   [Job 40:3–4a]

It remains only for Job to confess his humanness.

Then Job answered the Lord:

> I know that thou canst do all things
> and that no purpose is beyond thee.
> But I have spoken of great things which I have not understood,
> things too wonderful for me to know.　　　　　[Job 42:1–3]

Man cannot understand the ways of God. God's ways remain to man unpredictable. His actions do not fit into the neat categories in which Job's friends try to imprison them. And his actions do not necessarily coincide with man's concept of justice as Job had insisted they should.

Man's attitude toward God must be surrender. To man it is not given to understand the mystery of life. Suffering and death are past man's understanding. Man is called as a creature to trust his Creator, whose righteousness and justice must be as great as his awesome and inscrutable power. Leslie Weatherhead writes, "One thinks of a little boy whose father is a surgeon. One imagines an evil-intentioned person showing the boy his father operating, cutting the flesh of a helplessly unconscious victim. How could anyone explain? The boy has to believe from other evidence that his father is good, as well as [wise] and powerful, and await explanation." [17] Job now turns to God not to accuse God or to vindicate himself. Job now turns to God in trust.

> I knew of thee then only by report,
> but now I see thee with my own eyes.
> Therefore I melt away;
> I repent in dust and ashes.　　　　　[Job 42:5–6]

Chapter 20

DANIEL

The Persian Empire's domination of the Middle East was ended by Alexander the Great of Macedon. As a boy Alexander studied under Aristotle, the great Greek philosopher, and as a young man he dreamed of a world united by Greek language and culture. By the time of his death at age 33 (in 323 B.C.) he had nearly conquered the known world and had laid the foundations for spreading Greek civilization throughout his conquered lands.

After he died, his two most powerful generals divided his conquests between them. Seleucus founded the Seleucid dynasty at Antioch, the capital of the old Syrian Empire. Ptolemy founded the Ptolemaic dynasty at Alexandria in Egypt, a city remarkable for its Greek learning, library, and sophisticated cultural life.

As usual, Israel was caught between the two great powers of the north and south. At first it was under the Ptolemies. Though they ruled loosely, they were zealous Hellenizers. "Hellenization" (which derives its name from *Hellas*, Greece's ancient name) describes the effort to spread Greek language, philosophy, and culture to all parts of the world. Jews both in Israel and in Egypt were strongly influenced by Greek attitudes and only gradually became aware that their distinctive belief and ethic were threatened in the same way they had been earlier by Canaanite civilization. Consequently, a group emerged known as the Hasidim ("the loyal ones" or "pious ones") who adopted a deliberately anti-Hellenistic policy and who tried to preserve distinctive Jewish beliefs and customs in all their purity.

In 198 B.C. the Seleucids wrested control of Israel from the Ptolemies. Whereas the Ptolemies had been easy-going and respectful of Jewish customs, the Seleucids gradually adopted a hard-line policy of Hellenization. Antiochus IV Epiphanes (175–163 B.C.), sought to unify his empire by eliminating non-Greek practices. Antiochus called himself "the god Zeus manifest"

(*epiphanes* in Greek), and insisted that all his subjects worship
Zeus. He began by heavily taxing the Jews in Israel and selling
the high priesthood to the highest bidder, a Hellenizer. Later he
plundered the Temple at Jerusalem and made possession of the
Jewish Scriptures and observance of the Sabbath capital offenses.
In 168 B.C. he erected an altar to Zeus in the Temple and compelled the Jews to sacrifice swine upon it and to eat what was
sacrificed, though swine was to the Jews an unclean animal.

In the village of Modein, Mattathias, a priest, courageously
refused to offer such an abominable sacrifice. When a fellow Jew
went forward with a Syrian soldier to offer the sacrifice, Mattathias killed them both, then fled with his sons to the hills to form
a guerrilla movement to oppose Antiochus' policy. He soon died,
to be succeeded by his son Judas who, because of his remarkable
ability as a fighter, quickly gained the title Maccabeus ("The
Hammer"). By 165 B.C. Judas Maccabeus had driven the Seleucids out, restored and rededicated the Temple, and gained for
the Jews nearly a century of independence which was ended only
by the Roman conquest of 63 B.C. under Pompey.

THE BOOK OF DANIEL

The Book of Daniel was written by an unknown author living
in Israel during the persecution of Antiochus IV Epiphanes. The
author was a member of the Hasidim party and his book was
written to encourage his fellow Jews to remain loyal to Judaism
in the face of Antiochus' decrees.

Like the author of Job, the author of Daniel chose a figure of
legendary righteousness as the subject of his book. We know little
about the real Daniel, except that as early as 1300 B.C. a person
named Daniel was remembered in legend as a man of notable
goodness and courage. The author's account of Daniel is entirely
fictional. The Book of Daniel is the work of a superb storyteller
who spins romantic tales about Daniel in order to teach and encourage his fellow Jews to remain loyal to the faith under persecution.

The author places the story of Daniel in the setting of the King
of Babylon's court during the Exile, 586–538 B.C. Though Daniel
was written about 168–166 B.C., the author pretends he is writing
much earlier, during the Exile. His book therefore purports to
anticipate and predict events which, in fact, have already oc-

curred. His lack of accurate historical knowledge leads him to make a number of blunders about events between 586 and 168 B.C., though his accuracy improves as he writes about events nearer his own time. The accurate recording of history is obviously not his purpose in writing the book.

His purpose is to show to his fellow Jews under persecution that Yahweh is in control of history. His purpose in pretending to predict what has already happened is to show that God allows empires to rise and fall, and that, with successive empires, each worse than its predecessor, the end of history comes closer. The author clearly believes he is living at the end of human history, in the period of darkest darkness preceding the dawn of a new age in which God will establish his rule on earth.

The author is an apocalypticist. "Apocalyptic" comes from the Greek word for "uncover" or "reveal." Through symbols, visions, and stories, he endeavors to reveal to his contemporaries that the end is at hand and that if they remain faithful to God they will be vindicated when God establishes his kingdom on earth.

Though down the ages men wishing to predict the future have found the Book of Daniel a happy hunting ground, the author himself laid down no definite blueprint for the future. He was interested only in revealing that—despite appearances—God was even now, in the midst of Antiochus' terrible persecutions, sovereign over the universe. His conviction that God would demonstrate his sovereignty by appearing and establishing his kingdom expresses his faith in the ultimate triumph of God and the ultimate vindication of those who remain faithful to God.

Eric Heaton has written, "If the author of the Book of Daniel had been concerned to predict the date of the coming of the Kingdom of God as an event in the future, the disappointment of his expectations [when the Kingdom did not come immediately] would have exposed him as a complete failure and his work could be consigned to the limbo reserved for mistaken 'messianic' calculations. (Indeed, we may add, even if so limited a purpose had been rewarded with success, its religious significance to us after the event would hardly be [significant].) Since, however, our author was not concerned with anything so trivial, but with the moral and spiritual urgency of the crisis in which he and his fellow Jews were involved, he neither failed in his purpose nor did he wholly mislead his readers. In so far as he could not distinguish, in the crises of his times, between the decisive demand for faith and the immediacy of its complete fulfilment in history, he made a mistake. . . . But in so far as his hope was grounded, not in anything to which a date could be assigned, but in the 'living God . . . steadfast forever . . . [whose] kingdom is that which shall not be destroyed, and [whose] dominion shall never come to an end' (6:26), he taught . . . something which was true and fruitful not only then, but now and always." [18]

THE CONSOLING STORY OF DANIEL

The story of Daniel is placed in the context of the Exile, a time, like the author's own time, in which practicing Judaism was difficult and dangerous. Daniel and three companions are selected to be trained for the King of Babylon's service. Like the other trainees they are given the sumptuous food and wine appropriate to the king's palace. However, Daniel and his friends refuse this food because eating it would involve violation of Jewish dietary laws.

Then Daniel said to the guard whom the master of the eunuchs had put in charge of Hananiah, Mishael, Azariah and himself, 'Submit us to this test for ten days. Give us only vegetables to eat and water to drink; then compare our looks with those of the young men who have lived on the food assigned by the king, and be guided in your treatment of us by what you see.' The guard listened to what they said and tested them for ten days. At the end of ten days they looked healthier and were better nourished than all the young men who had lived on the food assigned them by the king. So the guard took away the assignment of food and the wine they were to drink, and gave them only the vegetables. [Dan. 1:11–16]

By this story the author subtly encourages his contemporaries to remain faithful to Judaism's dietary laws.

After three years, when all the trainees were examined, Daniel and his friends were found superior in wisdom to all the others. Oppressed peoples often feel inferior to their oppressors. The author of Daniel, however, attempts to rekindle national pride by recounting Daniel's successes.

When Nebuchadnezzar's dreams trouble him he calls the magicians and wise men of his court and asks them to tell him the content and meaning of his dream. After they fail, Daniel is brought to the king and, like Joseph earlier, he elucidates the king's dream: Babylonia and several other empires shall rise and fall; meanwhile God is secretly preparing to establish his kingdom.

'In the period of those kings the God of heaven will establish a kingdom which shall never be destroyed; that kingdom shall never pass to another people; it shall shatter and make an end of all these kingdoms, while it shall itself endure for ever. This is the meaning of your vision of the stone being hewn from a mountain, not by human hands, and then shattering the iron, the bronze, the clay, the silver, and the gold. The mighty God has made known to your majesty what is to be hereafter. The dream is sure and the interpretation to be trusted.'   [Dan. 2:44–45]

The author is telling his own contemporaries that Israel has long known the secret (hidden from others) that God is right now preparing to establish his sovereignty.

The king is impressed both by the God who has revealed the meaning of his dream, and by the people of that God to whom he has revealed it.

'Truly,' he said, 'your god is indeed God of gods and Lord over kings, a revealer of secrets, since you have been able to reveal this secret.' Then the king promoted Daniel, bestowed on him many rich gifts, and made him regent over the whole province of Babylon and chief prefect over all the wise men of Babylon. Moreover at Daniel's request the king put Shadrach, Meshach and Abed-nego in charge of the administration of the province of Babylon. Daniel himself, however, remained at court.   [Dan. 2:47–49]

If they thought Antiochus Epiphanes was bad, the author invites his contemporaries to compare him to the even more powerful Nebuchadnezzar.

King Nebuchadnezzar made an image of gold, ninety feet high and nine feet broad. He had it set up in the plain of Dura in the province of Babylon. Then he sent out a summons to assemble the satraps, prefects, viceroys, counsellors, treasurers, judges, chief constables, and all governors of provinces to attend the dedication of the image which he had set up. Then the herald loudly proclaimed, 'O peoples and nations of every language, you are commanded, when you hear the sound of horn, pipe, zither, triangle, dulcimer, music, and singing of every kind, to prostrate yourselves and worship the golden image which King Nebuchadnezzar has set up. Whoever does not prostrate himself and worship shall forthwith be thrown into a blazing furnace.' Accordingly, no sooner did all the peoples hear the sound of horn, pipe, zither, triangle, dulcimer, music, and singing of every kind, than all the peoples and nations of every language prostrated themselves and worshipped the golden image which King Nebuchadnezzar had set up. [Dan. 3:1–2, 4–7]

But Daniel's three friends remain true to God and refuse to worship the golden image. However, jealous non-Jews immediately come to the king to tell him of the three Jews' disobedience.

'There are certain Jews, Shadrach, Meshach and Abed-nego, whom you have put in charge of the administration of the province of Babylon. These men, your majesty, have taken no notice of your command; they do not serve your god, nor do they worship the golden image which you have set up.' Then in rage and fury Nebuchadnezzar ordered Shadrach, Meshach and Abed-nego to be fetched, and they were brought into the king's presence. Nebuchadnezzar said to them, 'Is it true, Shadrach, Meshach and Abed-nego, that you do not serve my god or worship the golden image which I have set up? If you are ready at once to prostrate yourselves when you hear the sound of horn, pipe, zither, triangle, dulcimer, music, and singing of every kind, and to worship the image that I have set up, well and good. But if you do not worship it, you shall forthwith be thrown into the blazing furnace; and what god is there that can save you from my power?' [Dan. 3:12–15]

The three men's answer to Nebuchadnezzar has been called the greatest statement of faith in the Old Testament.

Shadrach, Meshach and Abed-nego said to King Nebuchadnezzar, 'We have no need to answer you on this matter. If there is a god who is able to save us from the blazing furnace, it is our God whom we serve, and he will save us from your power, O King; but if not, be it known to your majesty that we will neither serve your god nor worship the golden image that you have set up.' [Dan. 3:16–18]

"If anyone can deliver us, Yahweh can. And we believe he *will*. But if it is part of his purpose *not* to deliver us, we *still* won't deny him. God is to be served because he is God, not because he will rescue us."

Then Nebuchadnezzar flew into a rage with Shadrach, Meshach and Abed-nego, and his face was distorted with anger. He gave orders that the furnace should be heated up to seven times its usual heat, and commanded some of the strongest men in his army to bind Shadrach, Meshach and Abed-nego and throw them into the blazing furnace. Then those men in their trousers, their shirts, and their hats and all their other clothes, were bound and thrown into the blazing furnace.

Then King Nebuchadnezzar was amazed and sprang to his feet in great trepidation. He said to his courtiers, 'Was it not three men whom we threw bound into the fire?' They answered the king, 'Assuredly, your majesty.' He answered, 'Yet I see four men walking about in the fire free and unharmed; and the fourth looks like a god.'

[Dan. 3:19–21, 24–25]

This fourth figure symbolizes the presence of God among his suffering people.

Nebuchadnezzar approached the door of the blazing furnace and said to the men, 'Shadrach, Meshach and Abed-nego, servants of the Most High God, come out, come here.' Then Shadrach, Meshach and Abed-nego came out from the fire. And the satraps, prefects, viceroys, and the king's courtiers gathered round and saw how the fire had had no power to harm the bodies of these men; the hair of their heads had not been singed, their trousers were untouched, and no smell of fire lingered about them.

Then Nebuchadnezzar spoke out, 'Blessed is the God of Shadrach, Meshach and Abed-nego. He has sent his angel to save his servants who put their trust in him, who disobeyed the royal command and were willing to yield themselves to the fire rather than to serve or worship any god other than their own God. I therefore issue a decree that any man, to whatever people or nation he belongs, whatever his language, if he speaks blasphemy against the God of Shadrach, Meshach and Abed-nego, shall be torn to pieces and his house shall be forfeit; for there is no other god who can save men in this way.' Then the king advanced the fortunes of Shadrach, Meshach and Abed-nego in the province of Babylon.   [Dan. 3:26–30]

The author's contemporaries could not have missed the point: Yahweh is more powerful than the greatest of all idols. Those who endure torture to remain faithful to Yahweh are rewarded in the end.

Next the author ridicules Antiochus Epiphanes' arrogance by means of a story about Nebuchadnezzar, who envisions himself as nearly a god:

At the end of twelve months the king was walking on the roof of the royal palace at Babylon, and he exclaimed, 'Is not this Babylon the great which I have built as a royal residence by my own mighty power and for the honour of my majesty?' The words were still on his lips, when a voice came down from heaven: 'To you, King Nebuchadnezzar, the word is spoken: the kingdom has passed from you. You are banished from the society of men and you shall live with the wild beasts; you shall feed on grass like oxen, and seven times will pass over you until you have learnt that the Most High is sovereign over the kingdom of men and gives it to whom he will.' At that very moment this judgement came upon Nebuchadnezzar. He was banished from the society of men and ate grass like oxen; his body was drenched by the dew of heaven, until his hair grew long like goats' hair and his nails like eagles' talons. [Dan. 4:29–33]

The most powerful king on earth goes berserk and acts like an animal; only after seven years of humiliating degradation is he restored to sanity.

At that very time I returned to my right mind and my majesty and royal splendour were restored to me for the glory of my kingdom. My courtiers and my nobles sought audience of me. I was established in my kingdom and my power was greatly increased. Now I, Nebuchadnezzar, praise and exalt and glorify the King of heaven; for all his acts are right and his ways are just and those whose conduct is arrogant he can bring low. [Dan. 4:36–37]

Even the most powerful earthly rulers can be brought to nothing by the Lord of the universe.

After Nebuchadnezzar dies, Belshazzar his son became king.

Belshazzar the king gave a banquet for a thousand of his nobles and was drinking wine in the presence of the thousand. Warmed by the wine, he gave orders to fetch the vessels of gold and silver which his father Nebuchadnezzar had taken from the sanctuary at Jerusalem, that he and his nobles, his concubines and his courtesans, might drink from them. So the vessels of gold and silver from the sanctuary in the house of God at Jerusalem were brought in, and the king and his nobles, his concubines and his courtesans, drank from them. They drank wine and praised the gods of gold and silver, of bronze and iron, and of wood and stone.   [Dan. 5:1–4]

Nothing horrified the Jews of the author's own time more than the sacrilegious use which Antiochus Epiphanes made of the Temple and its sacred vessels. Belshazzar is here shown mocking the true God by using holy things for profane and orgiastic purposes.

Suddenly there appeared the fingers of a human hand writing on the plaster of the palace wall opposite the lamp, and the king could see the back of the hand as it wrote. At this the king's mind was filled with dismay and he turned pale, he became limp in every limb and his knees knocked together.   [Dan. 5:5–6]

He called all the wise men of his court together but none could read the handwriting on the wall. Then his mother suggested calling Daniel. Ushered into the king's presence, Daniel delivers a stern lecture reminiscent of the prophets of old.

'My lord king, the Most High God gave your father Nebuchadnezzar a kingdom and power and glory and majesty; and, because of this power which he gave him, all peoples and nations of every language trembled before him and were afraid. He put to death whom he would and spared whom he would, he promoted them at will and at will degraded them. But, when he became haughty, stubborn and presumptuous, he was deposed from his royal throne and his glory was taken from him. He was banished from the society of men, his mind became like that of a beast, he had to live with the wild asses and to eat grass like oxen, and his body was drenched with the dew of heaven, until he came to know that the Most High God is sovereign over the kingdom of men and sets up over it whom he will. But you, his son Belshazzar, did not humble your heart, although you knew all this. You have set yourself up against the Lord of heaven. The vessels of his temple have been brought to your table; and you, your nobles, your concubines, and your courtesans have drunk from them. You have praised the gods of silver and gold, of bronze and iron, of wood and stone, which neither see nor hear nor know, and you have not given glory to God, in whose charge is your very breath and in whose hands are all your ways. This is why that hand was sent from his very presence and why it wrote this inscription. And these are the words of the writing which was inscribed: *Mene mene tekel u-pharsin.* Here is the interpretation: *mene*: God has numbered the days of your kingdom and brought it to an end; *tekel*: you have been weighed in the balance and found wanting; *u-pharsin*: and your kingdom has been divided and given to the Medes and Persians.' Then Belshazzar gave the order and Daniel was robed in purple and honoured with a chain of gold round his neck, and proclamation was made that he should rank as third in the kingdom.

That very night Belshazzar king of the Chaldaeans was slain, and Darius the Mede took the kingdom, being then sixty-two years old.

[Dan. 5:18–31]

Again, the author is summoning his contemporaries to take heart; the sacrilegious idolaters, who are now so puffed up and apparently powerful, will be brought low.

The author's last and best story is about Daniel in the lion's den. Jealous of Daniel's high position, the Persian leaders plot his downfall.

Then the chief ministers and the satraps began to look round for some pretext to attack Daniel's administration of the kingdom, but they failed to find any malpractice on his part; for he was faithful to his trust. Since they could discover no neglect of duty or malpractice, they said, 'There will be no charge to bring against this Daniel unless we find one in his religion.' These chief ministers and satraps watched for an opportunity to approach the king, and said to him, 'Long live King Darius! All we, the ministers of the kingdom, prefects, satraps, courtiers, and viceroys, have taken counsel and agree that the king should issue a decree and bring an ordinance into force, that whoever within the next thirty days shall present a petition to any god or man other than the king shall be thrown into the lions' pit. Now, O king, issue the ordinance and have it put in writing, so that it may be unalterable, for the law of the Medes and Persians stands for ever.' Accordingly King Darius issued the ordinance in written form.

[Dan. 6:4–9]

Men of every age, but especially of the author's own time, are tempted to abandon devotional practices when they are inconvenient, dangerous, or likely to be ridiculed. With remarkable calm, Daniel carries on the regular disciplined life of prayer as if nothing had happened: following ancient custom he continues to pray aloud publicly.

When Daniel learnt that this decree had been issued, he went into his house. He had had windows made in his roof-chamber looking towards Jerusalem; and there he knelt down three times a day and offered prayers and praises to his God as his custom had always been. His enemies watched for an opportunity to catch Daniel and found him at his prayers making supplication to his God. Then they came into the king's presence and reminded him of the ordinance. 'Your majesty,' they said, 'have you not issued an ordinance that any person who, within the next thirty days, shall present a petition to any god or man other than your majesty shall be thrown into the lions' pit?' The king answered, 'Yes, it is fixed. The law of the Medes and Persians stands for ever.' So in the king's presence they said, 'Daniel, one of the Jewish exiles, has ignored the ordinance issued by your majesty, and is making petition to his god three times a day.' When the king heard this, he was greatly distressed. He tried to think of a way to save Daniel, and continued his efforts till sunset; then those same men watched for an opportunity to approach the king, and said to him, 'Your majesty must know that by the law of the Medes and Persians no ordinance or decree issued by the king may be altered.' So the king gave orders and Daniel was brought and thrown into the lions' pit; but he said to Daniel, 'Your own God, whom you serve continually, will save you.' A stone was brought and put over the mouth of the pit, and the king sealed it with his signet and with the signets of his nobles, so that no one might intervene to rescue Daniel.

The king went back to his palace and spent the night fasting; no woman was brought to him and sleep eluded him. At dawn, as soon as it was light, he rose and went in fear and trembling to the pit. When the king reached it, he called anxiously to Daniel, 'Daniel, servant of the living God, has your God whom you serve continually been able to save you from the lions?' Then Daniel answered, 'Long live the king! My God sent his angel to shut the lions' mouths so that they have done me no injury, because in his judgement I was found innocent; and moreover, O king, I had done you no injury.' The king was overjoyed and gave orders that Daniel should be lifted out of the pit. So Daniel was lifted out and no trace of injury was found on him, because he had put his faith in his God. By order of the king Daniel's accusers were brought and thrown into the lions' pit with their wives and children, and before they reached the floor of the pit the lions were upon them and crunched them up, bones and all.

Then King Darius wrote to all peoples and nations of every language throughout the whole world: 'May your prosperity increase! I have issued a decree that in all my royal domains men shall fear and reverence the God of Daniel;

> for he is the living God, the everlasting,
> whose kingly power shall not be weakened;
> whose sovereignty shall have no end—
> a saviour, a deliverer, a worker of signs and wonders
> in heaven and on earth,
> who has delivered Daniel from the power of the lions.'

So this Daniel prospered during the reigns of Darius and Cyrus the Persian.   [Dan. 6:10–28]

The willingness of one man to risk his life to testify to God's presence in the world results in the proclamation to the whole world that Yahweh "is the living God, the everlasting."

DANIEL'S VISIONS

The author concludes with a vision of the end of history. The vision is an encouragement to those under persecution: the sufferings of the present are nothing in comparison to the vindication of all the faithful which is about to take place. With a barrage of symbols—"the scenery of eternity"—this vision views the whole sweep of history from Nebuchadnezzar to Antiochus Epiphanes from the perspective of its impending end.

The vision is of four beasts: a winged lion, a bear, a leopard, and a monster with ten horns. These beasts represent the four empires which successively oppressed the Jews (Babylonia, Media, Persia, and Greece).

In my visions of the night I, Daniel, was gazing intently and I saw a great sea churned up by the four winds of heaven, and four huge beasts coming up out of the sea, each one different from the others.

The first was like a lion but had an eagle's wings. I watched until its wings were plucked off and it was lifted from the ground and made to stand on two feet like a man; it was also given the mind of a man. Then I saw another, a second beast, like a bear. It was half crouching and had three ribs in its mouth, between its teeth. The command was given: 'Up, gorge yourself with flesh.' After this as I gazed I saw another, a beast like a leopard with four bird's wings on its back; this creature had four heads, and it was invested with sovereign power. Next in my visions of the night I saw a fourth beast, dreadful and grisly, exceedingly strong, with great iron teeth and bronze claws. It crunched and devoured, and trampled underfoot all that was left. It differed from all the beasts which preceded it in having ten horns. While I was considering the horns I saw another horn, a little one, springing up among them, and three of the first horns were uprooted to make room for it. And in that horn were eyes like the eyes of a man, and a mouth that spoke proud words.   [Dan. 7:2–8]

The beasts are arraigned before the heavenly court presided over by God ("the Ancient in Years," that is, the God who reigns absolutely over *all* the ages). Compared to the transcendent majesty of God—whom human words are inadequate to describe —the beastly empires are nothing.

> I kept looking, and then
> thrones were set in place and one ancient in years took his seat
> his robe was white as snow and the hair of his head like cleanest wool.
> Flames of fire were his throne and its wheels blazing fire;
> a flowing river of fire streamed out before him.
> Thousands upon thousands served him
> and myriads upon myriads attended his presence.
> The court sat, and the books were opened.   [Dan. 7:9–10]

Since Antiochus Epiphanes (perceived as one of the horns of the horned monster) is the Jews' most immediate persecutor, our author pictures him as the first to be obliterated:

Then because of the proud words that the horn was speaking, I went on watching until the beast was killed and its carcass destroyed: it was given to the flames. The rest of the beasts, though deprived of their sovereignty, were allowed to remain alive for a time and a season.
[Dan. 7:11–12]

The sovereignty which the beasts had presumed to exercise is God's alone and he now delegates it to "one like a man," who represents the remnant of Israel that had remained faithful to God through all the persecutions.

I was still watching in visions of the night and I saw one like a man coming with the clouds of heaven; he approached the Ancient in Years and was presented to him. Sovereignty and glory and kingly power were given to him, so that all people and nations of every language should serve him; his sovereignty was to be an everlasting sovereignty which should not pass away, and his kingly power such as should never be impaired.   [Dan. 7:13–14]

God "hath put down the mighty from their thrones and hath exalted the humble and meek."

The vision is of a new creation. As Adam was given dominion over the beasts at the creation (see Chapter 17), so now the true and tested Israel is given dominion over the imperial beasts. Yet this faithful Israel will not exercise dominion for its own glory, but will be God's agent, uniting all mankind in the new creation God is bringing into being.

But as the author writes the vindication has not yet occurred. The inevitable question therefore arises: what about those faithful saints who have died for the faith and who are *now* dying in Antiochus' persecution? The author of Daniel could not believe that God's "purpose in creation and his nature as love would be frustrated by the extinction of the creatures to whom he gave life, at a stage when they are obviously far removed from what he would have them become. . . . The blood of the martyrs and the infamy of the apostate Jews cried aloud for their appropriate reward. In these circumstances, the writer took the fateful step of affirming that both classes (the superlatively righteous and the superlatively wicked) would awake from their sleep in the grave on the Last Day and receive what they deserved." [19]

But at that moment your people will be delivered,
  every one who is written in the book:
  many of those who sleep in the dust of the earth will wake,
  some to everlasting life
  and some to the reproach of eternal abhorrence.
  The wise leaders shall shine like the bright vault of heaven,

and those who have guided the people in the true path
shall be like the stars for ever and ever.   [Dan. 12:1c–3]

With this ringing affirmation of an "after-life," we reach the
Old Testament's greatest assertion of God's steadfast love and
justice. Those who live and die for God in this life are ultimately
and mysteriously vindicated by him beyond history, beyond all
the injustices and sufferings of human life. "He who endures to
the end shall be saved."

NOTES

1. *The Layman's Bible Commentary,* vol. 3, pp. 51–52.
2. For a different interpretation see "Manna" in *The Interpreter's Dictionary of the Bible.*
3. Anderson, *The Living World of the Old Testament,* second edition, p. 59.
4. Greeley, *The Sinai Myth,* pp. 205–06.
5. *The Layman's Bible Commentary,* vol. 6, p. 131.
6. Cooper, *David,* p. 193.
7. James, *Personalities of the Old Testament,* pp. 184–85, abridged.
8. J. S. Bezzant, *Objections to Christian Belief,* London: Constable, 1968, pp. 110–11.
9. Quoted in D. M. G. Stalker, *Ezekiel,* London: SCM Press, 1968, p. 25.
10. *Ibid.,* p. 46.
11. Israel I. Mattuck, *The Thought of the Prophets,* p. 88.
12. C. R. North, *Isaiah 40–55,* London: SCM Press, 1952, p. 93.
13. Anderson, *op. cit.,* p. 427.
14. Greeley, *op. cit.,* pp. 26–27.
15. Dentan, *The Knowledge of God in Ancient Israel,* p. 68.
16. *The Layman's Bible Commentary,* vol. 14, p. 165.
17. Weatherhead, *The Busy Man's Old Testament,* p. 74.
18. E. W. Heaton, *The Book of Daniel,* London: SCM Press, 1956, pp. 91–92.
19. *Ibid.,* pp. 241–46.

BOOKS FOR FURTHER READING

ABRIDGED BIBLES

A Shorter Oxford Bible. New York: Oxford University Press, 1951.
God Who Saves Us, A Bible for Secondary Schools. New York: Herder and Herder, 1968.
Readings from the Bible (Selected by Mary Ellen Chase). New York: Macmillan, 1952.
The Bible Reader. New York: Bruce, 1969.
The Dartmouth Bible. Revised edition. Boston: Houghton Mifflin, 1965.

COMMENTARIES

Bible Guides. 12 vols. on the Old Testament. New York: Abingdon Press.
Buttrick, George A., ed. *The Interpreter's Bible.* 6 vols. on the Old Testament. New York: Abingdon Press.
The Cambridge Bible Commentary. 18 vols. on the Old Testament. Cambridge: Cambridge University Press.
The Layman's Bible Commentary. Vols. 1–15. Richmond: John Knox Press.
Torch Bible Commentaries. 20 vols. on the Old Testament. London: SCM Press.

GENERAL BOOKS

Alves, Colin. *The Covenant.* Cambridge: Cambridge University Press, 1957.
Anderson, Bernhard W. *The Living World of the Old Testament.* Second edition. Englewood Cliffs: Prentice-Hall, 1966.
Bright, John. *A History of Israel.* Second edition. Philadelphia: Westminster, 1972.
Buber, Martin. *On the Bible.* New York: Schocken Books, 1968.
Chase, Mary Ellen. *The Bible and the Common Reader.* Revised edition. New York: Macmillan, 1955.
Cooper, Duff. *David.* London: Rupert Hart-Davis, 1962.
Dentan, Robert C. *The Knowledge of God in Ancient Israel.* New York: Seabury Press, 1968.

Fosdick, Harry Emerson. *A Guide to Understanding the Bible*. New York: Harper's, 1938.

Greeley, Andrew M. *The Sinai Myth*. Garden City: Doubleday, 1972.

Guthrie, Harvey H., Jr. *God and History in the Old Testament*. New York: Seabury Press, 1960.

Heaton, E. W. *The Old Testament Prophets*. Baltimore: Penguin Books, 1958.

Jackson, Warren W. *Legend, Myth and History in the Old Testament*. Wellesley Hills: Independent School Press, 1970.

James, Fleming. *Personalities of the Old Testament*. New York: Scribners, 1943.

Orlinsky, Harry M. *Understanding the Bible through History and Archeology*. New York: KTAV Publishing, 1972.

Rattey, B. K. *A Short History of the Hebrews*. Second edition. Oxford: Oxford University Press, 1964.

Weatherhead, Leslie D. *The Busy Man's Old Testament*. Nutfield, Surrey: Denholm House Press, 1971.

Yates, Gilbert. *Introduction to the Old Testament*. London: Epworth Press, 1965.

REFERENCE WORKS

Black, Matthew and H. H. Rowley, eds. *Peake's Commentary on the Bible*. Edinburgh and New York: Nelson, 1962.

Buttrick, George A., ed. *The Interpreter's Dictionary of the Bible*. 4 vols. New York: Abingdon, 1962.

Walton, Robert C., ed. *A Source Book of the Bible for Teachers*. London: SCM Press, 1970.